BEHAVIORAL ECONOMICS

BEHAVIORAL ECONOMICS

James Allison

PRAEGER

PRAEGER SPECIAL STUDIES • PRAEGER SCIENTIFIC

Library of Congress Cataloging in Publication Data

Allison, James (James W.)
  Behavioral economics.

  Bibliography: p.
  Includes indexes.
  1. Economics — Psychological aspects.   I. Title.
HB74.P8A535   1983   330'.01'9   83-8058
ISBN 0-03-063400-8

Published in 1983 by Praeger Publishers
CBS Educational and Professional Publishing
a Division of CBS Inc.
521 Fifth Avenue, New York, NY 10175 USA

© Praeger Publishers

3456789 052 987654321

Printed in the United States of America
on acid-free paper

Preface

In the late 1960s I started a series of experiments intended to test a theory of what I then called reinforcement—the process that somehow leads the laboratory rat, allowed to press a lever for food, to press the lever far more often than it would in the absence of food reward. Bombarded by one experiment after another, the initial theory underwent a radical transformation in the familiar cycle of revision, rejection, total reconstruction, and more revision. Sufficiently content with the latest version to share it with my undergraduate psychology students, I cast about for some way to relate the phenomenon at hand to the world outside the laboratory: If we have a theory that tells us how to get the rat in its cage to work more than it really wants, maybe what we have is a theory of labor in a microcosm. But I could get little further than that without further education. Intending to study one or the other during my next sabbatical leave, I picked two fields that seemed most pertinent: the physiology of exercise and economics. When the time finally arrived, external circumstances made economics the more convenient alternative. Accordingly, I devoted most of that sabbatical year, 1976/77, to the independent study of economics.

A complete novice, I started with a few books on the history of economics and began to pick my way through a recent edition of Paul Samuelson's superb introductory text. Early on, I saw my first downward-sloping demand curve. The sight delivered a shock of recognition whose reverberations have not quite died, even now. My acute sensitivity came from two personal sources: a theory that predicted such a curve and many actual examples based not on the behavior of millions of anonymous consumers in the economic marketplace but on the behavior or individual humans and animals tested experimentally in the psychological laboratory.

I quickened my pace, reported what I had learned at an October colloquium at the University of Illinois, moved on to other books and primary sources in the literature of economics, and felt now and again some new and agreeable shock.

I soon discovered that several other investigators had taken much the same trip, and seen much the same sights, at about the same time or even long before: S. E. G. Lea, H. Rachlin, L. Green, R. Winkler, J. H. Kagel, R. C. Battalio, R. L. Basmann, W. R. Klemm, B. Castro, and K. Weingarten. No doubt there were many others; I hope they will forgive my inadvertent failure to mention them by name. This book attempts to describe some of these sights, and others we might behold in the future, in language accessible to students of psychology and economics as well as to the resolute layman.

Economists generally divide their field into two subfields, micro- and macroeconomics. They do not necessarily agree on the proper contents of each, and many feel that any such division is unfortunate and arbitrary.

The typical university bulletin might describe <u>microeconomics</u> somewhat as follows: principles of economics; scarcity, opportunity cost, competitive market pricing, and conditions of full employment; the problems of poverty, pollution, excise taxes, rent controls, and farm subsidies.

<u>Macroeconomics</u> might have the following sort of description: fluctuations in the levels of aggregate employment, income, and prices; measurement and explanation of total economic performance; monetary and fiscal policy; inflation; unemployment; economic growth in underdeveloped countries.

This book deals mainly with a small, select portion of micro-economics. Much of economics lies beyond the immediate reach of experimental psychology, and much of that territory does not appear here.

I have tried to clear the main text of technical and mathematical details, moving many to the chapter notes; some readers will think I should have tried harder. As I can promise no future improvement, I defend myself with sophistry: No reader will finally complain who studies a little harder before rendering final jundment.

I give heartfelt thanks to my wife, Tomi, and my daughters, Devon and Leigh, who supported the whole endeavor both psychologically and economically. Without their cheerful encouragement, that full sabbatical year at half pay might have been a half year at full pay instead, and rather less memorable. For their comments on an early draft of the manuscript, I give special thanks to Kevin Moore, Erwin Concepcion, and my most persistent critic, Edda Thiels.

Contents

List of Figures

Chapter 1

Overview

Thorstein Veblen, the foremost maverick among the economists of his time, had a fervent admiration for the Darwinian scheme of evolutionary biology. Running against the mentalistic current of contempory economic theory, he longed for an approach to economics that would seem more akin to natural science and less akin to armchair speculation. We find a symptomatic statement in the archives of the year 1898; even the title sounds plaintive: "Why Is Economics Not an Evolutionary Science?"

> The modern scientist is unwilling to depart from the test
> of causal relation or quantitative sequence. When he asks
> the question, Why? he insists on an answer in terms of
> cause and effect. He wants to reduce his solution of all
> problems to terms of the conservation of energy or the
> persistence of quantity. That is his last recourse.
> [Veblen 1898, p. 377]

A young psychologist, Edward L. Thorndike, published his doctoral dissertation in the same year (Thorndike 1898). The published work later gained fame for its account of Thorndike's experiment with the hungry cat inside a puzzle box, whose dish of food was outside—food the cat could get by pulling a string that unlatched the door, opening the way out. Thorndike kept a trial-by-trial record of the time it took each cat to make its escape. His records revealed a fairly steady increase in the speed of escape from one trial to the next, and thus a steady improvement in performance as training progressed.

Learning involves the modification of behavior through experience, an accurate description of Thorndike's observations of the cat's escape from the puzzle box. A term formerly reserved for the human manifestation of unique intelligent rationality, learning was supposed

1

to involve some mental process—insights arising suddenly from the search of assorted hunches and ideas, a conscious, deliberate, and logical process. Thorndike could accept the intelligence of cats and other animals, but he could not accept the mental bias of psychological theory any more readily than Veblen could accept its counterpart in economics. Instead, Thorndike proposed that learning in the cat consisted of the automatic formation of an association between the stimulus situation (S) and the correct response (R). The cat learns a specific response to a certain situation; when the cat is returned to that stimulus situation, it performs that response automatically, mechanically, and unthinkingly. The response reflects the formation of a compelling S-R bond as a result of experience.

Thirteen years later, Thorndike stated his position in his law of effect, where "effect" refers to satisfactions or discomforts attendant on the response:

> Of several responses made to the same situation, those which are accompanied or closely followed by satisfaction to the animal will, other things being equal, be more firmly connected with the situation, so that, when it recurs, they will be more likely to recur; those which are accompanied or closely followed by discomfort to the animal will, other things being equal, have their connections with that situation weakened, so that, when it recurs, they will be less likely to occur. The greater the satisfaction or discomfort, the greater the strengthening or weakening of the bond. [Thorndike 1911, p. 244]

"Satisfaction" and "discomfort" had mentalistic overtones that Thorndike sought to evade through objective behavioral definitions. A satisfier was a state of affairs the animal "does nothing to avoid, often doing such things as attain and preserve it." An annoyer was a state the animal avoids or abandons (Thorndike 1911).

One may wonder what would have happened if these two malcontents had come together in collaboration: indefatigable E. L. Thorndike, behavioral scientist, versed in the ways of the laboratory experiment; prickly Thorstein Veblen, theory-rich and data-poor, ready for a natural science of economics.

Psychology, a science of behavior with a strong tradition of laboratory experimentation, has shown little interest, and no sustained interest, in the economic side of behavior. On the other side, many distinguished economists frankly admire the progress of the laboratory sciences, but emphatically deny the feasibility of an experimental approach to economics patterned after the model of the laboratory sciences. Some turn pale, indifferent, or disdainful at any suggestion that laboratory experiments with animals might reveal something of value about basic economic processes. I hope that this book will make it a little harder for students of psychology and students of economics to continue their customary ways of mutual ignorance, indifference, or disdain. In addition, I hope Thorndike and Veblen would approve.

The next three chapters lay the psychological foundation for the economic material covered in the rest of the book. Students of economics should finish these chapters with a better understanding of behavioral experiments in the psychological laboratory, their relation to economic behavior, and the psychological theories of that behavior. Students of behavioral psychology, now securely footed on the bedrock of the reinforcement concept, should finish these chapters in a different state: less secure than now, and more receptive to an economic view of their familiar behavioral experiments.

Chapter 2 introduces the contingency schedule, illustrates its use in the psychological laboratory, and identifies its basic element, the response-contingent reward, in behavioral rules and regulations of life outside the laboratory. It deals with the reward as a reinforcing agent, a contemporary outgrowth of Thorndike's law of effect. The chapter includes an extensive account of David Premack's theory of reinforcement—probability-differential theory—and examines the impact that Premack's work has had upon the concept of reinforcement.

Chapter 3 deals with response deprivation, an antecedent condition whose discovery came directly from Premack's work. It relates the further development of the response deprivation concept in the hands of other theorists; documents the behavioral influence of the response deprivation condition; and shows how the flow of research has eroded the concept of response reinforcement.

The work on response deprivation spawned a new generation of theories that start with a close analysis of the behavioral constraints imposed by any particular kind of contingency schedule. These theories make no use of response reinforcement as an explanatory concept. They attempt to explain the behavioral effects of the schedule as an adaptive response of one sort or another to the external structural constraints of the schedule.

Chapter 4 deals with two members of the new generation, minimum-deviation theory and conservation theory. These particular theories provide a convenient transition to the final portion of the book, which unfolds the interpretation of response-contingent rewards as economic goods or commodities. We see there how we can derive from each theory some of the fundamental laws of microeconomics, laws that govern the behavior of consumer or laborer. Chapter 5 deals with theory, data, and analytic concepts from the economics of consumer demand; Chapter 6 with the economics of labor supply.

Each of these chapters presents an economic view of a large number of experiments drawn from the psychological literature.

Chapter 7 suggests new points of correspondence that might emerge from further research. It touches incidentally on the role of economic concepts in ecological analyses of the predator's search for food in its natural habitat. It touches more purposefully on the nascent field of experimental economics, whose continued growth will surely enlarge the mutuality of economics and experimental psychology. Chapter 8 concludes with an overview that should seem less controversial in retrospect than it does in prospect.

Chapter 2

Reinforcement

CONTINGENCY SCHEDULES

After I administered the final examination, a student gave me
a yellow felt scroll emblazoned with her pithy summary of the course:
"Life Is Just One Big Contingency Session!" Undoubtedly more than
that, everyday life nevertheless is closely constrained by specific
rules and regulations, often remarkably subtle, that stand out all too
clearly once we understand their general form, the contingency
schedule. My student had learned her lesson well.

As an introductory example, consider the colloquial expression
of one of the rules that govern the life of a young academic in a
research-oriented university: Publish, or perish. In other words,
if the newly hired instructor wishes permanent employment in the form
of academic tenure (awarded at the end of a lengthy trial period), the
instructor must start a program of research and publish its results
in the scholarly press; otherwise, the instructor will have to seek employment elsewhere at the end of the trial period.

This example contains the crucial elements of our key general
rule, the contingency rule: Event B will occur only if event A occurs
beforehand. Event B is contingent, dependent, conditional, or consequent on something else, event A. Those who publish (event A) may
receive tenure (event B), but those who do not, surely will not. Publication is necessary, but not sufficient, because the implicit contract
typically includes other conditions of tenure, such as adequate teaching and good citizenship. The example may also illustrate the influence a contingency can have upon our everyday behavior. What would
we expect to find if we compared the rate of publication in a research-
oriented university with the rate of publication in a small college whose
primary mission is teaching? Among the tenured faculty of a research-

oriented university, what would we expect to find if we compared the rates of publication just before and just after tenure?

Imagine a family seated at the dinner table. In response to the boy's reluctance to finish his spinach, the mother tries to influence his behavior by announcing a rule: no spinach, no dessert. But the boy would like a more complete contract: Do you promise me dessert if I finish my spinach? If his mother agrees, the boy will get dessert if, and only if, he eats the spinach. Eating the spinach is both necessary and sufficient for his getting the dessert. If no spinach, then no dessert (eating spinach is necessary); if spinach, then dessert (eating spinach is sufficient).

This contingency might or might not work as the mother hopes it will. If we tried to make a prediction, we might conclude that the boy's response to the contingency would depend on various imponderables. How intensely does he detest spinach and like vanilla ice cream? How much does he value his independence, rebelling at obvious efforts to manipulate his behavior? Later we shall examine several theories that try to remove the imponderables, theories that try to tell us whether a particular contingency will or will not induce the person to do what we want.

Universities publish catalogs that specify what a student must do to graduate with a Bachelor of Arts degree. The degree requirements include the satisfactory completion of a certain number of courses, distributed among various disciplines, admission to which is contingent upon the payment of tuition. Students who fail to complete the requirements may not collect their degrees. How much tuition would a university collect if students could get their degrees without taking any courses? Would class attendance suffer if students could pass their courses without attending class? How much can we depend on intrinsic rewards, the rewards we get from learning itself? Why does the educational system depend so heavily on extrinsic rewards, the degrees contingent on completion of course requirements?

How much labor would management get if paychecks were not contingent on work? If paychecks were free for the asking, the worker might still furnish some labor if the work were intrinsically interesting, but probably not enough to satisfy management; that is why management pays, to induce us to work more than we would if pay were not contingent on work.

Who can seriously doubt the power of the work-for-pay contingency? In a moment of rash enthusiasm, a colleague once told me that he liked his job enough to do it gladly for nothing. This platitude has a more credible variation: If I were rich, I would gladly do this job for nothing. My well-paid colleague could have returned part of his monthly pay to the payroll department; to all appearances, he kept it all for himself. But he did take some time and trouble to get job offers from other universities—his way of negotiating an even higher salary for the work he undoubtedly loved, but perhaps less than he claimed in that moment of elation over the intrinsic rewards of his job.

A contingency schedule spells out the details of a particular contingency. If we decide to deliver a monthly paycheck only to those who have furnished some minimum amount of labor, we must also decide on the exact amount of labor required for each paycheck, and the exact amount of money to be delivered. If we decide to deliver food only if the rat presses a lever, we must also decide on the exact number of lever presses required for each delivery, and the exact number of food pellets in each delivery. These numbers constitute the contingency schedule. We refer to the number of lever presses specified by the schedule as the instrumental requirement, to acknowledge the lever-pressing behavior as a means of getting the food. If we think of the response-contingent food as a reward, we may refer to the number of pellets in each delivery as the magnitude of reward.

Contingency schedules may change our behavior in either direction, up or down. For example, suppose we present the hungry rat with a lever that serves no apparent purpose; in particular, no amount of lever pressing delivers any food. Over the course of a one-hour session, we find that the rat presses the lever five times. Thus, the rat's baseline rate of lever pressing is 5/hour. The rat may derive some intrinsic satisfaction from pressing the lever, but apparently not much.

The next day, we wire the lever to an automatic pellet dispenser. We program the apparatus to deliver an extrinsic reward in the form of one small food pellet, .045 grams each, every time the rat presses the lever. We find that the hungry rat performs 400 instrumental lever presses and eats 400 contingent food pellets over the course of the one-hour contingency session. Thus, our contingency schedule has increased the rate of lever pressing relative to the baseline rate, 400/hour versus 5/hour. If a schedule raises the rate of the response relative to some baseline rate, we say that the schedule reinforced or facilitated the response.

We might see the other kind of change if we wired the lever to a shocker instead of a pellet dispenser. By delivering a brief but intense foot shock through the metal floor each time the rat presses the lever, the schedule might decrease the rate of lever pressing, say to 2/hour versus 5/hour. If a schedule decreases the rate of responding relative to some baseline rate, we say that the schedule punished or suppressed the response.

One of the main reasons we study such schedules in artificial laboratory experiments is that analogous schedules, outside the laboratory, can have powerful effects upon everyday behavior. They may increase the rate of publication, spinach consumption, class attendance,

or work, relative to some baseline rate observed in the absence of
the schedule. But a particular schedule may or may not have the effects the scheduler hoped to achieve by taking the trouble to design and
enforce the schedule. This is the province of reinforcement theory:
How to make a schedule work in the manner intended.

THE REINFORCEMENT CONCEPT

Some schedules succeed in driving the instrumental response
above its baseline rate, and others do not. A theory of reinforcement
is a guess about what all successful schedules have in common, aside
from the fact that all such schedules raise the rate of instrumental
responding.

Guided by various models of associative learning, many theorists
focused their attention on two events, the instrumental response and
the contingent reward delivered soon after the response. If B always
follows A, the sight of A may come to remind us of B; we have learned
the association between A and B. If Pavlov feeds his dog each time
the bell rings, the dog may come to salivate in response to the bell
because the dog has learned the association between bell and food
(Pavlov 1927). If we feed the hungry rat each time it presses the
lever, the rat may come to press the lever more often because it has
learned the contingent relation between pressing the lever and the delivery of food.

However, this can be only part of the answer. If we take our
trained rat and give it all the food it can eat just before we return it
to the box wherein it received its training under the press-for-food
schedule, the rat will show little interest in the lever. But it has not
forgotten what it learned, as we would see if we kept it away from food
overnight and tested it tomorrow. Tomorrow the hungry rat will show
great interest in the lever. Thus, we cannot explain performance
solely in terms of what the animal has learned; sometimes it acts in
accordance with what it has learned, sometimes not (Atkinson 1964;
Hilgard and Bower 1975). Perhaps its motivational state plays a crucial role: Only if moved by hunger will the rat show what it has
learned—that food is contingent upon pressing the lever.

Many psychologists make no distinction between learning and
performance; they prefer to think of the animal's current motivational
state as one of the variables that determine whether the contingent
event will raise the rate of the instrumental response. These psychologists tend to eschew the terminology of reward as prescientific
chatter; they prefer to interpret the effect of the contingent event in
terms of a unitary strengthening process, a response-strengthening
process. If the schedule increases the rate of the instrumental re-

sponse, the contingent event is a <u>reinforcer</u>, a strengthening agent that increased the rate by fortifying the instrumental response. If the schedule has no effect upon the rate of the instrumental response —for reasons that would include a lack of hunger—then the contingent event is simply not a reinforcer.

Those who advocate this radical behaviorist view embody a scientific version of existentialist philosophy: We are what we do. They show relatively little interest in behavioral potential, little interest in the possibility that we may leave the lever alone even though we know that food will come at the first press of the lever as surely as night follows day. What counts is what we do, not what we know or could do.

Harmless enough as metaphor, the response-reinforcement language has literal connotations that can prove troublesome. If we believe too literally that repeated application of a contingent reinforcer adds lasting strength to a response, as a steel strut adds strength to a bridge, we may be shocked to discover how quickly the response can return to its original level once we discontinue the schedule. Do not be surprised if extensive training under the spinach-dessert schedule has no discernible effect on the intrinsic delights of spinach, and no discernible effect on the boy's eating habits. How much spinach does he eat on his solitary vists to his grandmother's house?[1]

PROBABILITY-DIFFERENTIAL THEORY

In 1959 David Premack published a theory of reinforcement that held center stage for over a decade. Ironically, Premack's theory plays an ancestral role to contemporary theories that threaten to replace the very concept of response reinforcement.

It would be hard to match the elegant simplicity of Premack's proposal: <u>A contingent behavior will reinforce an instrumental behavior if, and only if, it has a higher probability than the instrumental behavior.</u>

Notice the emphasis on behavior. It is not the contingent delivery of food that reinforces instrumental lever pressing, but rather, a particular behavior—eating—made possible by the instrumental behavior. If eating is more probable, eating will reinforce lever pressing; otherwise, it will not. Indeed, if any behavior B is more probable than any behavior A, then B will reinforce A. The theory has genuine predictive power: To predict whether a particular contingency schedule will or will not reinforce the instrumental behavior, we need merely measure beforehand the probabilities of the two behaviors controlled by the schedule.

Premack suggested that we could measure the probabilities by means of a <u>paired baseline</u> condition, one that allows free performance of the two behaviors throughout the entire course of the baseline recording session. By measuring the total amount of time spent in the performance of each behavior, we measure their relative probabilities.

A typical paired baseline session would start with the presentation of two items, a lever and an unlimited supply of food pellets, and end one hour later with the withdrawal of lever and food. If the rat spends more time eating than pressing the lever, eating is more probable, and should in theory reinforce lever pressing.

Next we test the prediction by means of a one-hour contingency session that starts with the presentation of the lever alone. The schedule requires a certain amount of instrumental lever pressing for each contingent delivery of a little food and should, in theory, produce more lever pressing/hour than we saw in the paired baseline condition. The spinach-dessert contingency will work as the mother hopes it will if, and only if, the boy with free access to both spends more time eating dessert than spinach.

Premack's theory seemed to provide a wonderfully simple explanation of several well-known facts about reinforcement. Why might food reinforce lever pressing in the hungry rat, but not in the satiated rat? Because paired baseline measurements would reveal eating as the much more probable response in the hungry rat, but not in the satiated rat; the satiated rat would show little interest in either the food or the lever.

The theory also succeeded where others had failed. According to one such theory, food could reinforce the behavior of a hungry rat because food would reduce the rat's biological need for food; it would not reinforce the behavior of a satiated rat because such a rat has no current need for food. But why does the rat, fully satiated on food and water, press a lever so avidly for contingent saccharin solution, a sweet-tasting fluid that has no nutritional value whatever? Although rats thrive nicely without saccharin, they happen to spend more time drinking than pressing when given free access to saccharin and lever. We may ask why they do; but we must also recognize that the question is totally irrelevant to an evaluation of Premack's theory, whose only business is to predict whether a particular contingency schedule will or will not reinforce the instrumental response.

Notice too the deliberate omission of "preference," "likes," "dislikes," "pleasant," and "unpleasant" from our account of the probability-differential theory. In applying the theory we neither know nor care whether the more probable of the two behaviors is also the more preferred, pleasant, or likable. Most students spend more time in class than in musical concerts, but the same students might well prefer music to class, or find it more pleasant. All we need to know is the relative amount of time allocated to two measurable activities under the paired baseline condition.

Premack's theory did well on two additional dimensions of excellence: its ability to predict new phenomena and to disturb conventional views of the old. Before Premack, theorists generally partitioned the world into two mutually exclusive categories, the reinforcers and the reinforceables. Class membership was fixed and absolute: Reinforcers may strengthen, but cannot get strengthened; reinforceables may get strengthened, but cannot themselves strengthen something else. A few years after the publication of his theory, Premack (1963) reported one of the truly seminal experiments in the history of reinforcement theory, an experiment that thoroughly shattered the old categories.

One of the experimental subjects, a monkey named Chicko, was tested in paired baseline sessions that allowed free performance of three different manipulatory behaviors: H—moving a horizontal lever from side to side, D—opening and closing a small door fitted to a wall of the cage, and P—pushing and releasing a spring-loaded plunger. Chicko had free access to these devices, two devices per session, in a series of paired baseline sessions: H versus D, D versus P, and H versus P. The baseline measures showed H to be more probable than D, D more probable than P, and H more than P.

From three different behaviors we can create six different contingencies. One of the six would require Chicko to work the door instrumentally for the contingent chance to work the horizontal lever. We call this the DH contingency and list all six contingencies in the same manner, the instrumental member followed by the contingent member of each pair:

1. DH +
2. PH +
3. PD +
4. HD −
5. HP −
6. DP −

According to the theory, each of the first three contingencies should reinforce the instrumental member, because each contingent member had the higher probability in the paired baseline condition: H was more probable than D or P, D more probable than P. The positive signs in the list signify the prediction of a reinforcement effect, more instrumental responding in contingency than in baseline. Chicko's performance in the contingency phase of the experiment confirmed each of these three predictions. Thus, it seems that a reinforcer need not be something Chicko can smell, taste, drink, chew, or swallow, and it need not be some vital commodity without which Chicko would expire.

None of the last three contingencies should reinforce the instrumental member; there, each contingent member had the lower baseline probability—D less probable than H, and P less probable than H or D. The negative signs in the list signify the prediction of no reinforcement effect. Chicko's performance confirmed these three predictions as well as the first three.

Examine carefully the total pattern of these six results. If we attended to 1, 2, 4, and 5, we might assign behavior H to the old reinforcer category: H seems to reinforce anything and everything (1 and 2), but seems not to be reinforceable (4 and 5). If we attended to 2, 3, 5, and 6, we might assign behavior P to the old reinforceable category: P is easily reinforced (2 and 3), but reinforces nothing (5 and 6). Our old categories remain safely intact.

But what about behavior D? Two of the results give contradictory readings: 3 says D is a reinforcer, but 4 says no. Two others prove equally troublesome: 1 says D is reinforceable, but 6 says no.

The old categories cannot deal with Chicko's D results. Those results defy classification by any theory of reinforcement that attempts to assign a particular behavior to one category or the other on the basis of any intrinsic property the behavior seems to possess when viewed in splendid isolation. We cannot specify a reinforcer, and we cannot specify a reinforceable, by writing down the name of a particular behavior. We do no better by listing its possible consequences to the organism—need reduction, drive reduction, satisfaction, or pleasure. Will eating serve as a reinforcer? Drinking? Pressing a lever that delivers electrical stimulation to the septal area of the brain, the pleasure center? Chicko's results and Premack's theory say that it all depends: Eating, drinking, or pressing the septal lever will reinforce another response if they happen to be more probable than that other response; otherwise, they will not.

Look once again at the list of Chicko's results with the following question in mind: If behavior B reinforces behavior A, can A reinforce B? If we tried to answer the question inductively, by inspecting Chicko's six results, we would say no: H reinforced D, but D failed to reinforce H, and so on through the list.

But if we tried to deduce an answer from Premack's theory, we might get a different answer. Imagine two different experimental conditions, x and y. Under condition x, B is more probable than A; under condition y, A is more probable than B. According to the theory, B should reinforce A under condition x, but A should reinforce B under condition y. Such results would constitute an experimental demonstration of the reversibility of the reinforcement relation. How might we reverse the relative probabilities so as to test the predicted reversibility of the reinforcement relation?

Different individuals may spend different amounts of time on the same activities. Such differences—part of the stuff that makes human personality—can even be seen among laboratory rats from the same inbred strain. In a large sample of rats that have all gone without food for 22 hours, some may spend as much as 85 percent of their time in a food chamber as opposed to chambers offering a play object or a conspecific, while others may spend as little as 12 percent of their their time in the food chamber (Allison 1964).[2]

Premack (1959) took advantage of individual differences in children to test the predicted reversibility of the reinforcement relation. The paired baseline condition offered free access to a candy dispenser and a pinball machine, both wired for free operation. Some children proved to be "eaters"—their eating was more probable than their playing of the pinball machine—and others proved to be "players"—their playing was more probable than their eating. As the theory would predict, eating reinforced playing among the eaters, and playing reinforced eating among the players. Thus, Premack managed to demonstrate the reversibility of the reinforcement relation by sorting eaters into condition x, players into condition y.

But we should also be able to demonstrate reversibility of the reinforcement relation within one and the same individual. According to the theory, what we need is some pretest condition x that makes A more probable than B in the paired baseline session, and a different pretest condition y that somehow makes B more probable than A. If we test the individual with contingency schedules under the same pretest conditions, A should reinforce B under condition x, and B should reinforce A under condition y. These two results would illustrate the reversibility of the reinforcement relation within the same individual through the direct experimental manipulation of the individual's baseline probabilities.

Premack (1962) attempted that kind of reversibility by testing rats inside a running wheel, a cylindrical cage that rotated on a horizontal axis. One of the two flat walls rotated about a fixed disk in the center of the wall, and a retractable water tube was mounted on the disk. The opportunity to run was controlled by means of a brake mounted on the wheel: The wheel rotated freely or froze firmly in place when the experimenter released or applied the brake.

Pretest condition x allowed each rat to run as much as it pleased, but no chance to drink, during the several hours that preceded each test session. When the rats were finally given the chance to run and drink as much as they pleased in the paired baseline test session, with free access to both behaviors, drinking proved more probable than running. The next step in the experiment reestablished pretest condition x—unrestricted running, but no drinking—and tested the rats under a run-to-drink contingency. The results showed that drinking reinforced running, in line with Premack's theory as well as its competitors.

Pretest condition y allowed each rat to drink as much as it pleased, but no chance to run, during the several hours that preceded

each test session. When the rats finally had the chance to drink and
run without constraint in the paired baseline test session, running
proved more probable than drinking. After reestablishing pretest
condition y—unrestricted drinking, but no running—the rats were
tested with a drink-to-run contingency. The results showed that running reinforced drinking, in line with Premack's theory but out of line
with its major competitors.

Thus, if drinking is more probable than running, as it was under
condition x, drinking reinforces running; if running is more probable
than drinking, as it was under condition y, running reinforces drinking. It seems that we can reverse the reinforcement relation by
manipulating the individual so as to reverse the individual's baseline
probabilities. It seems, too, that we can use the classic reinforceables to reinforce the classic reinforcers: Playing can reinforce
eating, and running can reinforce drinking.

A SEMINAL FAILURE

After a long string of successes, Premack reported in 1965 an
experiment that failed to support the probability-differential theory.
We are about to see how an isolated failure can prove even more en-
lightening than success.

Almost to the last detail, the new experiment resembled his old
condition x experiment, where the run-to-drink contingency reinforced
running: The rats were thirsty at the time of the test sessions, and
drinking was more probable than running; again the contingency schedule required a few seconds of instrumental running for each contingent
access to the water tube. But in the new experiment, drinking failed
to reinforce running; instead, the rats spent no more time running
during the contingency session than they had done in the paired baseline session. How to explain the failure?

If we have every reason to expect a reinforcement effect, but
see no such effect after a few sessions of training under the schedule,
we may be inclined to blame the failure on insufficient training, and
run one more training session the next day. Sometimes it works;
this time, it did not. After a large number of training sessions, Premack looked elsewhere for the answer.

In casting about for an explanation, he discovered a small but
crucial difference between the old schedule and the new. The old
schedule required a relatively large amount of instrumental running
per second of contingent drinking—so large that if the rats had performed only their baseline amount of running, they would have fallen
far short of their baseline amount of drinking. The new schedule happened by chance to be more generous than the old; by performing

merely the baseline amount of running, the rats tested under the new schedule could achieve their baseline amount of drinking.

In the terminology developed by later investigators (Allison and Timberlake 1973), the old schedule deprived the rats of drinking, but the new schedule did not. The next chapter defines this <u>response deprivation condition</u> more precisely and examines its role in the individual's response to the behavioral constraints imposed by the contingency schedule.

NOTES

1. Contingency schedules may leave a variety of residual effects. For example, a behavior may lose some of its intrinsic attraction if we must perform it instrumentally for some contingent extrinsic reward. An anecdotal example is the professional athlete who claims to have enjoyed his sport until he started getting paid for his play. In a typical experimental example (Deci 1975), each person is asked to work on some puzzles; experimentals receive $1 for each of the four puzzles solved within a time limit, but controls do the same puzzles for no pay. Afterward, the experimenter says that the person need do no more puzzles and leaves the room on some pretext for an eight-minute period during which the person has free access to the puzzles and other activities. The measure of intrinsic motivation is the amount of time the person spends working the puzzles during the eight-minute free-time period. In one such experiment, unpaid controls averaged 208.4 seconds on the puzzles; paid experimentals, only 108.6 seconds. The conditions responsible for this effect are not understood, because there are too many experiments in which the contingent receipt of the extrinsic reward failed to alter the intrinsic attraction of the instrumental behavior (Arkes and Garske 1982, pp. 334-38). In one such experiment, the person performed each of two different tasks for the chance to perform the other task—an arrangement that should have decreased the intrinsic attraction of each task. Instead, intrinsic measures taken before and after the contingency phase revealed no significant change in the intrinsic attraction of either behavior (Podsakoff 1980). Sometimes the extrinsic reward seems to increase the intrinsic attraction of the instrumental behavior. In one such example (Allison 1976), thirsty rats pressed a lever for each contingent opportunity to drink and drank for the next chance to press the lever. Intrinsic measures were recorded before and after the contingency phase, in baseline sessions that offered the rat free access to the lever and the drinking tube. The baseline measures showed that the rats spent significantly more time pressing the lever after the contingency phase than before; there was no significant change

in time spent drinking. Thus, extrinsic reward may increase, decrease, or have no effect upon the intrinsic attraction of the instrumental behavior. At present there is no consensus on the true source
of these variations.

    2. These individual differences in time spent with freely avail-
able food were correlated with individual differences in instrumental
performance for food. Rats that spent a relatively large amount of
time with free food also ran relatively fast to a goal box baited with
food at the end of a straight runway and made relatively few errors in
learning which arm of a T-maze, left or right, contained food reward
at the end of the arm.

Chapter 3

Response Deprivation

SCHEDULE CONSTRAINTS

The kind of schedule discussed in Chapter 2 has a technical name, the fixed-ratio schedule. The distinguishing characteristic of a fixed-ratio schedule is the requirement of a fixed amount of instrumental responding, I, for each chance to perform the contingent response. Normally, such schedules also allow a fixed amount of contingent responding, C, each time the individual completes the instrumental requirement, I.

Pressed by final examinations, a student might attempt some self-modification of behavior: "I promise myself 10 minutes with a trashy magazine of my choice each time I accumulate 30 minutes of time reading this textbook; I swear on my honor to leave those magazines alone until I have done my 30 minutes of study." This is a fixed-ratio schedule—some would call it a cumulative time schedule—self-imposed, with $I = 30$ minutes of study, and $C = 10$ minutes of recreational reading. Experimental evidence suggests that children and adults can modify their behavior substantially by means of the self-imposed contingency schedule (Bandura 1969; Bandura and Perloff 1967).

If we let the schedule run for a constant duration, such as one hour per session, the total amount of responding in any particular session depends on the number of times the individual completes the instrumental requirement. Notice that the schedule itself can force no response from the individual; on the contrary, it leaves the individual complete freedom simply to ignore the lever, the food pellet, the spinach, the dessert, the textbook, the magazine, or the chance to make the running wheel go round. But it does set an upper limit on the amount of contingent responding the individual can do, relative to the amount of instrumental responding. Faithful adherence to the

17

schedule would permit no more than one-third of a minute of recreational reading per minute of study, as 10 minutes of recreational reading/30 minutes of study = one-third. In conjunction with the session duration, the schedule also places a limit on the total amount of responding the individual could achieve, even if the person devoted the entire session to the behaviors controlled by the schedule. In a four-hour session, the most heroic student could achieve no more than 180 minutes of study and 60 minutes of recreational reading. No doubt the actual totals would be considerably smaller, given the inevitable lapses of attention and the weary glances out the window.

The contingent behavior is usually something the individual would probably do without any outside coaxing. The instrumental behavior is usually one the individual would gladly desert in favor of the contingent behavior. For example, suppose we test a well-trained rat with a fixed-ratio schedule that requires $\underline{I}$ = 10 lever presses for each food pellet. Having just completed the tenth of the required lever presses, the hungry rat would leave the lever immediately, move to the food trough, eat the pellet, take a short break, and return to the lever. But the schedule itself forces no desertion of the lever, and no eating. The rat does not desert the lever in favor of the food because of the behavioral constraints imposed by the schedule; it does so because the hungry rat finds food more attractive than the lever.

The point merits further elaboration. Suppose we counted the total number of pellets actually eaten over the course of the session and the total number of lever presses. We would probably see close agreement between two ratios: the behavioral ratio, total pellets eaten/total presses; and the upper limit set by our schedule, 0.1 pellets/press (1 pellet/10 presses = 0.1 pellets/press). For example, the rat might have eaten 100 pellets and pressed the lever 1,000 times, a behavioral ratio of 100/1,000 = 0.1 pellets/press. But the schedule itself forces no such agreement. The schedule itself would not prevent the rat from pressing the lever 1,000 times, but eating only 1 of the 100 pellets earned—a behavioral ratio of only 0.001 pellets/press. But we can devise a schedule where behavioral constraints will guarantee close agreement between behavioral and schedule ratios. This is the reciprocal contingency schedule (Allison 1971).

In a reciprocal schedule, the individual must complete $\underline{I}$ units of behavior $\underline{i}$ for the chance to perform the other behavior, as usual; but, having gained that chance, the individual must complete $\underline{C}$ units of behavior $\underline{c}$ for another chance at behavior $\underline{i}$. For example, if we retract the lever upon the tenth press of the lever, and wait until the rat has finished eating the food pellet before presenting the lever once again, we have a reciprocal contingency schedule with $\underline{I}$ = 10 lever presses and $\underline{C}$ = 1 food pellet. By retracting the lever, we minimize any behavioral overshooting of the schedule requirement, $\underline{I}$ = 10 lever presses; by waiting for the rat to finish the pellet, we minimize any behavioral undershooting of the other requirement, C = 1 pellet. That is how the reciprocal schedule guarantees close agreement between our two ratios: the schedule ratio, C/I, and the behavioral ratio, the total amount of behavior c actually observed/total amount of behavior i actually observed.

Panel A in Figure 3.1 illustrates the behavioral constraints of a reciprocal schedule. Our hypothetical schedule requires I seconds of wheel-running for C seconds of drinking and C seconds of drinking for the next chance to run. We start the session with the wheel free to turn, but the water tube retracted. As soon as the rat accumulates

FIGURE 3.1

Behavioral Constraints of a Reciprocal Contingency Schedule

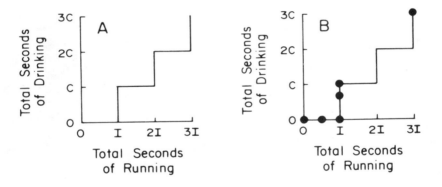

I seconds of running, we brake the wheel and present the water tube; as soon as it accumulates C seconds of drinking, we retract the tube and release the brake. The horizontal axis scales total running time; the vertical axis, total drinking time. The line that resembles a staircase in profile view shows the path the rat must follow during the course of the reciprocal contingency session.

The six points on the staircase line in panel B show a few of the many things the rat might actually do under the constraints of our schedule. Moving from left to right, the point in the lower left corner shows that the rat might stay at the origin (0, 0) throughout the entire session, neither running nor drinking. Second, the rat might perform only half of the I requirement, running for I/2 seconds and then quitting for the rest of the session, never gaining access to the tube.

Third, the rat might complete the requirement in full, I seconds of running, but ignore its chance to drink and spend the rest of the session doing something else, such as sleeping on the floor of the braked wheel. Fourth, the rat might drink only part of what it had earned, say two-thirds of C seconds, rather than the full C seconds. Fifth, the rat might drink for the full C seconds, then go to sleep on the floor of the unbraked wheel. Sixth, the rat might run and drink without pause throughout the entire session, for a total of $3C$ seconds of drinking and $3I$ seconds of running.

A nonreciprocal schedule would place many fewer constraints upon the rat's behavior. Suppose the experimenter cannot afford to equip the apparatus with all of the fancy bells and whistles: The wheel has no brake, and the apparatus lacks the electronic gadgetry one needs to record automatically the time spent drinking from the tube. The experimenter settles for a clock that cumulates running time, plus a clock-motor arrangement that presents the water tube after I seconds of running and retracts the tube C seconds later, whether the rat drinks or not.

If the experimenter hopes the rat will follow the staircase path defined by I and C, these hopes must come from something besides the constraints of the schedule. Figure 3.2 illustrates the behavioral constraints of this nonreciprocal schedule; the schedule keeps the rat on or below the staircase line, but denies little of the behavioral space below the staircase. Again, the points in Figure 3.2 show only a few of the many different things the rat might actually do in response to the constraints of this schedule. If the rat adheres to the staircase

FIGURE 3.2

Behavioral Constraints of a Nonreciprocal Contingency Schedule

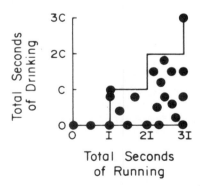

line, it probably does so for reasons other than the constraints imposed by the schedule. For example, imagine two rats whose small, cell-like home cages offer little opportunity for exercise. Which one would follow the staircase line more closely: the thirsty rat or the one whose home cage offers free access to water? No doubt the thirsty rat would follow the staircase line more closely, never ignoring the chance to drink water.

How does the individual learn about the constraints of a particular schedule? The attentive, credulous human can learn simply by hearing our description of the schedule. For example, "By pressing x on the computer's keyboard 50 times, you can make the computer display a line of poetry on the screen; you can make that line disappear by typing that exact line on the keyboard, after which another 50 x's will make the computer display the next line of the poem."

The rat can learn by experiencing directly the constraints of the schedule; that is, by actually performing the I units of behavior i and the C units of behavior c prescribed by the schedule. If we have reason to think that the rat might give up on either behavior too soon to experience the constraints of the schedule, we might start with relatively small values of I and C. We can gradually work up to larger values while holding their ratio constant: 2 seconds of i for 4 seconds of c in the first training session, 5 and 10 in the next session, 8 and 16 in the next.

Figure 3.3A shows the constraints of two reciprocal schedules with equal C/I ratios. The fine-toothed staircase has smaller verti-

FIGURE 3.3

Behavioral Constraints of Two Reciprocal Schedules with the Same
C/I Ratio but Different Values of C and I

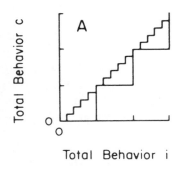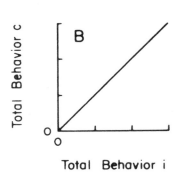

Total Behavior i   Total Behavior i

cal rises—$\underline{C}$—and horizontal runs—$\underline{I}$—than the coarse-toothed staircase, but the same slope as the other. The slope of the staircase function is the ratio rise over run, $\underline{C}/\underline{I}$. Notice that as we decrease $\underline{I}$ and $\underline{C}$ while holding $\underline{C}/\underline{I}$ constant, our staircase approaches a smooth, straight line with slope = $\underline{C}/\underline{I}$. To ease the tasks of drawing and understanding such figures, we will generally use straight lines like the one in Figure 3.3B. But keep in mind that the straight line representation is only a convenient, continuous approximation of the discontinuous path the individual actually follows over the course of the contingency session.

RESPONSE DEPRIVATION: AN ANTECEDENT CONDITION

Chapter 2 ended with a verbal definition of the response deprivation condition. To identify that condition, we start by measuring the paired baseline amounts of two behaviors, the totals observed when the individual can perform both behaviors without constraint. Next we impose certain constraints by establishing a contingency schedule. Mindful of these constraints, we now ask one hypothetical question about each of the two behaviors controlled by the schedule. Suppose the individual, performing under our schedule, were to perform only the paired baseline amount of behavior $\underline{i}$. How much of behavior $\underline{c}$ would that allow? If behavior $\underline{c}$ would surely fall short of its paired baseline amount, the schedule deprives the individual of behavior $\underline{c}$; otherwise, it does not. With the help of our graphic representation of schedule constraints, we can easily see whether a schedule does or does not deprive the individual of a particular behavior.

By way of illustration, suppose we put Wallace into ice cream paradise, a two-hour baseline session that offers free, unconstrained access to an unlimited supply of vanilla and strawberry cones. We observe that our growing lad eats five vanilla and ten strawberry cones. The unfilled circle in Figure 3.4 represents Wallace's basepoint, the number of vanilla and strawberry cones eaten under the paired baseline condition.

The next day, we switch Wallace to a reciprocal contingency schedule: We tell him that he must eat one vanilla cone for each chance to eat strawberry and two strawberry cones for another chance at vanilla. Line A in Figure 3.4 represents the constraints of this schedule.

One day later, we tell Wallace that we have changed our minds; today, he gets only one strawberry cone for each vanilla cone. Line B represents the constraints of our new schedule. Still later, we test him with a third schedule that allows five strawberry cones for each vanilla cone, a schedule represented by line C.

FIGURE 3.4

Behavioral Constraints of Three Reciprocal Schedules in Relation
to the Paired Basepoint

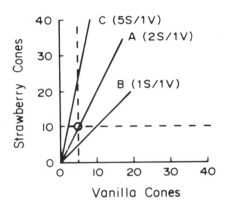

Ask yourself two questions about each of these three schedules.
First, does the schedule deprive Wallace of eating strawberry cones?
Second, does it deprive him of vanilla?

Notice that line A passes <u>through</u> the basepoint, five vanilla and
ten strawberry cones. If Wallace were to eat only the baseline number of vanilla cones—five—the schedule would allow the baseline number of strawberry cones, ten. Thus, the schedule represented by
Line A does not deprive Wallace of strawberry. Neither does it deprive him of vanilla: By eating only the baseline number of strawberry
cones, Wallace can eat the baseline number of vanilla cones.

Line B passes <u>beneath</u> the basepoint, and the schedule it represents thereby deprives Wallace of strawberry. If he were to eat only
five vanilla cones, the line B schedule would allow only five strawberry—five short of the baseline number, ten strawberry cones. But
it does not deprive him of vanilla: If he were to eat only ten strawberry, the schedule would allow ten vanilla cones—five more than the
baseline number.

Because line C passes <u>above</u> the basepoint, the line C schedule
deprives Wallace of vanilla, but not strawberry. If he ate only ten
strawberry cones the schedule would allow only two vanilla, three
short of the baseline number. If he ate only five vanilla cones the
schedule would allow 25 strawberry, well above his baseline consumption of strawberry cones.

It is easy to prove algebraically what Figure 3.4 demonstrates
geometrically: <u>Any particular schedule will deprive the individual of</u>

neither behavior, one behavior, or the other. No schedule can deprive the individual of both behaviors. If the line of schedule constraint passes through the basepoint, the schedule deprives the individual of neither behavior. If it passes beneath the basepoint, the schedule deprives the individual of the behavior scaled on the vertical axis, but not the behavior scaled on the horizontal axis. For reciprocal fixed-ratio schedules, if the constraint line passes above the basepoint the situation reverses—the schedule deprives the individual of the behavior scaled on the horizontal axis, but not the one scaled vertically. Geometric logic allows no other possibilities: The line of schedule constraint must pass through, beneath, or above the basepoint. [1]

The time has come to test your understanding of the response deprivation condition. Upon testing Wallace with schedule B, suppose we find that he responds to its constraints by eating ten vanilla and ten strawberry cones over the course of the two-hour contingency session. Does the schedule deprive him of strawberry?

Many readers will answer incorrectly. The correct answer is yes: Response deprivation is an antecedent condition whose presence or absence cannot be inferred from the individual's actual response to the schedule constraints. To say in advance whether a schedule deprives the individual of a behavior, we need only measure the basepoint, draw in a line that represents the behavioral constraints of the schedule we expect to enforce during the contingency phase of the experiment, and note its relation to the basepoint. Schedule B deprives Wallace of strawberry, regardless of his actual behavior during the contingency training phase; it does so because the constraint line passes beneath the basepoint. In the hypothetical example used in our test of comprehension, the schedule deprived Wallace of strawberry, facilitated vanilla eating (a behavioral effect of the schedule), and had no behavioral effect upon strawberry. Had he eaten only seven of each, we would say that the schedule facilitated the consumption of vanilla and suppressed strawberry.

Figure 3.5 presents a simple key to the vocabulary we shall use in describing the actual response to the constraints of a schedule. The broken lines through the basepoint divide the space into four quadrants. Should we find the individual in the upper right quadrant at the end of the contingency training session—for example, points 5 and 9— we say that the schedule facilitated both behaviors in relation to the basepoint, driving each one above its baseline level. Should the individual end in the lower left quadrant—for example, point 1—we say that the schedule suppressed both behaviors. In the lower right quadrant, the schedule facilitated behavior i and suppressed behavior c (for example, point 3). In the upper left, it facilitated c and suppressed i (for example, point 7). If the individual ends on the horizontal (vertical) broken line, the schedule had no effect on behavior c (i) in relation to the baseline total (points 4, 6, 2, and 8).

FIGURE 3.5

Possible Responses to the Behavioral Constraints of Two
Reciprocal Schedules

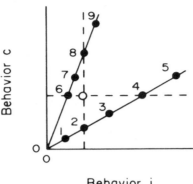

Readers who understand the analysis of the reciprocal fixed-
ratio schedule in terms of response deprivation should be able to gen-
eralize the analysis to any other kind of schedule. As a demonstration,
suppose we intend to test Wallace with nonreciprocal fixed-ratio schedules. Such schedules themselves may take various forms, but suppose
ours has the following specifications. Each time he finishes I vanilla
cones, we tell him two things. First, he may now eat as many as C
strawberry cones as his reward, and he can eat them any time he
wishes, now or later; those C cones will always be "on deposit" in
his "bank" of earned strawberry cones. Second, he may continue to
eat vanilla; indeed, he can eat as many extra vanilla cones as he
pleases.
    Under this nonreciprocal fixed-ratio arrangement, each of the
constraint lines in Figure 3.4 confines Wallace to the space on or below the line. Accordingly, the line B schedule deprives him of strawberry but not of vanilla, just as it did in the case of the reciprocal
schedule. And the line A schedule deprives him of neither, just as
it did in the case of the reciprocal schedule.
    But the line C schedule is a different matter. If Wallace were
to eat the baseline number of strawberry cones, the line C schedule
would allow him to eat the baseline number of vanilla cones, more
than that, or less than that. Thus, the nonreciprocal form of the line
C schedule does not deprive Wallace of vanilla, whereas the reciprocal form does deprive him of vanilla. In neither case does it deprive

him of strawberry. Thus, in their nonreciprocal form neither schedule A nor schedule C deprives Wallace of either behavior.

Toward the end of the next section we shall see how we could
use two line C schedules, one reciprocal and one nonreciprocal, to
test two alternative theories of the individual's response to schedule
constraints: probability-differential theory and response deprivation
theory.

BEHAVIORAL EFFECTS OF THE
RESPONSE DEPRIVATION CONDITION

It was Premack's two experiments on the run-to-drink contingency that first called attention to response deprivation as an antecedent condition, and its possible role in the organism's response to
the constraints of a schedule. Figure 3.6 presents a schematic representation of those two experiments. The location of the basepoint
represents the fact that drinking had a higher probability than running
in both experiments. Line A represents the schedule used in the earlier of the two experiments—a schedule that deprived the rats of
drinking and facilitated running. Line B represents the schedule used
later—one that did not deprive the rats of drinking and did not facilitate running.

Those two experiments suggested that response deprivation may
play an important role in the behavioral effects of a schedule but left

FIGURE 3.6

Schematic Representation of Premack's Two Experiments on the
Run-to-Drink Contingency

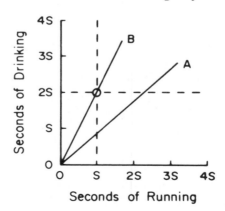

unclear the exact character of that role. The results would leave us free to conclude—as Premack himself suggested—that the earlier experiment facilitated running because of two antecedent conditions. First, drinking was more probable than running. Second, the schedule deprived the rats of drinking. In other words, maybe each of those two antecedent conditions is necessary; if our experiment lacks either one, the schedule will not facilitate running. The earlier experiment happened to include both conditions, and the later experiment happened to lack the response deprivation condition; but the experiment may fail in the absence of either antecedent, the probability-differential condition or the response deprivation condition.

Other theorists hit upon a simpler possibility (Eisenberger, Karpman, and Trattner 1967). Perhaps the earlier schedule facilitated running, and the later one did not, simply because the earlier schedule deprived the rats of drinking, and the later one did not. Although drinking was more probable than running in both experiments, maybe the probability-differential condition had nothing to do with the facilitation of running.

We might test the importance of the probability-differential condition by examining what happens when we remove that condition. Figure 3.7 illustrates one way of removing it. Because the line that represents the schedule passes beneath the basepoint, the schedule deprives the individual of the behavior scaled on the vertical axis. But that behavior is less probable than the other. Now, if the prob-

FIGURE 3.7

Facilitation Test of the Relative Importance of Two Conditions, Probability-Differential and Response Deprivation

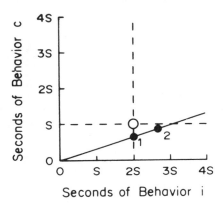

ability-differential condition is necessary, a low-probability response cannot facilitate a high-probability response, so the schedule represented in Figure 3.7 should not facilitate the high-probability behavior scaled on the horizontal axis. In other words, if the probability-differential condition is necessary, the individual should perform behavior i for no more than 2S seconds, the limit marked by point 1 in Figure 3.7. But if the response deprivation condition is sufficient, a schedule that deprives the individual of a low-probability behavior should indeed facilitate the high-probability behavior. In other words, if response deprivation is sufficient, the individual should perform behavior i for more than 2S seconds, as illustrated by point 2 in Figure 3.7.

The first experimental test of these two contrasting predictions appeared in 1967. Eisenberger, Karpman, and Trattner tested 25 high school students with an apparatus that allowed free access to a lever and a knob in a paired baseline session. A total of 12 of the 25 spent more time manipulating the knob than the lever; their 12 knob times ranged from 23 to 132 seconds and had a mean of 70; their 12 lever times ranged from 6 to 85 seconds and had a mean of 33. The schedule used in the subsequent contingency session deprived each of these 12 students of the low-probability behavior (lever) and, indeed, facilitated the high-probability behavior (knob). These results suggest that the probability-differential condition is not necessary after all: A schedule that deprives the individual of a low-probability response may facilitate the high-probability response, in the manner illustrated by point 2 in Figure 3.7.

If the results seem counterintuitive at first glance, bear in mind that the less probable behavior is not necessarily unattractive. If the person performs the less probable behavior at all during the paired baseline session, it probably holds some intrinsic attraction.

But what about the earlier experiments that seemed to confirm the importance of the probability-differential condition? According to Eisenberger and his colleagues, the schedules used in those earlier experiments facilitated the low-probability response simply because they happened to deprive the individual of the high-probability response. If a schedule is to facilitate a behavior, it is necessary and sufficient that the schedule deprive the individual of the other behavior. The probability-differential condition is neither necessary nor sufficient.

To understand the impact of the results reported by Eisenberger and his colleagues, consider their practical implications for the control of behavior. If we wish to see more of a particular behavior, we need not search for some other behavior more probable than the one we hope to facilitate. If the schedule deprives him of strawberry, Wallace will eat more vanilla; it does not matter whether strawberry has a higher baseline probability than vanilla, a lower probability, or the same probability as vanilla. (But if he never eats strawberry, can we devise a schedule that deprives him of strawberry?)[2] Is it hard to measure the time spent eating, as the probability-differential approach requires us to do? How should we define eating; do we include the time spent swallowing, the time spent savoring the after-taste?[3] No matter: To identify the response deprivation condition, we need not measure the time spent eating; we can use any unit of measurement that happens to be convenient, such as the sheer number of cones consumed. Moreover, the vertical and horizontal axes can use entirely different units, such as volumetric intake on the vertical axis, and number of lever presses on the horizontal axis. If the schedule line passes beneath our measured basepoint, the schedule deprives the individual of drinking; otherwise, it does not. Thus, the response deprivation approach vastly expands the practical possibilities for the control of behavior by means of contingency schedules. But is it more nearly correct than an approach based on probability-differential theory?

Many subsequent experiments have confirmed the irrelevance of the probability-differential condition. Much of this work follows the tactic illustrated by Figure 3.7. The schedule deprives the individual of the low-probability behavior, but appears to facilitate the high-probability behavior. The earliest confirmation appeared in 1973, in a series of experiments that offered rats two saccharin solutions with different concentrations. In the paired baseline condition, the rats spent more time drinking the sweeter of the two solutions. Contingency schedules that deprived the rats of the other solution facilitated their drinking of the sweeter solution (Allison and Timberlake 1973, 1974).

In pondering those particular results, one may wonder whether the contingency schedule itself made any essential contribution to the observed increase in the high-probability response. If Wallace eats ten strawberry and five vanilla cones in the paired baseline condition, maybe he would eat more than ten strawberry in a single baseline condition that offers an unlimited supply of strawberry, but no vanilla, cones. If strawberry were partly substitutable for vanilla, Wallace might eat more strawberry in the single baseline condition than in the paired baseline condition. We would hesitate to call that sort of increase a facilitation effect, because it is not a response to the constraints of a contingency schedule. But the rat study excluded that possibility by means of a control experiment that compared the paired baseline level of each behavior with its single baseline level. The control experiment revealed no more drinking of the sweeter solution under the single baseline condition than the paired baseline condition. Thus, it seems that the contingency schedule made a significant contribution to the observed increase in the high-probability response relative to the paired baseline level. Another experiment in the same series confirmed the role of response deprivation as a necessary condition; there, a schedule that did not deprive the rats of the low-probability response failed to facilitate the high-probability response.

A brief account of three additional studies will convey some notion of the variety of experiments that have demonstrated the irrelevance of the probability-differential condition. In the first study (Mazur 1975) the paired baseline condition allowed rats to drink sucrose solution—sugar water—or run in the activity wheel. The contingency schedule deprived the rats of running—the low-probability response—and facilitated drinking, the high-probability response.

The second study (Klajner 1975) offered adult humans the opportunity to play with a lever or a spring-loaded plunger. Like Premack's Chicko, the humans spent more time with the lever than the plunger in the paired baseline condition. The contingency schedule deprived them of the low-probability plunger response and facilitated the high-probability lever response. (I presume that Premack would have seen similar results with Chicko had his schedule deprived Chicko of the low-probability plunger response.)

The third study (Konarski, Johnson, Crowell, and Whitman 1980) may win the reader's prize for counterintuitive results. It offered grade school children the chance to color in their coloring books or work simple mathematical problems. Under the paired baseline condition, coloring was more probable than mathematics. The contingency schedule deprived the children of mathematics and facilitated coloring. Various control conditions showed that it was indeed the contingent mathematics reward that was responsible for the increase in coloring relative to the paired baseline level.

We can also compare the two approaches in terms of their contrasting predictions for the reversibility phenomenon defined in Chapter 2. According to probability-differential theory, behavior $\underline{B}$ will facilitate behavior $\underline{A}$ if $\underline{B}$ is more probable than $\underline{A}$; but if $\underline{A}$ is more probable than $\underline{B}$, $\underline{A}$ will facilitate $\underline{B}$. In contrast, the response deprivation hypothesis implies that we should be able to demonstrate reversibility without reversing the baseline probabilities—indeed, without changing them at all.

Figure 3.8 illustrates this technique. Line 1 represents a reciprocal contingency schedule that deprives the individual of behavior $\underline{B}$ and should therefore facilitate behavior $\underline{A}$, as illustrated by point 1. Line 2 represents another reciprocal schedule, one that deprives the individual of $\underline{A}$ and should therefore facilitate $\underline{B}$, as illustrated by point 2. Thus, the response deprivation hypothesis implies that we should be able to demonstrate reversibility merely by changing the requirements of the reciprocal contingency schedule. Once again, the response deprivation approach seems the more flexible and con-

FIGURE 3.8

Reversibility Test of the Relative Importance of Two Conditions,
Probability-Differential and Response Deprivation

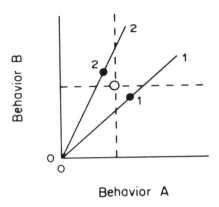

The first experiment designed in the pattern of Figure 3.8 appeared in 1974. Timberlake and Allison (1974) tested several rats in a running wheel equipped with a brake and a retractable drinking tube filled with a saccharin solution. A reciprocal schedule that deprived the rats of drinking facilitated running; another reciprocal schedule deprived the same rats of running and facilitated drinking. A few years later, Wozny (1979) reported similar results: Schedules that deprived the rats of drinking plain water generally facilitated running, and schedules that deprived them of running generally facilitated drinking. Wozny included various control conditions that showed that the facilitation effects proceeded from the constraints of the reciprocal contingency schedules. Noncontingent constraints on performance of either response had little or no effect upon performance of the other response.

venient. We can facilitate either behavior we choose by selecting the appropriate schedule requirements; we need not change the person's baseline probabilities, and we need not sort individuals in terms of their characteristic baseline probabilities.

Experiments with humans have demonstrated the same kind of reversibility. Heth and Warren (1978) tested college students with an apparatus that offered two particular kinds of sensory stimulation, visual and auditory. By pressing one button the person could see a brief visual display, a matrix of varicolored lights flashing in random sequence. By pressing another button, the person could listen to a segment of a musical recording played through stereophonic headphones. Some persons were tested with a reciprocal contingency schedule that deprived them of seeing, and the schedule facilitated listening. Others were tested with a schedule that deprived them of listening, and the schedule facilitated seeing.

Podsakoff (1980, 1982) recorded similar results with college students who could pull a trigger atop a control stick from a World War II fighter plane or perform a pursuit rotor task. The pursuit rotor task involves a metal disk on the perimeter of a turntable that rotates at a constant speed, and a metal pointer mounted with a swivel joint at the end of a long wand. The task is to follow the rotating disk with the floppy metal pointer, a fairly challenging job. Reciprocal schedules that deprived the person of "pursuit" facilitated "pull"; schedules that deprived the person of "pull" facilitated "pursuit."

Konarski, Crowell, Johnson, and Whitman (1982), dealing with mathematics and reading tasks performed by educable but mentally retarded children, have also demonstrated this kind of reversibility. Regardless of the baseline probabilities, each schedule facilitated the target behavior if, and only if, it deprived the child of the other behavior.

What about the other kind of reversibility, the kind that comes about through a reversal of the baseline probabilities? Figure 3.9 shows how the response deprivation hypothesis can account for that kind of reversibility as well. In the hypothetical example of Figure 3.9, drinking is more probable than running under condition x, but running is more probable than drinking under condition y. Under

FIGURE 3.9

Reversibility through Changes in the Baseline Probabilities
Explained in Terms of Response Deprivation

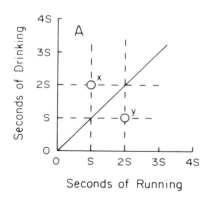
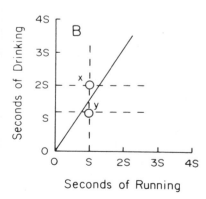

condition x the reciprocal contingency schedule deprives the rats of drinking and should therefore facilitate running; under condition y the schedule deprives them of running and should therefore facilitate drinking. Figure 3.9B shows that we need not go so far as to reverse the baseline probabilities: Although drinking is more probable under both conditions, the schedule still deprives the rats of drinking under condition x but of running under condition y.

This section opened with Premack's suggestion that two antecedent conditions are necessary and sufficient for the facilitation of a response: The other response must be more probable, and the schedule must deprive the individual of the more probable response. The experiments reviewed in this section contradict that claim, suggesting that the probability-differential condition is neither necessary nor sufficient. To test your understanding of their bearing on the two-antecedent hypothesis, Figure 3.10 repeats the design of an experiment that attempts to demonstrate reversibility by changing the requirements of the reciprocal contingency schedule. Ask yourself how the individual should respond to the constraints of each schedule if both antecedents were necessary.

If both were necessary, schedule x should facilitate behavior A, but not behavior B. Why? Because B is more probable than A, and schedule x deprives the individual of B, but not of A. Points 1 and 2 illustrate two different results that would confirm this prediction. The prediction would be confirmed by any point that fell to the right of the vertical broken line and on or below the horizontal broken line. No

FIGURE 3.10

Facilitation Test of the Necessity of Two Antecedent Conditions, Probability-Differential and Response Deprivation

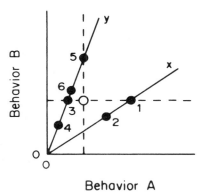

Behavior A

other result would confirm the prediction. Notice that the response deprivation hypothesis and the two-antecedent hypothesis make exactly the same predictions for schedule x. It is schedule y that distinguishes the two hypotheses.

If both antecedents were necessary, schedule y should fail to facilitate either behavior. It cannot facilitate B, because B is more probable than A. It cannot facilitate A, because the schedule does not deprive the individual of B. The prediction would be confirmed by any point that fell on or below the horizontal line and on or left of the vertical line. Points 3 and 4 illustrate two such results; no other result would confirm the prediction.

In contrast, the response deprivation hypothesis predicts that schedule y will facilitate B but not A: Schedule y deprives the individual of A, but not of B. This contrasting prediction would be supported by any point that lay above the horizontal line and on or to the left of the vertical line, as illustrated by points 5 and 6. No other result would confirm the prediction.

As one further test, suppose schedule y were a nonreciprocal schedule rather than a reciprocal schedule. Recall that a nonreciprocal schedule would allow the individual to follow practically any path on or below line y. Would the nonreciprocal schedule y deprive the individual of either behavior? The correct answer is no, because the nonreciprocal schedule would allow the individual to follow a path through or near the basepoint. Accordingly, the nonreciprocal schedule y should not facilitate behavior B, nor should it facilitate behavior A. I know of no experiment that has tested those predictions, but it could prove most informative: In the unlikely event that the probability-differential condition is necessary and sufficient, the experiment should facilitate behavior A, but not behavior B.

AVERSIVE EVENTS

How much would you pay to be free of polluted air, garbage, cans and bottles littering the highway, excessive noise or silence, excessive heat or cold, excessive moisture or dryness? Consider the popularity of environmental-protection laws and the human's response to sensory deprivation.[4] Consider the sales of air conditioners, umbrellas, heaters, and humidifiers. Individuals may place some value on the absence of certain events or conditions; indeed, the rat may press a lever for food because the food frees it from hunger. How can we understand such phenomena in terms of response deprivation?

Imagine a box with wooden walls and a floor made of steel rods connected to a source of electric shock. One of the wooden walls is equipped with two levers side by side. We put a rat inside the box, and start the paired baseline session by turning on the shock. The rat can rid itself of shock for exactly as long as it holds lever c down; the other one, lever i, is totally ineffective. Its paired baseline behavior suggests that the rat places some value on shock-free time, because it spends nearly all of the session holding lever c down.

Next we establish a contingency schedule that deprives the rat of shock-free time. In the contingency session, shock-free time is contingent on instrumental holding of lever i: Lever c is now ineffective unless the rat first holds lever i. Holding lever i in the presence of foot-shock "primes" lever c; having held lever i, the rat can then move over to lever c and secure some shock-free time by holding it down. After it has exhausted that shock-free time, the rat must return to lever i and hold it instrumentally for some additional shock-free time on lever c.

We select the schedule requirements so as to guarantee that the rat cannot secure its baseline amount of shock-free responding by holding lever i no more than it did in the paired baseline session. Our schedule thus deprives the rat of shock-free responding. We find that the rat responds to the constraints of our schedule by holding lever i much longer than it did in the baseline session. Thus, a schedule that deprives the rat of the shock-free response facilitates the other response (Timberlake and Allison 1974).

In principle, aversive events or conditions are the same as any others. The key to this application of the response deprivation approach is to link a specific behavior to the absence of the event or condition we presume to be aversive.

HOW MUCH RESPONSE DEPRIVATION?

Some schedules satisfy the response deprivation condition, and others do not; of those that do, some do it more than others. Figure 3.11 illustrates these quantitative variations in response deprivation.

Reciprocal schedule x does not deprive the rat of behavior B: If the rat performs the paired baseline amount of behavior A, it must also perform its paired baseline amount of behavior B. Letting RD_B signify the amount by which the schedule deprives the rat of behavior B, $RD_B = 0$ for that particular schedule.

Under schedule y, baseline performance of A would leave the rat short of its baseline amount of B. Figure 3.11 shows y' as the measure of this shortfall. For schedule y, $RD_B = y'$, appreciably greater than 0. Schedule z would involve a still greater shortfall and therefore more response deprivation, $RD_B = z'$.

Within limits, schedules that involve a relatively large amount of response deprivation generally produce relatively large facilitation

FIGURE 3.11

Quantitative Variations in Response Deprivation

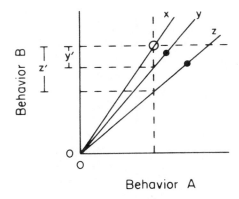

effects (Timberlake and Allison 1974), an empirical relation illustrated by the two points on lines y and z. For example, schedules
that deprived the rat of a relatively large amount of shock-free responding produced a relatively large amount of lever i holding. A
later chapter discusses possible reasons for this relation and reasons
for its limits.

Two schedules may involve different requirements, but the same
amount of response deprivation. To show why, we return to the staircase representation of the behavioral constraints imposed by a fixed-
ratio schedule. The fine-toothed x-function in Figure 3.12 has smaller
runs and rises than the coarse-toothed y-function, but both functions
have the same rise/run ratio. And the two schedules they represent
impose equal amounts of response deprivation: $RD_B = x' = y'$.

Schedules like x and y in Figure 3.12, which involve equal
amounts of response deprivation, generally produce equal facilitation
effects (Allison and Timberlake 1973, 1974), as illustrated by the point
in the lower right quadrant. For example, a schedule that requires
100 instrumental licks of the sweeter saccharin solution for 10 contingent licks of the other saccharin solution produces about the same lick
totals as schedules that require 200 for 20, 300 for 30, or 400 for 40.
Under each of these four different schedules, the rats total about 1,000
licks at the sweeter solution, 100 at the other. A later chapter describes some exceptions to this rule and possible reasons for those
exceptions.

FIGURE 3.12

Different Schedule Requirements but Equal Amounts of Response
Deprivation

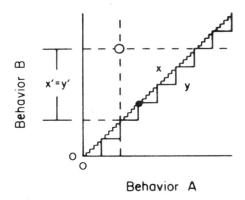

IMPLICATIONS FOR THE
REINFORCEMENT CONCEPT

In describing the typical behavioral effects of response deprivation, I have studiously avoided the language of response reinforcement.
A schedule that deprives the individual of behavior $\underline{B}$ "facilitates" behavior $\underline{A}$—a theoretically neutral term that signifies a rise in $\underline{A}$ above
its paired baseline level, and nothing more than that. I do not say that
the schedule "reinforced" $\underline{A}$—a term laden with connotations about the
theoretical process responsible for the rise in $\underline{A}$, a response-strengthening process.

My avoidance of "reinforcement" reflects something more than
academic fastidiousness. The theories that stem from Premack's
work make the reinforcement concept unnecessary in some cases, untenable in all other cases. Figure 3.13 illustrates the logic behind
this conclusion.

The box in the figure represents an exhaustive set of possibilities; the dividing line partitions the set into two mutually exclusive
subsets. The top line in the box represents an antecedent condition,
response deprivation. It shows again what we have already seen, that
any particular schedule either does (left side) or does not (right side)
deprive the individual of behavior $\underline{B}$.

The middle line refers to the effect of the antecedent condition.
If the response deprivation hypothesis is correct, the schedule will

FIGURE 3.13

Implications for the Concept of Response Reinforcement

	$RD_B > 0$	$RD_B = 0$
Antecedent Condition:		
Effect Upon Behavior A:	Facilitation	No Facilitation
Status of Reinforcement Concept:	Unnecessary	Untenable

facilitate behavior A if it deprives the individual of B (left side); otherwise, it will not (right side).

The bottom line shows the logical implications for the concept of reinforcement. Should the schedule prove to facilitate behavior A, the concept of reinforcement is unnecessary. Why? Because we can predict and explain the facilitation effect in terms of antecedent response deprivation. Should the schedule fail to facilitate A, the concept of reinforcement is untenable: Because the evidence reveals no rise in A above its paired baseline level, the evidence supports no claim that B reinforced A, or that the schedule reinforced A.

If we place no value on parsimony—explanation by means of the smallest number of assumptions—we may still interpret facilitation as a reinforcement effect, but the evidence itself requires no such claim: The language of reinforcement is totally absent from the definition of response deprivation. Notice, too, that the response deprivation hypothesis predicts and explains both of the effects shown in the box. We thereby finesse the problem of explaining why contingent behavior B does and does not have the power to strengthen instrumental behavior A automatically—a dilemma for the classic view of a reinforcing agent.

Because the classic view makes no distinction between learning and performance, it makes no allowance for the possibility that the individual may still have learned the contingent relation between A and B under a schedule that failed to facilitate A. The response deprivation hypothesis relates to performance, not learning; it assumes that the individual somehow learns the terms of the schedule by experiencing the constraints of the schedule and leaves the question of how learning occurs to another body of theory, learning theory. In the felicitous words of a distinguished colleague, "Animals don't learn responses; they learn the facts."[5] Those words are reminiscent of another classic concept that many contemporary psychologists seem to have forgotten, the concept of latent learning (better called latent performance). In the original demonstration of latent learning (Blodgett 1929), hungry rats suddenly took a fast, direct route to the food-baited goal box at the end of a complex maze after several slow, meandering strolls to the unbaited goal—as if they had already learned the layout of the maze but failed to act on their knowledge until motivated to do so by the sudden prospect of food at the end of the maze.

Is the learning assumption plausible? Perhaps this question is best answered by another question: How can one prove that the individual did not learn the contingent relation between $\underline{A}$ and $\underline{B}$? A failure to act as if one had learned something can easily mislead the outside observer. Blodgett's rats acted as if they had learned little or nothing until he baited the goal box with food; but, on the very next run, they behaved most knowledgeably.

Adorned by no distinction between learning and performance, the stark connectionist notion of a backward-acting agent, adding strength automatically to the instrumental response, faces many other difficulties—enough to make one wonder how it still enthralls so many students of psychology. Mature psychologists, imprinted on the concept during a critical period of their graduate training, may have some excuse—more so than the typical undergraduate I encounter, who has the advantage of less formal training but comes to my classroom equally enthralled. I give each of my classes the following test, with the same result each time.

Suppose we train our thirsty rat to press a lever for water. We start each training session by presenting the lever alone. In each one-hour session the rat presses the lever instrumentally for the contingent chance to drink. Over some 20 consecutive training sessions we observe several hundred instances of the following sequence: The rat presses the lever; the lever retracts, and the water tube appears simultaneously; the rat immediately leaves the lever and drinks; the tube retracts, and the lever reappears simultaneously; after a brief pause, the rat presses and drinks once again. Recall what you learned in introductory psychology: For the thirsty rat, drinking acts as a reinforcer of the preceding response. Then why did our schedule facilitate the lever-pressing response, driving it far above the paired baseline level measured beforehand? The typical answer: Because the contingent drinking strengthened the instrumental lever-pressing response. Drinking is a reinforcer.

Our twenty-first session returns the rat to the original paired baseline condition. We start the session by presenting lever and water tube simultaneously. If training has added strength to the lever-pressing response, how should the rat behave at the start of our posttraining baseline session? The typical answer: The rat should first press the lever.

What actually happens is quite different (Allison 1976). The rat typically starts the session by darting to the water tube; after a few thousand licks, almost without pause, the rat deserts the tube, grooms, explores, goes to the lever, and presses it several times—generally more than it did in the original paired baseline session. After several hundred more licks the rat may repeat the same sequence: groom, explore, then visit the lever for several additional presses. After a little reflection, the class generally agrees that although the session total may leave the impression that training strengthened lever pressing, the impression is mistaken; the behavioral sequence that generates the total belies the strengthening notion.

Analogous behavior in a human would seem sensible enough: If the boy sees that the dessert is suddenly free for the asking, why eat the spinach? He may wonder what would happen if he did eat the spinach, but how many of us would indulge that curiosity before eating the dessert?

Similarly, the thirsty rat may indulge its curiosity about the current function of the lever, but not until it has taken advantage of an unexpected windfall, several thousand licks at the free water tube. The discovery does not take long: Over the course of a few more paired baseline sessions, its total lever pressing gradually returns to the original baseline level. Thus, a typical "extinction" curve may not reflect the gradual weakening of a response through the omission of the reinforcer that strengthened it, but rather, an active learning process, learning the rules of the new game. It is well known that animals become more adept at recognizing the new rules as they gain more experience with the training-extinction-training-extinction sequence (Mackintosh 1974, pp. 441-42).

Because many of the students who have learned that water is a reinforcer know that saccharin is too, they can easily predict the results of another experiment (Allison and Timberlake 1975). Suppose we conduct a series of paired baseline trials, one trial per day, over 18 consecutive days. Each baseline trial starts with the simultaneous presentation of two metal tubes, side by side, one empty and the other filled with saccharin solution. We retract the empty tube as soon as the rat makes one lick at it—1 E-lick—and we retract the saccharin tube as soon as the rat makes 100 S-licks. We place no constraint on the order in which the rat completes the two response requirements, 1 E-lick and 100 S-licks; each trial ends with the retraction of the second tube, whether it be the empty or the saccharin tube.

Each baseline trial allows the rat to display one of several behavioral patterns. The two that actually occur most frequently, on nearly 90 percent of the trials, are the ES pattern—1 E-lick followed by 100 S-licks—and the SE pattern, 100 S-licks followed by 1 E-lick. Reasonably enough, the SE pattern occurs about twice as often as the ES pattern, 61 percent versus 28 percent. (We rarely see a third kind of pattern, SES, where the rat makes one or more S-licks, then the E-lick, and finally the rest of the S-licks.)

Which of these two patterns should the rat be more likely to repeat on the very next trial? If we suppose that 100 S-licks are more reinforcing than 1 E-lick, the answer follows immediately. In the ES pattern, the S-lick reinforcer should operate on the preceding E-lick, raising its strength. It should gain more strength than the S-licks would gain from the SE pattern. Accordingly, the rat should be more likely to repeat the ES pattern than the SE pattern.

But the results contradict that prediction. The rats actually show little inclination to repeat the ES pattern, shifting instead to some other pattern on the very next trial, a shift that happens about 74 percent of the time. They are much more likely to repeat the SE pattern, shifting to some other pattern only about 32 percent of the time.

Maybe the ES pattern occurred too rarely to cause any significant strengthening of the E-lick. To test that possibility, we switch the rats to a contingency training schedule. Each contingency training trial starts with the presentation of the empty tube alone; upon 1 E-lick the empty tube retracts and the saccharin tube appears, retracting in turn and ending the trial upon the hundredth S-lick. We conduct 27 of these ES training trials, 1 trial per day: On 27 consecutive occasions the rat performs 1 E-lick, moves immediately to the saccharin tube and performs 100 S-licks. The rat's behavior during the training phase gives us some reason to believe that the ES pattern enforced on each trial has truly strengthened the instrumental E-lick: The rat completes the E-lick much faster now than it did in the paired baseline phase, one form of the facilitation effect.

We probe for further evidence of reinforcement by returning the rat to the original paired baseline condition, expecting to find the ES baseline pattern more popular now than before. Instead, we find the ES baseline pattern no more popular now than before; if anything, it is a little less popular now.

I could cite many additional experiments, with humans as well as animals, where the behavioral pattern enforced and "reinforced" over a prolonged period of training disappeared as soon as the constraints of the schedule were lifted (Ayllon and Azrin 1965; Baer 1962; Holstein and Hundt 1965; Wasik 1968). What about the gradual improvement in instrumental performance as training proceeds? Rather than a gradual strengthening of the instrumental response as the effects of reinforcement accumulate, it may signify a gradual learning of the rules of the contingency game. Animals must generally learn these rules by experiencing the schedule; humans may learn more efficiently by listening to instructions. For example, if we tell the human beforehand that the schedule will require 180 key presses to escape electric shock to the other hand, we can actually eliminate the characteristic learning curve: The person will complete the 180 presses on the very first trial as quickly as on any subsequent trial (Dreyer and Renner 1971).

Other work with humans has shown that one may learn a response that was never "reinforced" just as well as another response that was frequently "reinforced." If we are trying to teach the person that some arbitrary symbol is worth a certain amount of reward, we do just as well by merely telling the person so as we do by actually giving the person that amount as a tangible reward for guessing it correctly (Estes 1969).

Finally, the logic of reinforcement and punishment favors prompt application of reinforcer or punisher to the response we hope to strengthen or weaken; but humans sometimes do much better when the reinforcer or punisher comes long after the response. Buchwald (1969) has reported several examples. In a typical experiment, the person is shown a list of several "stimulus" words, one word at a time. Each stimulus word has a correct response, either the digit 3 or the digit 5, and the person's job is to guess which digit goes with each word. In the immediate outcome condition the experimenter says "right" or "wrong" immediately after each of the person's guesses. This training trial is followed by a test trial in which the experimenter presents each stimulus word again, and the person attempts again to make the correct response to each word. The logic of reinforcement and punishment would lead us to expect a greater tendency to repeat responses the experimenter called "right" on the training trial than responses the experimenter called "wrong." Indeed, the typical person repeated about 53 percent of the responses called "right" and only 46 percent of those called "wrong."

During the training trial for the delayed outcome condition, the experimenter remains silent after each of the person's guesses. But during the test trial, the experimenter presents each stimulus word and says simultaneously whether the person's previous response to that word was "right" or "wrong." Thus, the outcomes are delayed rather than immediate. Despite the delay, the typical person still repeated a greater percentage of "right" responses than "wrong." Moreover, the delayed "right" produced even more response repetition than the immediate "right" (70 percent versus 53 percent), and delayed "wrong" produced even less response repetition than immediate "wrong" (32 percent versus 46 percent).

Buchwald notes that to perform correctly on the test trial under the immediate condition, the person must recall correctly two pieces of information from the training trial: the person's response to the test word ("3" or "5") and the immediate outcome of that response ("right" or "wrong"). In the delayed condition, recall of the outcome plays no role in performance; to perform correctly, all the person need recall is the previous response to the test word. Thus, the logic of the reinforcement-punishment model favors prompt application of "right" or "wrong," but Buchwald's results are unsympathetic to that model. They are more sympathetic to a problem-solving model that attends to the storage and processing of pertinent information.

Reinforcement, where is thy strength?[6]

RESISTING BEHAVIOR CONTROL

It seems that prolonged training under a press-for-water contingency schedule fails to convert the rat into a lever-pressing robot, insensible of any change in the rules of the game. Our conclusion may lead some readers to wonder about the behavior observed while the schedule remains in force. Perhaps a particular contingency schedule can alter the behavior of an acquiescent person but fail against a more rebellious type.

The implicit question has no definitive answer at present. But the evidence suggests that it would be a serious mistake to underestimate the schedule's ability to influence our behavior and overestimate our ability to resist its influence.

Bernstein (1973; Bernstein and Ebbesen 1978) paid three adults to live in his laboratory individually 24 hours per day. In three separate tests a 19-year-old female undergraduate, a 39-year-old housewife, and an unemployed male construction worker, age 26, lived there for 21, 34, and 21 consecutive days, respectively. The large basement room, 20 feet by 30 feet, offered many of the amenities of an ordinary apartment—tables; chairs; couch; bed; refrigerator; reading matter; stereo tape system; utensils for cooking, eating, and drinking; and a bathroom with shower a few steps down the hallway. The observer viewed the person from an adjoining room equipped with a one-way mirror/window, various recording devices, and a two-way intercommunication system. After recording the paired baseline levels of various everyday behaviors of the person's choice, Bernstein studied the response to contingency schedules that deprived the person of one of the two behaviors.

Figure 3.14 shows a typical result. Under the paired baseline condition, with 1,200 minutes in each daily observation session, the person had free access to two activities: sewing—the more probable behavior—and reading Scientific American magazines, the less probable behavior. The subsequent schedule deprived the person of sewing. Its constraints are represented by the line sloping upward from

FIGURE 3.14

Facilitation of Reading and Suppression of Sewing by a Schedule
That Deprived the Person of Sewing

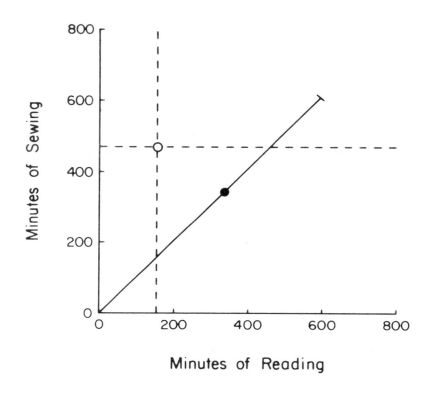

Minutes of Reading

the origin; the upper end of the line shows the maximum amount of
each behavior the person could achieve by devoting the entire contingency session, also 1,200 minutes long, to the two behaviors controlled
by the schedule.

Bernstein took some care to make sure that the person understood the rules of the contingency schedule: If you want to sew, you
must read instrumentally, but the choice is entirely yours—you must
decide for yourself whether to read or not, and the pay you receive
for your service in this experiment does not depend in any way upon
your response to any schedule, as long as you obey the rules of the
schedule: A certain amount of sewing is contingent upon a certain
amount of instrumental reading. Bernstein signaled the availability
of sewing by means of a light: The light went on when the person had

completed the required amount of reading, off when the person had completed the contingent allotment of sewing.

The point on the line of constraint shows the person's response to the schedule. This schedule, which deprived the person of sewing, had two effects: It facilitated reading and suppressed sewing. Because sewing was more probable than reading, we cannot pinpoint the antecedent condition responsible for the facilitation effect: response deprivation, probability-differential, or both.

Figure 3.15 shows another typical result, this time with 900-minute sessions. There the schedule deprived the person of a composite behavior, sewing or knitting. Again the schedule had two effects: It facilitated the less probable behavior—studying Russian—and suppressed the more probable behavior, sewing or knitting.

Try to imagine yourself as a participant in Bernstein's experiment. Why should a schedule that deprives you of sewing or knitting induce you to do more than your normal, baseline amount of reading or studying? Surely you can live without sewing or knitting; biological survival requires neither. You could, of course, choose to defy the

FIGURE 3.15

Facilitation of Studying and Suppression of Sewing or Knitting by a Schedule That Deprived the Person of Sewing or Knitting

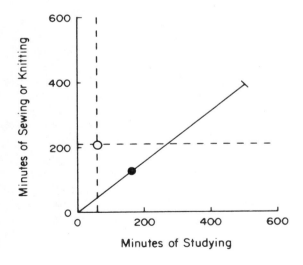

schedule in any number of ways; it should be easy enough to read or study at or below the paired baseline level of that behavior.

At the end of the experiment, Bernstein interviewed each one to see whether the person had made any conscious effort to resist the influence of the contingency schedules. Did the schedules exert their effects despite conscious efforts to the contrary? The interviews revealed that each person had tried to resist the schedule by not performing the instrumental response. One said that she objected to the constraints imposed by the schedule, preferring freedom of choice. Another said that she tried to show that she could resist: On one occasion she earned, but deliberately ignored, the chance to sew; after 11 hours of no sewing, she finally sewed for the number of minutes she had earned and immediately returned to the instrumental behavior. According to her interview, the prospect of further life without sewing was worse than the feeling of giving in to the schedule. The male reported that one schedule left him so furious that Bernstein would have received a punch in the mouth if he had happened to enter the room that day. Yet, their daily journals and their interviews showed that they found the experiment neither particularly stressful nor pleasant.

On Bernstein's evidence, the contingency schedule may alter our behavior despite conscious efforts to the contrary. Countervailing efforts may have some effect, but we cannot say how much without further evidence. [7]

SUPPRESSION

In Bernstein's experiment, schedules that deprived the person of behavior $\underline{B}$ had two effects: facilitation of $\underline{A}$ and suppression of $\underline{B}$. Notice that the response deprivation hypothesis would predict the facilitation of $\underline{A}$, but would not necessarily predict the suppression of $\underline{B}$. All it predicts for $\underline{B}$ is that the schedule will not facilitate $\underline{B}$. Thus, the response deprivation hypothesis would tolerate the suppression of $\underline{B}$, but it would also tolerate performance of $\underline{B}$ at its paired baseline level—no effect upon $\underline{B}$ (see Figure 3.10, points 1 and 2).

But Bernstein's results are typical: Schedules that deprive the individual of $\underline{B}$ generally produce both effects, facilitation of $\underline{A}$ and suppression of $\underline{B}$. Accordingly, the next chapter turns to a new group of theories, theories capable of predicting and explaining both effects.

NOTES

1. Much of the literature expresses the response deprivation condition in terms of algebraic relations rather than geometric rela-

tions. The algebraic version denotes O_c and O_i as the amount of each behavior in the paired baseline condition—sometimes called the free operant condition, hence the "O" notation. Then if $C/I = O_c/O_i$, the schedule deprives the individual of neither response. Why? Because the line of schedule constraint has a slope, C/I, which guarantees that the line will pass through the basepoint: It has the same slope as a line that must pass through the basepoint, a line whose slope is O_c/O_i. Similarly, if C/I is less than O_c/O_i, the line passes beneath the basepoint, depriving the individual of behavior c, but not behavior i. The reverse is true if C/I is greater than O_c/O_i.

2. If Wallace never eats strawberry, the basepoint will lie on the horizontal axis, so no line of schedule constraint can pass beneath the basepoint. It follows that if Wallace never eats strawberry, we can devise no contingency schedule that deprives him of strawberry.

3. For an empirical approach to the problem of deciding when one behavior has stopped and another kind of behavior has begun, see Allison and Castallan (1970) and Machlis (1977).

4. Humans paid handsomely to do absolutely nothing aside from lying in bed with their eyes covered by translucent lenses, ears covered with earphones, hands enclosed in loose-fitting tubular cuffs that prevent normal somesthetic perception, soon find the monotony sufficiently intolerable to end the experiment voluntarily (Bexton, Heron, and Scott 1954). For evidence of the rat's response to stimulus change, see Dember (1956).

5. Frank Restle, personal communication, 1979.

6. Animals often display foraging strategies that seem to confute the response-reinforcement concept. In the context of foraging, the response-reinforcement concept implies a "win-stay" strategy: The foraging animal should tend to repeat a successful food-getting behavior. But foraging animals often display a "win-shift" strategy, visiting a new location instead of returning to the place where they found food most recently. For examples involving the rat, see Olton (1979); several related examples appear in Kamil and Sargent (1981). On hummingbirds and Siamese fighting fish as win-shift strategists, see Cole et al. (1982) and Roitblat, Tham, and Golub (1982). Menzel and Juno (1982) report evidence more favorable to the reinforcement concept.

7. For a discussion of "voluntary" factors in classical (Pavlovian) conditioning, see Kimble (1961, pp. 104-6). In a typical experiment on eyelid conditioning, the person learns to blink in response to a light that signals the imminent delivery of an air puff to the eye. Under special instructions ("Be sure you do not wink before you feel a puff"), humans typically reduce, but do not entirely eliminate, the conditioned response to the light (Norris and Grant 1948). Thus, the human may resist to some extent, but not entirely, the behavioral control of the conditioned stimulus. No doubt the resistance itself is sensitive to the rewards contingent on resistance.

Chapter 4

Performance Models

"At present, there exists no general account of what makes something a reinforcer" (Schwartz and Lacey 1982, p. 70). Here we examine several recent attempts to provide such an account. Although the several protagonists may disagree with one another, they would disagree more sharply with Schwartz and Lacey.

THE BEHAVIORAL BLISS POINT

Several theorists view the paired baseline condition as an Eden-like state that reveals the individual's behavioral ideal. Readers who prefer a secular vision of the same state may imagine the Big Rock Candy Mountain, with its cigarette trees and its soda water fountain. Given free access to an unlimited amount of each of two behaviors, with absolutely no external constraint on the order of their performance, the observed behavioral totals—the paired basepoint—supposedly reflect a behavioral or biological ideal, the preferred amount of each behavior, the peak of some hedonic hill of happiness. In short, the paired basepoint represents a kind of bliss point.[1] It is a point the individual will strive to attain, even under the constraints of a contingency schedule. Indeed, we can understand the individual's response to the constraints of any particular schedule by comparing those constraints with the paired basepoint. So say these theories (Allison 1981b; Rachlin and Burkhard 1978; Rachlin et al. 1981; Staddon 1979; Timberlake 1979a).

Figure 4.1 shows a reciprocal fixed-ratio schedule that deprives the individual of neither behavior. Because the line that represents the schedule goes right through the basepoint, the unfilled circle, the schedule would let the individual perform each behavior at its paired

FIGURE 4.1

A Reciprocal Fixed-Ratio Schedule That Deprives the Individual of
Neither Behavior and Fails to Facilitate or
Suppress Either Behavior

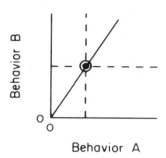

baseline level. Experiments with that kind of schedule generally show
that the individual responds to its constraints by performing at or near
the measured basepoint, as illustrated by the point inside the unfilled
circle. Thus, schedules that deprive the individual of neither behavior
generally fail to facilitate or suppress either one—a fact nicely aligned
with the view that the basepoint measures the individual's behavioral
ideal.

What about schedules that deprive the individual of one behavior
or the other? In 1979 Staddon published a minimum–deviation model
capable of explaining the facilitation and suppression effects often seen
with that kind of schedule.

Suppose the individual happens to place equal importance upon
the paired baseline level of each of the two behaviors. We test the
person with three different schedules: One deprives the person of
neither behavior, and the other two deprive the person of behavior B
or A. Figure 4.2A represents each of these three reciprocal fixed-
ratio schedules. During the contingency session, how far should the
person climb each of the three lines of schedule constraint so as to
minimize the deviation from the measured behavioral ideal?

If the person places equal importance upon the paired baseline
level of each behavior, the answer is given by Figure 4.2B. We construct the answer by drawing a perpendicular line from the basepoint
to the line of schedule constraint and placing a point at the intersection. The intersection point shows how much of each behavior the
person must perform so as to minimize the deviation from the baseline ideal. By climbing to a higher or lower point the person would

FIGURE 4.2

Illustrative Predictions from the Minimum-Deviation Model for
Performance under Three Reciprocal Fixed-Ratio Schedules

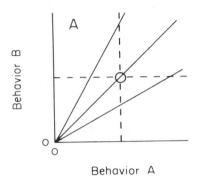

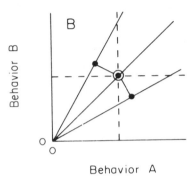

move too far from one baseline level or the other, and would thereby
fail to approach the ideal as closely as the constraints permit.

Notice that the model neatly predicts the typical effects of such
schedules. Schedules that deprive the individual of neither behavior
generally fail to facilitate or suppress either one. Schedules that deprive the individual of behavior B generally facilitate A and suppress
B. The model also predicts reversibility and assigns no fundamental
importance to the probability-differential condition: Schedules that
deprive the individual of A generally facilitate B and suppress A.

What if the individual happens to attach more importance to the
baseline level of B than the baseline level of A? If B were eating and
A were pressing a lever, we might expect the hungry rat to weigh
baseline B more heavily than baseline A in its adaptive response to
the constraints of our schedule.

We construct an illustrative answer in Figure 4.3A by drawing
slanted lines from the basepoint to the schedule lines that run above
or below the basepoint. If the schedule line runs above the basepoint,
our slanted line intersects the schedule line a little below the perpendicular and thereby assigns more weight to the baseline level of B
than the baseline level of A. If the schedule line runs below the basepoint, our slanted line intersects the schedule line a little above the
perpendicular. Figure 4.3B shows the opposite case, one in which
the individual assigns more importance to the baseline level of A than
B.[2]

We can test the model in more detail by comparing the response totals observed when we vary the schedule requirements. For example, what if we double each of the two requirements? This transformation fails to change the slope of the line of schedule constraint, the rise/run ratio. Accordingly, the minimum-deviation model would predict identical behavioral totals under two different schedules with the same rise/run ratio. As we saw in Chapter 3, such schedules often produce identical behavioral totals. But we should also pay some attention to a known exception to this rule.

The conventional test cage, even an unusually long one, places lever and drinking tube so close together that the rat need travel only a short distance in moving from one to the other. To the outside observer, the shortest possible trip may seem inconsequential. But suppose we lengthen the shortest possible trip by erecting a partition wall between lever and tube, forcing a long detour route around the far end of the wall. With the wall in place, the shortest possible trip covers a V-shaped route 48 centimeters long; with the wall removed, the shortest possible trip covers a straight-line route only 8 centimeters long.

We test the rat with three different reciprocal schedules that require 5 seconds of lever holding for 5 seconds of drinking, 10 for 10, and 20 for 20—schedules with different requirements but identical rise/run ratios, 1 second of drinking/second of holding.

FIGURE 4.3

Illustrative Predictions from the Minimum-Deviation Model for
Behaviors Weighted Unequally

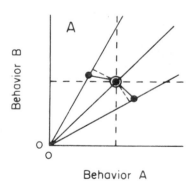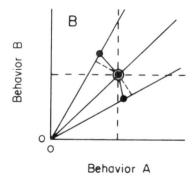

FIGURE 4.4

Time Spent Drinking as a Function of Time Spent Holding the
Lever and the Distance between Lever and Drinking Tube

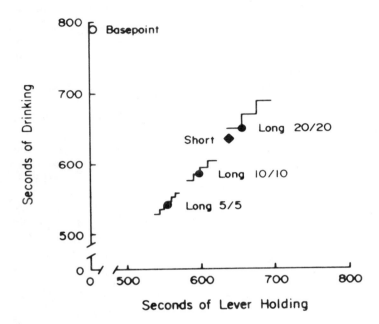

In the short-trip condition, we find that the three different
schedules generate essentially the same behavioral totals—about 635
seconds of holding, and 635 of drinking—as the minimum-deviation
model would predict.

Not so in the long-trip condition; there, the behavioral totals
increase systematically as we raise the schedule requirements from
5/5 to 10/10, and on to 20/20 (Allison, Miller, and Wozny 1979).

In interpreting these results, summarized in Figure 4.4, keep
this in mind: To reach some upper point on the schedule's staircase
function, the rat must take more trips up the 5/5 function than the
10/10 function, and more there than the 20/20 function. Maybe that
is why the rat, facing relatively long trips, settles for a lower final
point on the 5/5 function than the 10/10 function, and lower there than
the 20/20 function. Facing relatively short trips, it shows little con-
cern for the number of trips it must take, and therefore climbs to
about the same point on all three functions.

Maybe the minimum-deviation model could handle both conditions
by taking account of a third behavior, the behavior involved in travel-

ing between lever and tube. In terms of the minimum-deviation model, the results suggest that the rat assigns some weight to this third behavior when the shortest possible trip is relatively long, none when short. We would have to complicate our graphic representation of the model by resorting to three-dimensional space, scaling the number of trips on a vertical axis projecting upward from the origins of the two-dimensional planes in Figures 4.2 and 4.3. The third axis can be visualized by placing the point of a pencil at the origin and holding the pencil perpendicular to the page. Because the basepoint is now a point in three-dimensional space, it would float above the page to a height determined by the number of trips the animal took in the baseline session. (For analytic purposes, the algebraic form of the minimum-deviation model for more than two behaviors is much easier to deal with than the geometric form.)

The virtues of the model include its specific implications for changes in the slope of the schedule line. Figure 4.5 applies the model for two behaviors to five schedules whose lines of constraint have different slopes. The example assumes that the individual assigns equal weights to the baseline levels of the two behaviors. As we move from the first schedule through the fifth, we decrease the slope of the line. At the same time, the predicted A total rises steadily to a peak at

FIGURE 4.5

Illustrative Predictions from the Minimum-Deviation Model for
Performance under Five Reciprocal Fixed-Ratio Schedules

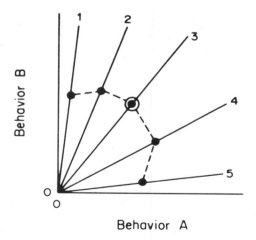

schedule 4 and declines as we move on to schedule 5; the predicted $\underline{B}$ total rises to a peak at schedule 2 and falls steadily thereafter.

Notice that the five behavioral totals predicted for these schedules describe a curvilinear relation between the total amount of $\underline{A}$ and the total amount of $\underline{B}$, the curve shown by the broken lines connecting the points on adjacent schedule lines. If the individual places some importance on the baseline level of each, the minimum-deviation model for two behaviors will always predict a curvilinear relation between the two behavioral totals, rather than a linear (straight-line) relation.

Accordingly, we can test the model by creating many different schedules whose constraint lines cover a wide range of slopes. If they cover only a narrow range of slopes we must interpret the test results with some caution, because a function that truly follows a genuine but gentle curve may seem straight—linear—over a short stretch of the curve.

A comprehensive search of the experimental literature would disclose many examples of the curvilinear function predicted by the model. One such example appears in Figure 4.6. Teitelbaum (1957) tested rats in daily 12-hour sessions under fixed-ratio schedules that differed in the number of lever presses required for each 90-milligram food pellet. Figure 4.6 presents the results for "dynamic hyperphagics"—so called because of experimental lesions in the brain that normally result in the overeating of freely available food, rapid weight gain, and ultimately a condition of pronounced obesity. The figure shows no paired basepoint, because none was recorded. The possible importance of the paired basepoint did not become apparent until much later, so experiments done at that time rarely included the measurement of the paired basepoint. Such measurement would surely have placed it near the upper left corner of the figure. But the missing basepoint is of no great consequence to our present purpose. Our present purpose should lead your eye over the bend in the function: As the slope of the schedule line decreases, the lever-press total rises and falls and the food-pellet total falls steadily. The curvilinear relation between total presses and total food illustrates the kind of function predicted by the minimum-deviation model.

But the same search would also disclose examples that seem to elude the grasp of the model. Figure 4.7 presents Teitelbaum's results for another group of rats, normal controls with no experimental brain lesions. The function in Figure 4.7 appears linear: As the slope decreases, both totals fall steadily and the food total appears to fall linearly as the lever-press total rises. Because the five schedules covered a broad range of slopes, we would probably hesitate to blame the apparent linearity on a too-narrow range of slopes.

The apparent linearity displayed by Teitelbaum's normal rats cannot be dismissed as an isolated example, because we know of simi-

FIGURE 4.6

Total Food Pellets as a Function of Total Lever Presses by Rats
Tested in the Dynamic Phase of Hypothalamic Hyperphagia

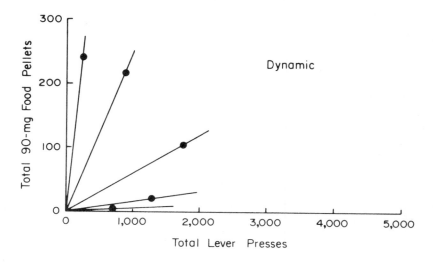

lar examples. Chapter 3 included a brief account of an experiment on reversibility, where humans pulled a trigger and performed a pursuit rotor task (Podsakoff 1980, 1982). Figure 4.8 presents the results in more detail. The schedules represented by the two shallow lines deprived the persons of the pursuit rotor behavior; each of those two schedules facilitated trigger behavior and suppressed pursuit rotor. The schedules represented by the two steepest lines deprived them of the trigger behavior; each facilitated pursuit rotor behavior and suppressed trigger. The remaining schedule deprived them of neither behavior and caused no statistically significant facilitation or suppression of either. But note the absence of any significant bend in the functional relation between the two behaviors: As the trigger total increased, the pursuit rotor total showed a strictly linear decrease.

The theoretical issue addressed by such experiments—Does the function truly curve, or not?—probably seems a little more complicated now than it did at first glance. But we can avoid those complications entirely by a slight change in tactics. Our new tactic opens the way to some experimental tests of the model's basic assumption—direct experimental tests of the assumption itself that do not turn on the curvilinearity deduced from the assumption.

FIGURE 4.7

Total Food Pellets as a Function of Total Lever Presses
by Normal Rats

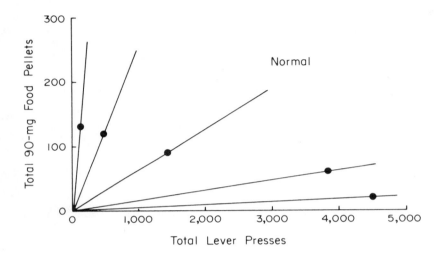

Figure 4.9 shows three schedule lines with different slopes, all passing beneath the basepoint. Imagine the basepoint as your own behavioral ideal, measured beforehand. Just before your contingency session begins, with behavior A instrumental and B contingent, the experimenter describes the three schedules and offers you a choice among them. Which one would you choose?

If the basepoint measures your behavioral ideal, you should choose the one with the steepest slope, the greater rise/run ratio. Why? Because that one would let you approach your basepoint more closely than either of the others. In general, if the steepest possible line still passes beneath the basepoint, you should seize any chance to select or produce the steepest line you can. Does it matter whether the schedules are reciprocal or nonreciprocal? Not in the least. In either case, each line of schedule constraint represents the steepest line attainable under that particular schedule.

I know of no such experiment, but the literature contains many experiments with <u>concurrent fixed-ratio schedules</u> that capture the essential features of Figure 4.9. Such schedules provide a choice between different ratios, usually two in number. For example, by pressing one lever twice, the rat can get 60 contingent licks at a water tube;

FIGURE 4.8

Total Time on the Pursuit-Rotor Task as a Function of
Total Trigger Pulls

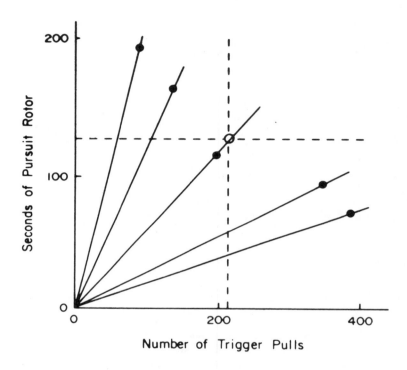

but another lever offers the 60 contingent licks for eight instrumental presses. The procedure allows the rat to press either lever as much or as little as it pleases throughout the one-hour session.

Figure 4.10 shows the typical performance of a rat tested with a reciprocal version of the concurrent fixed-ratio schedule (Allison 1981b; Shapiro and Allison 1978). Both of the schedule lines pass beneath the basepoint; the 60/2 ratio has a steeper slope than the 60/8 ratio available on the other lever, 30 licks/press versus 7.5. Exclusive responding on the 60/2 lever would keep the rat on the steepest line attainable; exclusive responding on the 60/8 lever would keep the rat on the shallowest line attainable. If it samples both levers extensively, the rat will end on some third line of intermediate slope. This particular rat, like all of the others tested in this experiment, sampled both levers extensively and thereby failed to approach the

FIGURE 4.9

Three Alternative Schedules That Deprive the Individual of
Behavior $\underline{B}$ in Varying Degrees

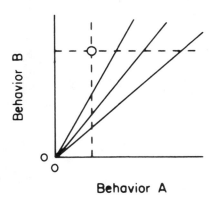

FIGURE 4.10

Total Water Licks as a Function of Total Lever Presses by a Rat
Tested with a Concurrent Fixed-Ratio Schedule

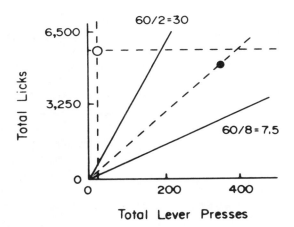

FIGURE 4.11

Total Food Pellets as a Function of Total Lever Presses by
Six Rats Tested with a Concurrent Fixed-Ratio Schedule

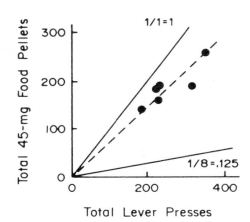

basepoint as closely as allowed by the constraints of the concurrent
fixed-ratio schedule.

The excessive deviation from the presumed behavioral ideal
probably did not result from any need to discover at the start of the
session which lever offered which ratio. These rats generally distributed their sampling throughout the session; because they did not
confine their sampling to an initial warmup period, a liberal allowance for initial sampling still revealed a substantial departure from
exclusive responding on the more favorable lever.

We can minimize the need to discover which alternative lever
offers which alternative ratio by testing the rat over a long series of
sessions while keeping each ratio on the same lever from one session
to the next. Figure 4.11 shows how six rats responded to that kind of
procedure under a concurrent schedule that offered one 45-milligram
food pellet for each lever press, or one pellet for eight presses.
Each of the six sampled the two levers extensively, following some
line of intermediate slope (Allison 1981b). The authors of this study
(Lea and Roper 1977) reported no basepoint, but similar experiments
leave no doubt that the basepoint would have fallen above the steepest
line attainable under the schedule.

Similar work (Herrnstein and Loveland 1975), with pigeons
pecking one wall key or the other for each 2-second access to grain,

suggests that the pigeon may approach the steepest line more closely
as the two extremes grow more divergent. Illustrative results from
one such experiment, which ended each session when the bird had
accumulated 120 seconds of access to grain, appear in Figure 4.12—
group means for five pigeons. The panel on the left shows that the
birds followed a line of intermediate slope when the schedule offered
2 seconds for 50 pecks, or 2 for 70. The middle panel shows that
they came closer to the steepest line attainable when the schedule offered 2 seconds for 40 pecks, or 2 for 80. The panel on the right
shows that when the extremes diverged still more, 2 seconds for 20
or 100 pecks, the birds adhered to the steepest line attainable (Allison 1981b).

In summary, the work with concurrent fixed-ratio schedules
raises some doubt about the basic assumption of the minimum-deviation model. Given an opportunity to do so, the animal may or may not
approach its presumed behavioral ideal as closely as it might. The
pigeon data may suggest a perceptual defense of the model. Maybe
the bird or the rat fails to follow the steepest line available because
it fails to see the objective difference between the two extreme lines.
But I would hesitate to interpret the reported failures as total failures
of discrimination, because the data generally revealed a decided
preference, though not an exclusive preference, for the more favorable of the two alternatives—the alternative which, if chosen exclusively, would have led the animal as close as possible to the paired
basepoint. If the animal preferred the more favorable alternative,
it must have seen some difference between the two alternatives.

FIGURE 4.12

Total Seconds of Access to Grain as a Function of Total Key Pecks
by Pigeons Tested with Concurrent Variable-Ratio Schedules

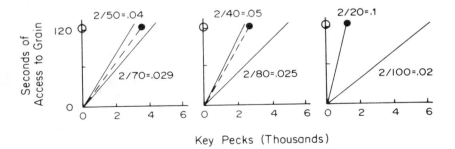

Key Pecks (Thousands)

FIGURE 4.13

Illustrative Predictions of the Minimum-Deviation Model for
Performance under Three Concurrent Fixed-Ratio Schedules

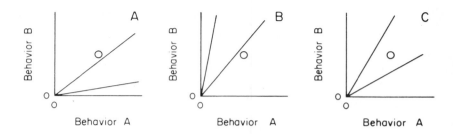

Further variations on the same experimental tactic would help
settle the issue. Figure 4.13 diagrams three concurrent fixed-ratio
schedules, reciprocal contingency style. The minimum-deviation
model implies that the individual should follow the steeper line in
panel A, but the shallower line in panel B. Confronted with the schedule shown in panel C, the individual should end at or near the basepoint,
on some line of intermediate slope. Thus, the model predicts exclusive responding on one alternative or the other for the schedules represented in panels A and B, but extensive sampling of both alternatives for the schedule represented in panel C.

To stage a still simpler attack on the same question, we might
abandon the concurrent schedule in favor of a simple fixed-ratio schedule of the nonreciprocal variety. With behavior $\underline{B}$ contingent on instrumental behavior $\underline{A}$, each of the nonreciprocal schedules in Figure 4.14
would let the individual follow practically any path on or below the line
of schedule constraint. In panels A and B the path actually chosen
should conform closely to the line of constraint; in panel C, the actual
path should fall substantially below the line of constraint, running
through or near the basepoint. I know of no experiment designed in
the manner illustrated by Figure 4.13 or 4.14.

One final variation on the simple fixed-ratio schedule will con-
solidate your understanding of the minimum-deviation model. Suppose
our schedule requires 20 instrumental lever presses for each contingent access to a water tube. Having gained access to the tube, the
rat can drink for as long as it pleases unless it quits drinking for five
minutes. Any five-minute pause causes the tube to retract, whereupon the rat must perform 20 more presses for its next chance to
drink. Unlike the standard schedule, where the experimenter fixes

FIGURE 4.14

Illustrative Predictions of the Minimum-Deviation Model for
Performance under Three Nonreciprocal Fixed-Ratio Schedules

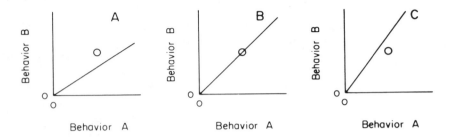

the size of each contingent reward, our schedule offers the rat an
optional magnitude of reward, much like a restaurant that charges a
certain price of admission for all you care to eat in one sitting.

Figure 4.15A diagrams the staircase constraints of this schedule. The schedule confines the rat to the horizontal axis from 0 to
20 lever presses, but denies little else; it allows the rat to occupy
practically any point in the space on or to the right of the vertical line
at the 20-press mark.

FIGURE 4.15

Behavioral Constraints of a Fixed-Ratio Schedule with an Optional
Magnitude of Reward

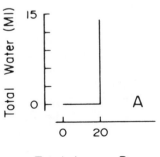

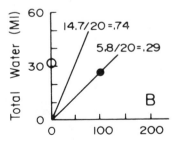

Suppose we know from another experiment that our rat can drink as much as 14.7 milliliters in one "sitting"—one bout of drinking that lacks a five-minute pause. We know, too, that in the paired baseline condition the rat drinks about 30 milliliters altogether, about 1.7 milliliters per bout, and presses the lever very little. How should the rat respond to the constraints of our schedule?

The answer appears in Figure 4.15B. We calculate the slope of the steeper line in the figure as follows: If the rat drinks 14.7 milliliters per access, as we know it can do, it will follow a path whose slope is 14.7/20, or .74 milliliters per lever press. By climbing the proper distance up this relatively steep line, the rat could come closer to the paired basepoint than it could by climbing any shallower line.

But the rat apparently rejects the paired basepoint ideal. As the figure shows, this rat actually chose to climb a much shallower line: 5.8/20, or .29 milliliters per lever press. This selection of a shallower line than the animal could have selected was typical of all of the four rats examined in this experiment (Marwine and Collier 1979), each one tested with 12 different lever-press requirements ranging from 1 press per access to 300 presses per access. We have similar results from an experiment (Collier, Hirsch, and Hamlin 1972) that offered an optional magnitude of food reward for instrumental lever pressing (Allison 1981b).

Perhaps the model could accommodate such results by resorting to three baseline measures weighted appropriately: total lever presses, total food or water intake, and the total number of meals or drinking bouts.

CONSERVATION MODEL 1

The act of eating an apple entails many different sensory, motor, and dietary consequences. Accordingly, we can conceptualize the act as a unique point in a multidimensional space whose dimensions include sweetness, moisture, odor, energy expenditure, protein, fat, calories, and various vitamins and minerals, among others. The act of eating a banana must comprise another unique point in the same multidimensional space; otherwise, how could we know apples from bananas? Thus, a person who expresses a preference for apples over bananas makes an evaluative comparison of their underlying characteristics, multiple dimensions of the sort listed above. More generally, we can conceptualize any two disparate acts, such as pressing a lever and drinking, as two distinct points in a space composed of various sensory, energetic, and nutritional dimensions or characteristics.

Maybe we should ask how much of some such dimension the organism gets from the two behaviors measured in the paired baseline condition. How far can we get by supposing that the organism conserves that quantity as it responds to the constraints of our contingency schedule (Allison 1976)?[3]

Consider a pet monkey that subsists on a diet composed mainly of small apples and large bananas. Each day the owner provides an unlimited supply of fruit, of which the monkey typically eats a total of six apples and eight bananas. Let us focus on one dimension, calories. How many calories does the monkey get by eating six apples and eight bananas in the daily paired baseline condition?

In dietetics, the calorie is the heat required to raise the temperature of one kilogram of water one degree Celsius—a totally arbitrary definition. Suppose we invent an equally arbitrary unit, the apple-calorie. We define an apple-calorie as the number of dietetic calories in one small apple. Dietetic tables of food values tell us that one large banana has roughly twice the caloric content of one small apple. It follows that the monkey gets 22 apple-calories from its baseline consumption of the two fruits, 16 apple-calories from the eight bananas, and 6 more from the six apples: $2(8) + 6 = 22$ apple-calories.

In more general notation, the monkey derives a total of $\underline{B}$ apple-calories from its baseline consumption of the two fruits:

$$\underline{B} = \underline{k}\underline{O}_i + \underline{O}_c$$

where $\underline{k}$ signifies the number of apple-calories in one banana, $\underline{O}_i$ signifies the number of bananas consumed in the paired baseline condition, and $\underline{O}_c$ signifies the number of apples consumed in the paired baseline condition.

Figure 4.16A summarizes the first part of our purely hypothetical, purely didactic example, plotting total apples on the vertical axis, bananas on the horizontal. The line with negative slope, running downward through the basepoint, is a constant-calorie line. Each point on that line represents a total of 22 apple-calories. The line intercepts the vertical apple axis at 22: If the monkey eats no bananas, it can get 22 apple-calories by eating 22 apples. It intercepts the horizontal banana axis at 11: Eating no apples, the monkey can get 22 apple-calories from 11 bananas, as $2(11) = 22$ apple-calories. The line specifies every combination of apples and bananas, fractional slices included, that comprises a total of 22 apple-calories. Notice that the slope of the line is $-\underline{k}$, its vertical intercept is $\underline{B}$, and its horizontal intercept is $\underline{B}/\underline{k}$.

Panel B portrays the constraints of three reciprocal fixed-ratio schedules. The shallow line of constraint arises from a spring frost

FIGURE 4.16

Constant Caloric Intake Derived from the Consumption of Apples
and Bananas

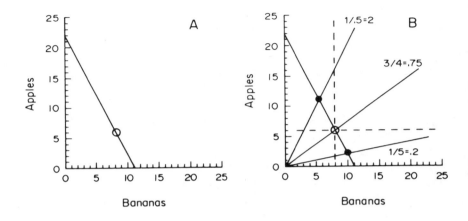

that nips the apples in the bud. The consequent shortage of apples
raises their retail price; the monkey's owner responds by buying
fewer apples and more bananas. At the same time, the owner abandons the profligate paired baseline feeding procedure and tries to cut
the monkey's apple consumption by resorting to a strategem, a reciprocal contingency schedule that allows only one apple for every five
bananas. How much of each fruit will the monkey eat in conserving
its baseline quantity, 22 apple-calories?

   We construct the answer by drawing an upward line of schedule
constraint with the proper positive slope, 1 apple/5 bananas = 0.2
apples/banana. Its point of intersection with our downward-sloping
line tells us how much of each the monkey will eat under the constraints
of this particular schedule in achieving the baseline quantity, 22
apple-calories. As shown in panel B, the anwer is ten bananas and
two apples.

   For an arithmetic solution of the same problem, think of the two
schedule requirements as a bundle of fruit, five bananas plus one
apple. Each bundle contains 11 apple-calories, as 2(5) + 1 = 11. The
monkey must eat two such bundles for 22 apple-calories; in eating
those two bundles, it eats ten bananas and two apples.

   In more general notation, each bundle contains k̲I̲ + C̲ apple-
calories, where k̲ signifies the number of apple-calories in one banana,
I̲ signifies the number of bananas in each bundle, and C̲ signifies the
number of apples in each bundle. How many such bundles, N̲, must
the monkey eat in achieving the baseline number of apple-calories?

The monkey can achieve the baseline number of apple-calories by selecting a value of $\underline{N}$ that satisfies the following conservation equation:

$$\underline{N}(\underline{kI} + \underline{C}) = \underline{kO}_i + \underline{O}_c = \underline{B}$$

Under this particular schedule, $\underline{N} = 2$, so $\underline{NI} = 10$ bananas and $\underline{NC} = 2$ apples.

The steepest line of constraint arises from civil unrest in a Latin American state that cuts the supply of bananas, raises their retail price, and leads the owner to buy fewer bananas and more apples. The owner's new schedule allows one apple for half of each banana; its constraint line has an upward slope of $1/0.5$, or 2 apples/banana, and intersects the constant-calorie line at 5.5 bananas and 11 apples. Arithmetically, the monkey must eat 11 bundles, each containing $2(0.5) + 1 = 2$ apple-calories, for a total of 5.5 bananas and 11 apples.

The third line of constraint passes through the basepoint. It might represent a schedule that allows 3 apples for every 4 bananas, a schedule that should generate the paired baseline totals: 8 bananas and 6 apples.

We have just seen an illustrative application of a conservation model, first published in 1976 (Allison 1976), for performance under the constraints of a simple fixed-ratio schedule, reciprocal contingency style. By reinterpreting the lines of constraint in Figure 4.16B, the reader can easily extend the model to many other schedules, including nonreciprocal schedules, concurrent schedules, and schedules that offer an optional magnitude of reward. Aside from a schedule that strictly confines the individual to a path that runs through the basepoint, this conservation model can tolerate a good deal of straying from the basepoint—behavioral deviations that the minimum-deviation model might find intolerable. Thus, the conservation model does not view the paired basepoint as a behavioral ideal; any point on the downward sloping line, including the paired basepoint, would satisfy the theoretical constraints of the conservation model. If the minimum-deviation model for two-behavior schedules sometimes errs in its predictions, the conservation model may avoid those errors by default.[4]

For further illustration of this difference between the two models, consider the constraints imposed by a widely used schedule that we have not yet discussed, the interval schedule. The typical interval schedule delivers the contingent reward upon the first instrumental response that occurs some specified time after the preceding delivery. In a fixed-interval schedule, the specified time is always the same. For example, we might start the fixed-interval 60-second schedule by presenting the rat with a lever. We record all lever presses that occur during the next 60 seconds, but we deliver no food until the first

FIGURE 4.17

Behavioral Constraints of a Fixed-Interval Schedule

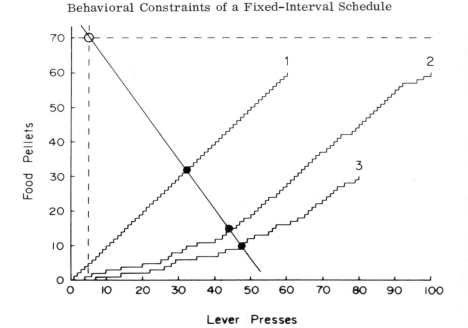

Lever Presses

lever press that occurs after the 60-second interval has elapsed. As soon as we deliver the food, we start timing the next 60-second interval. The receipt of food under a fixed-interval schedule resembles the receipt of a monthly paycheck from the payroll department. A paycheck comes upon the first visit to the payroll department after the first day of the month, but all other visits are futile.

Figure 4.17 portrays the constraints of a particular fixed-interval 60-second schedule. Over the course of a one-hour session the rat cannot get more than 60 food pellets. It may get fewer than 60 food pellets if it sometimes waits much longer than 60 seconds before pressing the lever once again. Staircase 1 shows the steepest path the rat could possibly follow: In climbing to the top of staircase 1 the hypothetical rat got 60 pellets for 60 lever presses, 1 pellet/ press. Only if blessed with an external clock or an exquisite sense of time could the rat actually get to the top of that staircase, wasting none of its lever presses during the interval between deliveries, and pressing the lever at the exact end of every 60-second interval.

Real rats typically follow a much shallower path, such as staircase 2 or staircase 3. In climbing to the top of staircase 2 the hypothetical rat managed to get all 60 pellets, but often pressed the lever before the 60 seconds had elapsed. Its 100 lever presses included 40 futile responses during some of the intervals between deliveries: 60 pellets for 100 lever presses, only 0.6 pellets/press. In climbing to the top of staircase 3, the hypothetical rat missed half of its opportunities for food delivery, getting only 30 pellets for 80 presses, about 0.4 pellets/press.

The line that slopes downward through the basepoint is a constant-quantity line that illustrates the predictions of the conservation model. Whatever staircase path the rat happens to follow, the conservation model predicts that the rat will climb that staircase until it meets the point of intersection between the staircase path and a conservation line with negative slope that passes through the basepoint. Thus, the three filled circles in Figure 4.17 show three results that would each conform to the conservation model. Notice that the conservation model would tolerate the lowest point, the one on staircase 3, even though that point strays much further from the basepoint than it need have done under the constraints of the schedule.

Take another look at Figure 4.16B and notice how the model relates to the antecedent response deprivation condition. A schedule that deprives the individual of either behavior should suppress that behavior and facilitate the other. If it does not deprive the individual of either behavior, it should neither suppress nor facilitate either one. Like minimum-deviation, the conservation model handles reversibility effects with ease and attributes no fundamental importance to the probability-differential condition.

Figure 4.18 shows in more detail how the model predicts that a schedule that deprives the individual of one behavior will suppress that behavior and facilitate the other. That prediction comes from a constant-quantity line that slopes downward through the basepoint. In the monkey example, the constant-calorie line slopes downward because both fruits have some caloric content. Its slope is -2 because each banana has twice the caloric content of each apple. Thus, each additional banana reduces by two the number of apples needed to make a total of 22 apple-calories: The slope, rise/run, is therefore $-2/1 = -2$.

If the two fruits had equal caloric content, the constant-calorie line would represent only 14 apple-calories $(8 + 6 = 14)$ and would fall more gently, with a slope of -1: Each additional banana reduces by one the number of apples needed to make 14 apple-calories. If each banana had only half the caloric content of each apple the constant-calorie line would fall more gently still, with a slope of $-1/2$. All of these variations appear in Figure 4.18. In each case, the model predicts that the schedule shown in the figure, which deprives the monkey of apples, will facilitate banana and suppress apple consumption.

FIGURE 4.18

A Family of Four Constant-Calorie Lines

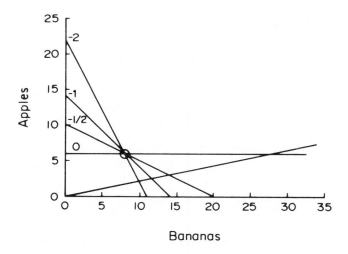

Bananas

To understand the final variation in Figure 4.18, imagine a new variety of banana that has no caloric value whatever. In that event, our constant-calorie line will be perfectly flat, with slope = 0, and will intercept the vertical apple axis at 6: Each additional banana reduces by 0 the number of apples needed to make 6 apple-calories. Consequently, the schedule should still facilitate banana consumption, but should not suppress apple consumption. Instead, the monkey should respond to every conceivable schedule by eating instrumentally whatever number of bananas it must eat to achieve its baseline apple intake, six apples. For the schedule shown in the figure, the model makes the following prediction about the slope of the constant-quantity line: As the slope decreases, the schedule's facilitation effect should grow larger, its suppression effect smaller.

The experimental literature contains some cases that look as if the constant-quantity line were flat (for example, Hogan, Kleist, and Hutchings 1970). Far more commonly, the results agree with a down-ward-sloping constant-quantity line.

In summary, this model assumes that the organism conserves, or holds constant, the total amount of some dimension that the two be-haviors controlled by the schedule might have in common with each other. Thus, if each entails some positive amount of that dimension, however small, then in performing more of either behavior the orga-

nism will perform less of the other as it progresses toward the constant dimensional quantity postulated by the model.

We can apply the model without naming the dimension specifically, and we need not assume that the same dimension governs all
cases. In the monkey example, caloric intake served as a convenient
didactic example in our exposition of the model. Energy would serve
as a universal example, because every conceivable behavior entails
the expenditure of energy. And the results of certain experiments
suggest that the individual may sometimes conserve the total amount
of energy allocated to the two behaviors controlled by the schedule.

One such experiment (Allison, Miller, and Wozny 1979) tested
the thirsty rat in 60-minute sessions with a reciprocal fixed-ratio
schedule that required a certain number of lever presses for a certain
number of licks at the water tube. The lever was mounted on a horizontal axle that served as a pivot; the far end of the lever, the end
outside the test cage, rested on top of an electromagnetic coil. By
varying the electrical current flowing through the coil, the experimenter could vary from one session to another the amount of force the
rat had to exert to depress the lever. The heavy condition required

FIGURE 4.19

Total Water Licks as a Function of Total Lever Presses and the
Force Required to Depress the Lever

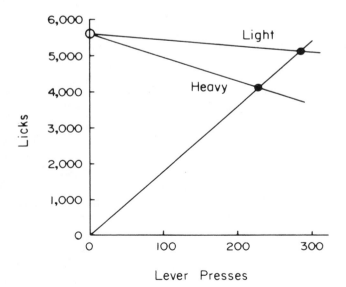

about three times as much force as the light condition. It follows
that the energy-conserving rat should perform more lever presses
and licks under the light condition than under the heavy.

The results appear in Figure 4.19 and support our expectation:
Under the light condition, the schedule produced more facilitation of
lever pressing, and less suppression of licking, than it did under the
heavy condition. The full experiment provided four different comparisons of heavy and light, two from each of the two rats tested,
each with results like those in Figure 4.19.

The results support, but cannot prove, the notion of energy conservation. They might support many alternative hypotheses, including the conservation of various psychological dimensions: utility,
satisfaction, or their colloquial relative, fun. We could seek direct
evidence of energy conservation by moving the test cage into the exercise physiology laboratory for on-line measurements of energy expenditure in terms of oxygen uptake—a perfectly feasible experiment
whose exact equivalent remains to be done.[5] Should the direct evidence favor the notion of energy conservation, we should still doubt
the governance of that dimension in all cases: No behavioral experiment can reveal a constant-quantity line that is perfectly flat if energy
conservation holds universally.[6]

Like minimum-deviation, the conservation model provides a
handy account of motivational variations in the response to schedule
constraints. Figure 4.20 shows why any experimental treatment
that results in more drinking or wheel running under the paired baseline condition, all else equal, should also result in more running and
drinking under the constraints of the reciprocal fixed-ratio schedule.
The likely candidates, some already verified (Allison, Miller, and
Wozny 1979; Timberlake and Allison 1974), include the classic motivational variables: incentive variations in the contents of the drinking
tube, or even in the width of its aperature; organismic variations in the
prior availability of exercise or water (that is, thirst). Such models
leave ample room for individual differences as well, differences that
might or might not appear in baseline measurements: If one rat, perhaps more adept than the other, somehow can manage to press the
identical lever more easily, their difference might appear solely in
the guise of constant-quantity lines with different slopes, much like
Figure 4.19.

Look again at Figure 4.4. Why should the rat, facing relatively
long trips between the lever and the drinking tube, climb to a higher
point along the 20/20 slope than the 10/10 slope, and higher there than
the 5/5 slope? Why should it behave so differently in the face of short
trips, climbing to about the same point on all three slopes? Maybe
such an experiment engages the conservation of energy. Its results
are what we would expect from the energy-conserving rat that expands

FIGURE 4.20

Behavioral Effects of Motivational Variables Explained in Terms of
Conservation Theory

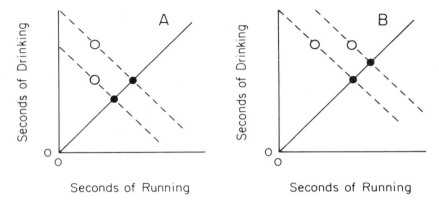

Seconds of Running

a negligible amount of energy on each short trip, but a substantial
amount on each long trip.

From Figure 4.16 on, all of our graphic representations of this
conservation model seem to predict a linear relation between the two
behaviors controlled by the schedule. As the total amount of behavior
A rises, the total amount of behavior B declines linearly, with a slope
equal to the slope of our constant-quantity line. This impression is
not quite accurate (Allison 1979b, 1981a). Actually, the model can
tolerate a spline function, two lines chopped and spliced end-to-end.
The top line segment in the spline function would slope downward from
left to right, but the bottom segment would reverse direction at the
joint, descending from right to left. To explain this subtle feature of
the conservation model, Figure 4.21 returns to the more accurate
staircase representation of three reciprocal fixed-ratio schedules.
Each schedule in panel A requires a certain number of instrumental
lever presses for each contingent food pellet. Schedule 1 requires
the largest number of presses per pellet, schedule 3 the smallest.

Suppose we first train the rat with schedules 3 and 2, then
switch to schedule 1. In panel A, schedule 1 requires so many lever
presses that the rat will arrive at the constant-quantity line, and
therefore quit responding, before it satisfies the instrumental requirement even once. In consequence, the rat will never see a response-contingent food pellet, but only a test cage equipped with a

FIGURE 4.21

Staircase Representation of Three Reciprocal Fixed-Ratio
Schedules in Relation to Conservation Model 1

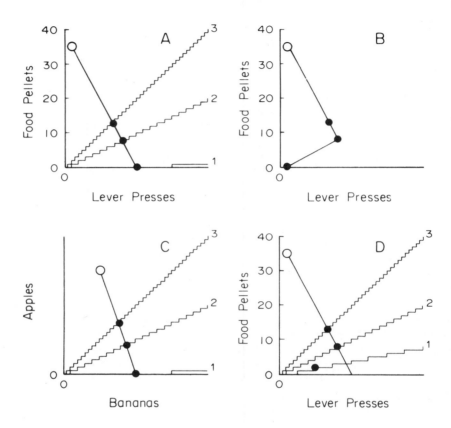

lever that seems totally ineffective as a means of securing food—the
operational equivalent of the single baseline condition, with a lever
freely available, but no food at all. For all practical purposes, each
such session is an "extinction" session. After a few of these sessions,
the rat should revert to the total number of lever presses it normally
performs under the single baseline condition. Because the single baseline level of lever pressing is typically low, the final results of all
three schedules would look like those shown in panel B: A spline function composed of two line segments, the top sloping down from left to
right, the bottom reversing direction at the joint, sloping down from
right to left.

But the model does not necessarily predict a spline function. We can easily imagine an instrumental behavior whose single basepoint might far exceed its paired basepoint. The monkey, given unlimited bananas but no apples, might eat more bananas than it does when both fruits are freely available. In that event, the results might resemble the simple linear function shown in panel C.

If this conservation model can handle both the simple linear result exemplified by Figures 4.7 and 4.8, and the nonlinear result exemplified by Figure 4.6, why go any further? Panel D shows why. Tested with schedule 1, the rat satisfies the instrumental requirement and eats the response-contingent pellet, perhaps many times; it therefore experiences the contingency condition, rather than the single baseline condition. Yet, the rat still quits responding before it reaches the constant-quantity line extrapolated from the other three points.

Several experiments have actually given results like those in panel D. For two examples, see the two lower points in Figure 4.6, where the schedules required 64 and 256 lever presses per pellet. Because these highly trained rats pressed the lever frequently enough to experience the terms of each of the two schedules, they must have quit responding for some reason other than failure to come into contact with the terms.

Conservation Model 1 plainly needs some repair work of the sort provided by model 2, published five years later (Allison 1981a).

CONSERVATION MODEL 2

To refresh your memory of Figures 4.6 and 4.7, recall that Teitelbaum's fat and lean rats responded quite differently to the very same schedules. On the schedule that offered the largest number of food pellets/press, the hyperphagic fat rats outperformed the normal lean rats, pressing the lever more frequently and eating more food. As the pellets/press ratio decreased, lean rats showed a steady increase in lever presses but a steady drop in food consumption; total pellets fell linearly as total presses increased, in the manner prescribed by Conservation Model 1. Fat rats behaved much the same way, but only up to a point; beyond that point, a further decrease in the pellets/press ratio resulted in a decrease in total presses rather than the increase shown before. Why did the fat rats stop climbing so soon up two lines of constraint that the lean ones climbed so easily? Why did they forge ahead of the lean on the two easiest schedules but lag so far behind on the two most difficult ones? How might we revise model 1 so as to explain more gracefully both the fat data and the lean?

A consumer demand equation (Awh 1976) relates the consumption of a particular commodity to the major independent variables that influence consumption. Faced with a sharp rise in the price of coffee, the grocery shopper may buy less coffee in favor of some readily available substitute, such as tea. In consequence, a demand equation for coffee might include as independent variables both the price of coffee and the availability of coffee substitutes. Such equations typically predict that consumers will buy less of commodity $\underline{Y}$ as its price rises and will buy less of $\underline{Y}$ as substitutes for $\underline{Y}$ become more readily available.

Why not apply a similar logic to Teitelbaum's rats? In a sense, the rat buys each food pellet at a particular behavioral price, such as 1 press/pellet, established by the constraints of the contingency schedule. Unlike the typical grocery store, the typical test cage offers no supply of some alternative food. But keep in mind that the rat carries at all times an alternative source of calories, food stored internally as body fat—a substitute for external food pellets, possessed in greater quantity by the fat rat than the lean. When external food is relatively cheap, say 1 press/pellet, the rat may buy food with abandon. At a much higher price, say 256 presses/pellet, the rat may buy less food and draw more heavily on its bodily stores of food, especially if the stores are relatively large.

We can conceptualize this substitution process as a third behavior, much like the third behavior involved in traveling between the lever and the drinking tube or the food trough. But there are several important differences. We can easily observe and record a trip; we cannot yet observe and record the specific "other" behaviors that the rat substitutes for eating. But we can hypothesize their existence, and we can also hypothesize that they, along with lever pressing, have something in common with eating. We can also hypothesize that these other behaviors grow more prevalent as the behavioral price of food rises, and more so among fat rats than lean. Conservation Model 2 allows for all of these hypothetical possibilities.

For application to the kind of experiment reported by Teitelbaum, a convenient mathematical version of model 2 is

$$\underline{N}(\underline{kI} + \underline{C}) + \underline{ji}(\underline{I}/\underline{C}) = \underline{kO}_i + \underline{O}_c = \underline{B} \qquad (4.1)$$

The left-hand side of the equation models the contingency session, and the rest models the paired baseline session. In the first parenthetical term on the left, $\underline{I}$ refers to the size of the run, the number of instrumental lever presses the schedule requires for each contingent food pellet. The size of the rise is $\underline{C}$, the one contingent food pellet received upon each completion of the $\underline{I}$th lever press. The third symbol is a scaling constant: $\underline{k}$ represents the amount of the dimension entailed in pressing the lever once, relative to the amount entailed in eating one food pellet. Thus, the sum $\underline{kI} + \underline{C}$ represents the amount of the dimensional quantity contained in one behavioral bundle, one run and one rise up the line of schedule constraint. The N in front of the parenthetical term is a dependent variable, the total number of runs and rises the rat completes over the course of the contingency session. By increasing N, the rat climbs ever higher up the line of schedule constraint, performing more lever presses and eating more pellets along the way.

In the second parenthetical term on the left, I/C refers to the number of presses/pellet, the behavioral price of food as established by the schedule. Two constants appear in front of that term. The constant i refers to the individual rat's tendency to substitute other behaviors; if our hypothesis is correct, i should be larger among fat rats than lean. The partial product, $i(I/C)$, expresses the total amount of this other behavior; thus, the model plainly hypothesizes that other behavior should increase as the price of food rises, and more so among the fat rats than the lean. The second constant, j, is another scaling constant, the amount of the dimension entailed by one unit of other behavior, relative to the amount entailed by eating one food pellet. Accordingly, the full product, $ji(I/C)$, expresses the total amount of the dimensional quality attributable to other behavior. Throughout the entire equation we use the food pellet as our arbitrary measure of the underlying dimension.

On the right-hand side, O_i signifies the total number of lever presses performed in the paired baseline condition; O_c, the total number of food pellets eaten. Thus, $kO_i + O_c$ represents the total amount of the dimension, measured in terms of food pellets, the rat derived from pressing and eating under the paired baseline condition. The left-hand side represents exactly the same total but acknowledges that the rat might derive some of that total from behavior other than pressing or eating. Notice why the right-hand side omits any reference to behavior other than pressing or eating. If the rat has free, unlimited access to lever and food, as it does in the paired baseline condition, it has no reason to substitute any other behavior for eating. To see the mathematical version of model 1, cross out the "other behavior" term on the left-hand side of equation 4.1, $ji(I/C)$.

We can fit equation 4.1 to Teitelbaum's data by multiple regression analysis, a statistical technique that shows how closely the data conform to the model, and also provides numerical estimates of the constants in the model equation: k, ji, and $(kO_i + O_c)$. Such analyses showed that the model fit the data very closely. They also revealed some sensible differences between dynamic and normal rats in terms of the numerical values the constants had to assume if equation 4.1 were to fit the two very different curves in Figures 4.6 and 4.7. The constant ji was positive and considerably larger among the dynamic group than among the normal, in support of the notion that other behavior increased with the price of food, and more so among the fat rats than among the lean. Another major difference turned up in the estimate of total food consumption in the paired baseline condition—over twice as large for the dynamic group as for the normal. Although Teitelbaum reported no paired baseline measure, the model thus told us that if they had been tested under the paired baseline condition, the dynamics would have eaten about twice as much food as the normals. That inference agrees nicely with observations that have often been made under free-feeding conditions, where dynamics typically eat two to three times as much as normals.

Model 2 fares better than model 1, but its improved performance comes at a cost, the cost of assuming an implicit substitution process. How could we bring this process out into the open?

Imagine a test cage equipped with three retractable metal tubes, a water tube on the left, saccharin on the right, and a dry tube in between. Each reciprocal contingency schedule requires a certain number of instrumental licks at the dry tube for 40 contingent licks at the water tube. The saccharin tube remains freely available throughout each two-hour session, a possible substitute for water. We raise the instrumental requirement across sessions, from 5 dry licks to 10, 20, 40, and 80, and thereby raise the behavioral price of water, dry licks/water lick.

Figure 4.22 shows the response of the one rat tested in this experiment. [7] Look first at the five filled circles. As the price of water rises from the top schedule to the bottom, the water total falls steadily;

FIGURE 4.22

Total Contingent Water Licks or Free Saccharin Licks as a
Function of Total Instrumental Licks at an Empty Tube

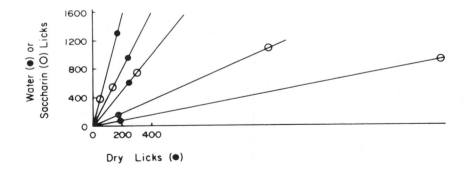

the dry total rises to a maximum and declines fairly steadily thereafter, much like Figure 4.6. At the same time, the rat shows a
fairly steady compensatory rise in total licks at the free saccharin
tube, as indicated by the five unfilled circles. In summary, the rat
seems more inclined to substitute saccharin for water as the behavioral price of water rises—an explicit substitution, observed and recorded directly, that conforms fairly closely to the implicit process
assumed when we applied model 2 to the Teitelbaum experiment.

PREVIEW

This chapter has presented some selected models and experiments from the psychological literature, chosen in part for their particular relevance to economic concepts, economic phenomena, and
economic theory.[8] The rest of the book will make their relevance
more apparent. By interpreting the constraints of a contingency
schedule in terms of a behavioral price, the chapter presented the
book's first major allusion to possible conceptual links between experimental psychology and economics. The next two chapters explore
these interdisciplinary connections in more detail. They focus on two
related subdivisions of microeconomics: the economics of consumer
demand and the economics of labor supply.

NOTES

1. In economics, the bliss point represents the greatest amount
of utility, or psychological satisfaction. For example, in a two-
dimensional space composed of apples and oranges, each point represents a certain number of apples and a certain number of oranges.
The consumer would find some of these points preferable to others.
For instance, the consumer might find two of each (2, 2) preferable to
one apple plus two oranges (1, 2). Mindful of storage costs, the consumer might prefer the (1, 2) combination to a (500, 500) combination.
If the consumer were asked to generate a preference order on all
points in the space, the first point on the list would represent the bliss
point. For an economic version of the bliss point in the context of
social welfare, see Awh (1976, pp. 448-51).

2. Applied to two behaviors, A and B, Staddon's model implies
that the organism will behave so as to minimize a weighted distance
function,

$$\underline{d}^2 = \underline{k}^2 (\underline{NA} - \underline{O}_a)^2 + (\underline{NB} - \underline{O}_b)^2$$

where $\underline{O}_a$ and $\underline{O}_b$ signify the paired baseline levels of the two behaviors, $\underline{A}$ and $\underline{B}$ signify the schedule requirements (run and rise), $\underline{N}$ signifies the number of times the organism completes the two requirements (the number of runs and rises), and $\underline{k}$ signifies the weight of behavior A relative to that of behavior B. The value of $\underline{N}$ that minimizes this distance function is

$$\underline{N} = (\underline{k}^2 \underline{AO}_a + \underline{BO}_b)/(\underline{k}^2 \underline{A}^2 + \underline{B}^2)$$

For further details see Wozny (1979), who also discusses formal relations between the minimum deviation model and one of the conservation models presented later in this chapter, Conservation Model 1.

3. Conservation models are common in the physical sciences. For a highly readable account of such models, see March (1978).

4. Conservation models for schedules other than the simple fixed-ratio schedule have appeared in a number of sources (Allison 1976, 1980; Shapiro and Allison 1978). Those models are for the "controlled-time" paradigm in which each experimental session has the same duration and the subject may vary the rate of responding (amount/time) by varying the total amount of responding from one session to another. Allison (1982) presents conservation models for the "controlled-amount" paradigm in which the experimenter ends each session as soon as the subject has completed a prescribed amount of responding. In that experimental paradigm the subject may vary the rate of responding (amount/time) by varying the time taken to complete the prescribed amount. The classic example is the straight runway experiment, where each trial ends as soon as the rat runs from start box to goal box and eats the food in the goal box. Because the distance between start box and goal box remains the same from one trial to the next, the rat can achieve a relatively high rate of instrumental responding, feet/second, by running relatively quickly from start to goal. This is essentially the same measure that Thorndike (1898) recorded in his experiment on the cat's escape from the puzzle box.

5. Morrison (1968) used this kind of methodology in an experiment whose results suggested the conservation of energy allocated to the rat's feeding and nonfeeding behaviors. Experiments on thermoregulatory behavior (Stern et al. 1979) suggest that the rat may conserve the heat from two different sources—microwaves of the sort used in microwave ovens and an infrared lamp. Shaved, refrigerated rats could press a lever to turn on the infrared lamp while exposed to microwave stimulation of various power densities (milliwatts per square centimeter). As the power density of the microwave stimulation increased, the rats showed a linear decrease in the proportion of session time they spent pressing the lever for infrared heat. My own

regression analysis of the data reported by Stern et al. (1979, foot-note 12) shows that $I = .33 - .0066M$, $r^2 = 1.00$, where I refers to infrared time and M refers to microwave power density. According to the model, when the microwave is turned off ($M = 0$), the rat should spend .33 of the session with the infrared lamp on; the value actually observed, .326, agreed closely with the value predicted.

6. Consider three different behaviors, such as eating apples (a), bananas (b), and cherries (c). If the same dimension is conserved among these three different behaviors, we should be able to predict the amount of responding under contingency schedules that involve a novel pair of behaviors. For example, suppose we have tested the animal with several banana-apple schedules that require a certain number of instrumental bananas for each contingent apple. We plot our results, apples against bananas, and see that the results form a linear function whose slope is $-k_{ab}$. Purely to ease the exposition, let us name the unknown dimension "calories." Thus, the number of apple-calories per banana is k_{ab}. Repeating this procedure for the cherry-banana pair, we plot bananas against cherries and see that the slope of the linear function is $-k_{bc}$. Thus, the number of banana calories per cherry is k_{bc}. From our two measured values of k, we should be able to predict the slope of the function for our novel pair, the cherry-apple pair. If

$$k_{ab} = \text{apple-calories/banana}$$

and

$$k_{bc} = \text{banana-calories/cherry}$$

then the product of these two ks should predict the animal's response to schedules involving the novel cherry-apple pair:

$$
\begin{aligned}
k_{ab}k_{bc} &= (\text{apple-calories/banana}) \, (\text{banana-calories/cherry}) \\
&= (\text{apple-calories/cherry}) \, (\text{banana-calories/banana}) \\
&= (\text{apple-calories/cherry}) \, (1) \\
&= \text{apple-calories/cherry} \\
&= k_{ac}
\end{aligned}
$$

Thus, if we test the animal under several schedules with our novel cherry-apple pair and plot apples against cherries, the results should form a linear function with a slope of $-k_{ac}$. This feature of the conservation model has been applied to one of the most recalcitrant problems in contemporary research on animal behavior: the problem of explaining why a contingent behavior may facilitate one instrumental behavior more readily than another, despite comparable basepoints and schedule requirements. For example, in the golden hamster, response-contingent food readily facilitates instrumental digging, scrabbling, or rearing, but does not readily facilitate face washing, scratching, or scent marking (Shettleworth 1975). In the context of our present example, suppose we find that $k_{ab} = k_{bc} = 2$. Reference to the family of constant-quantity lines in Figure 4.18 shows that if $k_{ab} = 2$, then the contingent eating of apples can readily facilitate the instrumental eating of bananas. But, by the same token, contingent apples will not facilitate so readily the instrumental eating of cherries, because $k_{ac} = k_{ab}k_{bc} = 4$. Thus, the model can potentially predict in advance that a contingent behavior that readily facilitates one instrumental behavior will not readily facilitate another. Indeed, if the predicted k is extremely large, it may prove practically impossible to detect any significant facilitation effect. For further discussion and a confirmatory experimental application of the model to four behaviors (pressing a heavy lever or a light lever for access to a narrow-gauge or broad-gauge water tube), see Allison, Miller, and Wozny (1979, pp. 24-30).

7. This unpublished experiment was conducted in my laboratory with the help of Kevin Moore, Douglas Forrest, and Sharyn Hoffman.

8. All of the selected models attempt to explain facilitation or suppression effects in terms of schedule constraints upon the response totals observed under the free-performance baseline condition. An alternative class of models would attend, instead, to constraints on the temporal distribution of behavior in the free baseline condition. For example, Dunham (1977) has proposed an optimal duration model whose general features can be outlined in terms of a schedule involving instrumental running for the contingent opportunity to drink. Suppose that in the paired baseline condition we have recorded not only total drinking time, but also the average duration of the drinking bout and the average duration of the pause between bouts. We also record, and perhaps manipulate, the duration of bouts and pauses during the contingency session. Dunham proposes that contingent drinking will facilitate instrumental running if the drinking bouts are shorter, or the pauses longer, than they were in the free baseline condition. Conversely, contingent drinking will suppress instrumental running if the drinking bouts are longer, or the pauses shorter, than they were in the free baseline condition. No comprehensive test of the optimal duration model has yet appeared in the experimental literature, and the model's possible economic import remains to be explored. I have also omitted the matching model (Herrnstein 1970) for choice between the alternative components of a concurrent schedule. This model pro-

poses that the relative frequency of responding on an alternative matches the relative frequency of reinforcement for responding on that alternative. For critical discussions of the matching model in the context of economics, see Schwartz and Lacey (1982, pp. 104-23) and Lea (1978).

Chapter 5

Consumer Demand

If food, water, saccharin, music, and a pursuit-rotor toy are not reinforcers, what are they? According to the models discussed in Chapter 4, such items are nothing special. When freely available without constraint, they simply engage the individual's behavior in varying degrees, depending on the intrinsic characteristics of item and individual and the latter's motivational state. A contingency schedule modifies behavior by placing certain external constraints on the individual's access to such items. The behavioral effects of the schedule are an incidental result of the adaptive response to schedule constraints. Theorists differ on the exact character of the adaptive response. Perhaps the organism approximates as nearly as possible the way it would behave if given free access to the behaviors constrained by the schedule. Perhaps the organism conserves some underlying dimension common to the behaviors constrained by the schedule. All of these theorists acknowledge the schedule constraints as a key determinant of the schedule's ability to modify behavior.

Our next task is to examine these constraints and their effects from the standpoint of economics. The examination will show that the laboratory rewards traditionally called reinforcers might well be viewed as economic goods or commodities. Accordingly, the models discussed in Chapter 4 might well be viewed as models of economic behavior. If the rat is engaged in a kind of economic behavior as it presses the lever for food, a psychological theory that purports to explain the behavior is a theory of economic behavior. By the same token, we should be able to apply to the same behavior a body of theory with which psychologists are generally unfamiliar, conventional economic theory. [1]

The first stage of the examination makes use of some simple integrative concepts from the economics of consumer demand. It explores similarities between laboratory rewards and economic goods on two different levels, definitional and empirical. First, we examine the definition of an economic good and ask whether a laboratory reward, such as a response-contingent food pellet, might satisfy the definition. Next, we examine some facts about economic goods—empirical laws that economists suppose they follow—and ask whether the rewards used in psychological experiments follow the same laws. If the fundamental similarities seem to outweigh any differences, we can hardly fail to see the mutual relevance of the two disciplines.

SCARCITY AND EXCHANGE

Some define an economic good as something the person is willing to buy in exchange for something else: in a culture that appreciates the convenience of money, your side of beef in exchange for some of my dollars. In a simpler barter economy, the exchange would involve no money or other such tokens, but a direct trade for other goods or services: your side of beef for my bushels of corn, your supper for my song.

We saw in the earlier chapters that humans and animals, subjected to the constraints of a contingency schedule, often seem willing to exchange some instrumental behavior in return for the chance to perform some contingent behavior. A direct barter exchange of one thing for another, the trade looks much like an economic transaction between subject and experimenter, the one who both designs and purveys the schedule. The subject/consumer trades a certain number of lever presses in exchange for one of the food pellets held in store by the experimenter/shopkeeper.

Like the human who works for money instead, later exchanging the money for other goods and services, various animals—chimpanzees, dogs, cats—have wits enough to work for artificial tokens that they later can exchange for food (Cowles 1937; Ellson 1937; Smith 1939; Wolfe 1936). Even if other animals do not, we cannot for that reason bar them from the world of economics. Humans were probably economic creatures long before they invented money, a great convenience but hardly a crucial element in trade. In the words of Adam Smith, father of economics, dated 1776, "The real price of everything, what everything really costs to the man who wants to acquire it, is the toil and trouble of acquiring it" (p. 36). Later economists have also referred to effort as the bedrock foundation of price (for example, Robbins 1930). If you ever have grown a tomato or bought one at market, you know something about the toil and trouble of producing a tomato, or the toil and trouble of getting the cash to buy one.

The terms of a contingency schedule often establish both the kind and the amount of toil and the kind and the amount of the thing received in turn. Consider the prearranged terms of some fixed-ratio schedules: 1 lever press for each .045-gram food pellet; 100 lever presses for each .045-gram food pellet; 100 lever presses for each .090-gram food pellet; 15 minutes of study for 20 minutes of sewing. Some experiments (see Kazdin 1977, for example) have used schedules that approximate the flexibility of a more advanced economy: "Mental patients on this ward who make their beds this morning will get 20 tokens apiece, which they can exchange for candy, cigarettes, or magazines in the hospital canteen, in accordance with the schedule of token prices posted there." This arrangement reflects in full the economist's conventional distinction between work and purchase (Castro and Weingarten 1970), a distinction missing from the "barter" schedules commonly used in psychological experimentation. Similar use has been made of tokens in the teaching of basic skills in the classroom: Learn this part of the alphabet for marbles exchangeable for toys or games of your choice (O'Leary 1978; Staats 1975).

The definitions often refer to economics as a problem of allocation, how to distribute scarce or limited resources. Thus, an economic good or commodity is relatively scarce; as food is generally scarce, but air is not, food is, but air is generally not, an economic good.

If you have ever tried to train a rat to press a lever for food, you probably know that successful training depends on the scarcity of food. Your laboratory instructor speaks of the need to "motivate" the rat before any attempt at training and probably means one or both of two things. If we make the rat go entirely without food for several hours before each session, we can guarantee that the rat will start each session in a motivational state of acute hunger. In terms of the performance models discussed in Chapter 4, hunger elevates the amount of eating the rat would do if it could suddenly eat all it pleased: Hunger raises the baseline level of eating. Alternatively, if we keep the rat on a meager daily ration, it eventually loses a significant amount of its body weight. At a constant 90 percent or 80 percent of its normal weight, for all practical purposes the rat is chronically hungry. From the rat's point of view, our motivational techniques impose one kind of scarcity relative to those days before the experiment when food was more abundant, a time when the home cage always contained an unlimited supply of food.

With or without that first kind of scarcity, all contingency schedules impose a second kind of scarcity: if no publications, then no tenure; no spinach, no dessert; no study, no passing grade; no lever presses, no food. Now the rat has some control over its access to food, but any contingency schedule still limits that access by imposing an instrumental response requirement: No food will come unless the rat presses the lever. Some schedules are assuredly more generous than others; a schedule that requires one press/pellet is more generous with food than one that requires ten presses/pellet; but all contingency schedules exact some behavioral price for the contingent reward, by definition of a contingency schedule.

Notice that each of these two kinds of scarcity can be identified in the animal's evolutionary habitat, as well as the artificial laboratory habitat created by the experimenter. Food is typically "patchy" in the wild—the abundance of food generally varies from one place to the next, and from one time to the next. Accordingly, the foraging animal may use much of its limited time and energy in the search for food, despite which it may often have to settle for meals that are smaller or less frequent than the meals it would eat if food were available without limit. Pressing a lever for food can be viewed as a kind of foraging behavior, although it differs superficially, and perhaps importantly, from the foraging behavior normally seen in the animal's evolutionary environment.

Some schedules impose a third kind of scarcity, and others do not. This third kind of scarcity is response deprivation. If the rat eats only 10 pellets and performs ten lever presses when both food and lever are freely available without limit, then a fixed-ratio schedule that requires one lever press for each 1-pellet delivery does not deprive the rat of eating: It could get 10 pellets, the paired baseline number, merely by doing the baseline number of lever presses, ten. If we elevate baseline eating by making the rat hungrier, say to 100 pellets, the same schedule will deprive the rat of eating: The ten baseline lever presses would gain 10 pellets, 90 short of baseline— our third kind of scarcity, response deprivation. Notice that if we choose not to make the rat hungrier, we can deprive the rat of eating by changing the terms of our schedule, say to five lever presses for each 1-pellet delivery. The ten baseline presses would gain only 2 pellets, 8 short of the baseline number.

As we saw in earlier chapters, response deprivation is a most effective kind of scarcity; it is an antecedent condition that generally induces the individual to do more than the baseline amount of the other response. Viewed in an economic context, this facilitation effect may have some use as a definition of work, or productive labor. If the rat has free access to everything, does it do any work (in the economic sense) as it does its baseline number of lever presses? Why should I take the trouble to corner the local supply of food and purvey a contingency schedule, unless I want more lever presses than the rat would do anyhow if left undisturbed in the baseline paradise?

What it does in paradise is not productive labor in the economic sense; what it does over and above that, in response to the constraints of my contingency schedule, is a different matter.

In summary, the response–contingent rewards employed in the psychological laboratory have many of the features that define an economic good or commodity in terms of scarcity and exchange. We may try to motivate the individual by supplying less than the individual would consume at will if the reward were freely available without limit. We require some behavior in exchange for the reward; and we may require so much of that behavior that the normal amount would bring less of the reward than the individual would consume freely. These definitional similarities prepare the way to the next stage of our examination, one that attends to empirical similarities between laboratory rewards and economic goods.

THE DEMAND LAW

All else equal, we can sell more beer, shoes, cars, or gasoline at a low price than at a high price. Economists refer to this simple inverse relation between price and quantity consumed as the demand law: As price ($\underline{P}$) rises, quantity ($\underline{Q}$) falls.

A specific example (Lancaster 1969) appears in Figure 5.1, which plots total watermelon consumption, in millions of tons per year ($\underline{Q}$), against the unit price of watermelons, cents per pound ($\underline{P}$): As $\underline{P}$ increased, $\underline{Q}$ decreased.

Students of economics will notice that Figure 5.1 reverses the conventional practice of economists, who normally plot $\underline{P}$ on the vertical axis and $\underline{Q}$ on the horizontal. Students of other disciplines will notice that the figure conforms to a more widespread convention that plots the dependent variable on the vertical axis and the independent variable on the horizontal.

In all economics, there is probably nothing more fundamental than the demand law, nothing that approaches more closely the status of an axiom. Indeed, many economists seem to regard this sensitivity to price as the principal empirical test of rationality (McKenzie and Tullock 1981), a test that one might pass while failing others of a religious or psychological character, such as the possession of a soul, a mind, clarity of thought, or a strong chess game. As a valid sign of rationality, obedience to the demand law depends on the assumption that we try to maximize utility, or psychological satisfaction. All else equal, as the price of apples rises do we buy fewer apples and more of some substitute, such as bananas? Such behavior can be derived mathematically from the hypothesis that we allocate our limited resources so as to maximize the utility gained from our

FIGURE 5.1

Watermelon Consumption as a Function of Price

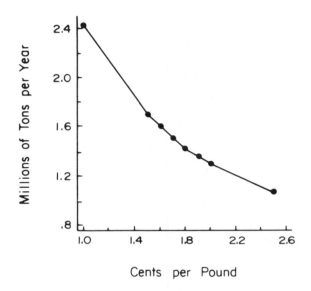

expenditures. (Under certain theoretical circumstances, the rational consumer might violate the demand law; these theoretical conditions are discussed later in the chapter under the heading of the Giffen good.)

In the eyes of the economist, every behavior has some sort of price—there is no such thing as a free lunch—and the total amount of any particular behavior should depend on its price, in accordance with the demand law. Several economists have shown how this simple principle might illuminate and unify many diverse aspects of human behavior that go far beyond the economist's traditional field, the field of commercial life (McKenzie and Tullock 1981). Should punishment deter crime? Of course it should. If we impose harsher punishments on convicted criminals, we raise the price and therefore reduce the amount of criminal behavior. The average criminal is not deranged, but just as rational as the average grocery shopper. Maybe that is why empirical studies of this issue generally show that punishment does tend to deter crime.

Should the government compel the auto industry to build safer cars? Maybe not—if we reduce the likelihood of personal injury in automobile accidents, we may reduce the personal cost of reckless driving, and thereby encourage reckless driving.

Should we press for a reform of our state's divorce laws? Think of the married couples who would be so much happier if they could afford the cost of a divorce. But, in cutting the cost of divorce, we also cut the cost of carelessness in choosing a marital partner. Maybe that is why the fraction of married women is relatively small in states where divorce is relatively costly: If the high cost of divorce encourages more careful selection of a mate, marriageable men and women may spend more time in the search for a spouse and thereby marry later than they would otherwise.

If obedience to the demand law lays claim to rationality, rats are no less rational than humans. Figure 5.2 shows a consumer demand function based on two rats tested with 14 different fixed-ratio schedules (Collier, Hirsch, and Hamlin 1972). Each schedule required a certain number of lever presses for each 45-milligram food pellet. The rats lived in their test cages 24 hours/day, with water freely available, and got all of their daily food by pressing the lever. The behavioral price of food ranged from 1 press/pellet up to 220 presses/pellet. The figure plots total grams of food consumed on the vertical axis and the unit price of food, lever presses/gram, on the horizontal. In accordance with the demand law, total food consumption (Q) generally decreased as the unit price of food (P) increased.

The unfilled circles show that goldfish also obey the demand law (Rozin and Mayer 1964). Each of the seven fish got food by striking an underwater target during each one-hour contingency session; each time the fish paid the behavioral price specified by the schedule, an automatic dispenser shot a waterproof food pellet into a ring floating

FIGURE 5.2

Total Food Consumed by Rat or Fish as a Function of the
Behavioral Price of Food

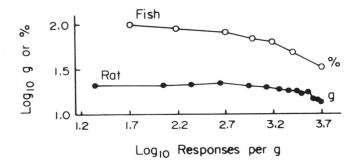

on the surface. The schedules specified seven different prices, responses/gram of food. As the behavioral price of food increased, total food consumption decreased.

I should note in passing that the original reports of these experiments presented the results rather differently. Throughout this chapter, practically all of the consumer demand functions based on laboratory experiments with contingency schedules represent old data subjected to new analyses intended to reveal the economic implications of the data (Allison 1979a). The original reports typically make no reference to laboratory rewards as economic goods, and focus on instrumental performance under a particular schedule, rather than the total amount of reward the animal received for its instrumental performance.

The fixed-ratio schedules of the psychological laboratory normally vary price by varying the instrumental requirement, while holding constant the magnitude of each contingent reward. For example, in the rat experiment of Figure 5.2, each contingent reward consisted of one 45-milligram food pellet. The experimenter varied the unit price of food by varying the number of lever presses required for each food pellet, ranging from 1 press to 220 presses. Thus, the unit price of food ranged from 22 presses/gram to 4,889 presses/gram (1/.045 = 22, and 220/.045 = 4,889). We could also raise the unit price of food by cutting the weight of the food pellet while holding constant the number of lever presses required for each pellet. Analogously, we can raise the unit price of candy by raising the price of the candy bar, or charging the old price for a smaller bar. The evidence suggests that the rat's consumption of food or water conforms to the demand law either way.

Figure 5.3 presents the case for water (Allison, Miller, and Wozny 1979). Six rats got all of their water in daily one-hour sessions. The point on the left in Figure 5.3 shows total time spent drinking under a baseline condition with lever and water ever present, along with food. The other nine points show time spent drinking under nine different schedules that varied the unit price of drinking in two different ways. Any particular schedule required either 10, 20, or 30 seconds of instrumental lever holding for each contingent access to water; it allowed in return either 20, 30, or 40 seconds of contingent drinking. By combining the three different "package prices" with the three different "package sizes," we get nine different schedules but only seven different prices, seconds of holding/second of drinking.

Some of the nine schedules vary the price of the package while holding the package size constant. For example, consider these three schedules: 10 seconds of holding/20 seconds of drinking, 20/20, and 30/20. These schedules charge 0.5, 1, and 1.5 seconds of holding/second of drinking.

FIGURE 5.3

Total Time Spent Drinking as a Function of the Behavioral Price
of Drinking

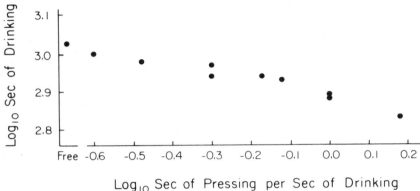

Some of the nine schedules vary the size of the package while
holding the price of the package constant. For example, compare
these three: 10 seconds of holding/20 seconds of drinking, 10/30,
and 10/40. These three schedules charge 0.5, 0.33, and 0.25 seconds
of holding/second of drinking. Notice that two pairs of the nine schedules have different requirements but identical prices: 10/20 versus
20/40, and 20/20 versus 30/30. Figure 5.3 shows that total drinking
generally decreased as the unit price of drinking increased; schedules
with different requirements but identical prices produced comparable
amounts of drinking.

Figure 5.4 shows more clearly that both types of price rise induced a drop in consumption. Moving from left to right, total drinking fell as the price of the package increased from 10 seconds of lever
holding to 20, and from 20 to 30, with the size of the package held
constant. Moving from the top curve to the bottom, total drinking fell
as the size of the package decreased from 40 seconds of drinking to
30 and from 30 to 20, with the price of the package held constant.[2]
As you may recall from Chapter 4, in this kind of experiment the
rat's consumption of water is also sensitive to another kind of cost,
the effort cost of the trip between lever and drinking tube (see Figure
4.4).

Some of the other schedules discussed in Chapter 4 give the consumer some control over the unit price of the good. Recall the restaurant that charges a fixed amount of money, $\underline{X}$ dollars, for all of

FIGURE 5.4

Total Time Spent Drinking as a Function of the Behavioral Price of
Access to Water and the Amount of Drinking Allowed per Access

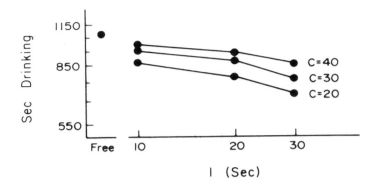

the food the diner chooses to eat in one meal, Q. The unit price of
the food is X/Q, but the seller cannot specify that price in advance:
The seller specifies X by printing it on the menu, but Q depends on
the consumer. In the same way, the fixed-ratio schedule with an optional magnitude of food reward allows the rat some control over the
unit price of food, a price we must calculate after the fact. The experimenter sets and may vary the price of admission to the food bin,
say from 1 instrumental press of the lever up to 5,120 presses; but
the rat sets the size of each contingent meal.

Even in this kind of arrangement, a cooperative price-setting
system, the rat's consumption of food or water still conforms to the
demand law. An illustrative demand curve for food appears in Figure
5.5, based on an experiment in which rats lived in their test cages
around the clock (Collier, Hirsch, and Hamlin 1972). The two points
on the left show two daily totals, food intake and meals, under a free-
feeding baseline condition with water also available. The remaining
points come from 12 different schedules that each required a certain
number of lever presses, X, for each access to the food bin, ranging
from 1 press to 5,120 presses. The bin stayed open until a ten-
minute pause in eating that defined the end of the meal, whereupon the
schedule required another X press(es) for the next admission to the
bin. On the horizontal axis we see the unit price of food, calculated
after the fact as total lever presses/total grams consumed for the
day; as unit price increased, total food intake decreased.

The price of the meal, X, also appears on the horizontal axis;
as the price of the meal increased, total meals decreased. Other

FIGURE 5.5

Total Food Consumption and Total Meals as Functions of
Behavioral Price

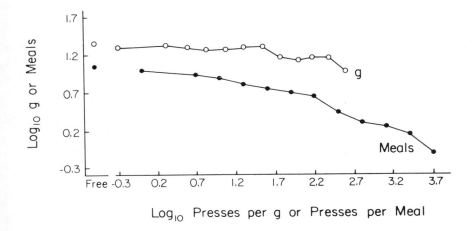

analyses showed that the rats took both larger and fewer daily meals
as the price of the meal increased; but, as the figure shows, these
compensatory increases in the size of the meal failed to hold food intake constant, and therefore failed to violate the demand law. Figure
5.6 shows comparable results from a similar experiment on the rat's
consumption of water (Marwine and Collier 1979). Volumetric intake
dropped significantly as the price of water increased. As the price
of the drinking bout increased the rat took fewer and larger bouts, but
the compensatory increase in bout size failed to achieve a constant
volumetric intake and therefore failed to violate the demand law.

Like the fixed-ratio schedule with an optional magnitude of reward, the interval schedule—much the more popular of the two—also
allows the consumer considerable control over the unit price of the
contingent reward, calculated after the fact. Figure 5.7 presents a
staircase representation of the behavioral constraints imposed by a
schedule that arranges a series of one-pellet food setups at periodic
intervals; the setups occur $\underline{T}$ seconds apart. (The same constraints
apply whether we fix $\underline{T}$ or vary it from one setup to the next; and the
same constraints apply across schedules that set different values for
$\underline{T}$, such as 10-second intervals for one schedule and 120-second intervals for another schedule.) The first press of the lever after the $\underline{T}$-
second interval has elapsed causes the automatic dispenser to deliver

FIGURE 5.6

Total Water Consumption and Total Drinking Bouts as Functions
of Behavioral Price

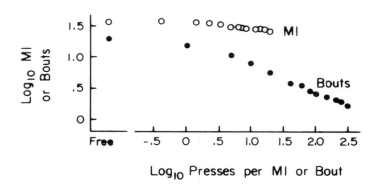

FIGURE 5.7

Staircase Representation of the Behavioral Constraints of an
Interval Schedule

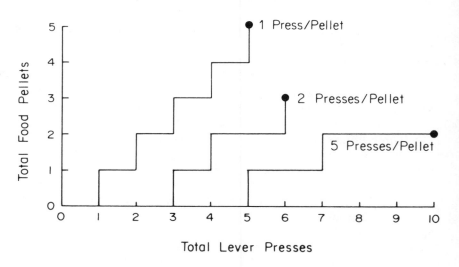

the contingent food pellet. Because any lever presses that occur during the T-second interval are ineffective, they serve only to raise the behavioral price of food above the lowest price attainable, one press/pellet. The top staircase function shows the path a rat might follow in consuming the food at the lowest price allowed by the schedule constraints: five presses and five pellets all told, for a unit behavioral price of one press/pellet. The rat cannot take any path above that one, but might follow any one of many paths below it, such as the middle path: six presses and three pellets all told, for a unit price of two presses/pellet. That is a higher price than the first, but not as high as the price the rat would pay if it followed the bottom path. Notice that the unit price of the food is the inverse of the slope: slope = pellets/press, price = presses/pellet, hence price = 1/slope.

Notice, too, that the hypothetical examples in Figure 5.7 conform to the demand law. The unit price of food, calculated after the fact, increases steadily as we move from the top path to the bottom, and total food consumption also decreases steadily.

But the constraints imposed by the schedule allow many other possible outcomes, some of which would violate the demand law. Figure 5.8 presents a linear representation of two interval schedules, both hypothetical, that differ only in the values they set for T, 7 seconds for one and 14 seconds for the other. The top line represents the lowest price attainable under the constraints of either schedule, one press/pellet. The slopes of the other two lines show that the rat happens to pay a higher price for food under the 14-second schedule than the 7-second schedule. Suppose that under the 7-second schedule, the rat performs as shown by the unlabeled point on the middle line. If it also performed on the 14-second schedule, as shown by point a, the rat would conform to the demand law: less food consumption at the higher price. But if it performed instead as shown by point b, the rat would violate the demand law: more food consumption at the higher price; more on the 14-second schedule than the 7-second schedule. How do rats actually behave in response to the constraints of an interval schedule?

In one such experiment (Allison 1980), rats pressed a lever for all of their water during a series of daily one-hour test sessions. Each rat was tested under two different reciprocal schedules, each of which required one lever press for every 25-lick access to the drinking tube. Both schedules arranged the drinking-tube setups at variable intervals; the setup intervals averaged 7 seconds on one schedule, 14 seconds on the other. The results appear in Figure 5.9A: The rats hit a higher behavioral price, presses/lick, on the 14-second schedule. They also performed fewer licks there than on the 7-second schedule, in agreement with the demand law.

Figure 5.9B adds two more data points to the two shown in panel A. The unfilled circle on the left shows total licks and lever

FIGURE 5.8

Linear Representation of the Behavioral Constraints of Two
Interval Schedules

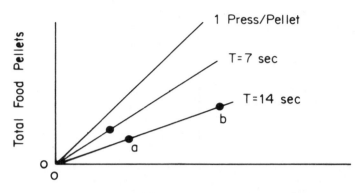

FIGURE 5.9

Total Water Licks as a Function of Total Lever Presses by Rats
Tested with Various Interval Schedules

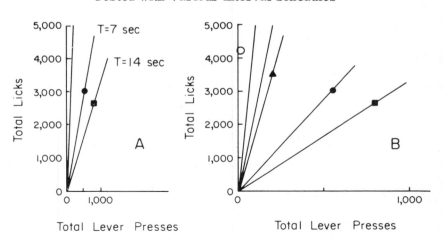

presses under the paired baseline condition, with free access to lever and tube. The filled triangle goes with the steeper line of schedule constraint; it shows the results of a 7-second schedule that required one press for every 50-lick access. Like Figure 5.9A, the results in 5.9B conform to the demand law. Notice that they also conform to Conservation Model 1: As total lever presses increased, total licks decreased linearly.

But why do rats pay more than they need to, more than the lowest price allowed by the structural constraints of the variable-interval schedule? They would probably do better with the help of an external clock that tells when the interval has elapsed—perhaps a light that comes on when each setup comes due. That kind of signal seems to improve the rat's performance under a fixed-interval schedule (Segal 1962); it probably reduces the number of ineffective, inflationary lever presses, but why does it not eliminate them entirely? A similar question pertains to the fixed-ratio schedule with an optional magnitude of reward; it, too, remains unanswered. If you will look again at Figures 4.10, 4.11, and 4.12, this time in terms of price and consumption, you will see that the question also pertains to the behavior of rats and pigeons under the constraints of the concurrent fixed-ratio schedule. Economists, take note: In failing to approach the paired basepoint ideal as closely as these three kinds of schedule would allow them to do, each in its own way, these animals may be telling us that they also fail to maximize utility.

In response to a significant rise in the price of home heating fuel, many of us would adjust to the onset of winter by turning the thermostat a little below last year's setting and donning more woolen clothing. As commercial heat grows more expensive, we consume less of it. Similarly, laboratory rats buy less heat as its behavioral price rises. Weiss and Laties (1960) clipped each rat's fur and put the rat into a test cage inside a ventilated refrigerator at 2° Celsius. The shorn, refrigerated rat could buy external heat by pressing a lever; each response activated a heat lamp at various intensities for various durations. The consequent rise in skin temperature was inferred from another experiment that measured the rise directly by means of subdermal thermocouples. Figure 5.10 expresses the unit price of heat as the number of lever presses/Celsius degree rise in skin temperature; as price increased, total heat generally decreased.

In the popular imagination, a drug addict is one who must get the usual amount of the drug at any price. In economic terms, the drug addict violates the demand law, consuming the same amount at all prices. The experimental literature exposes the popular image as a myth, showing that the consumption of various drugs, addictive and otherwise, declines as the behavioral price of the drug rises. One of the pertinent experiments (Weeks 1962; Weeks and Collins 1964)

FIGURE 5.10

Heat Consumption by Rats as a Function of the Behavioral
Price of Heat

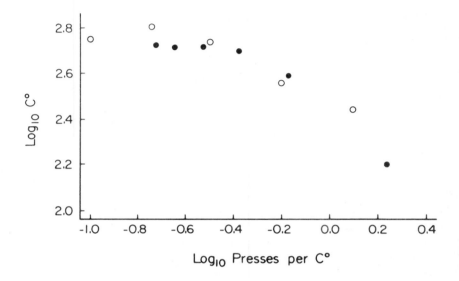

allowed rats to "mainline" morphine by pressing a lever for intravenous injections; the dosage ranged from 0.1 milligram of morphine/
kilogram of body weight up to 10 milligrams/kilogram. Figure 5.11A
expresses the price of morphine as the number of lever presses re-
quired/mg/kg and combines the results of two separate experiments:
As price increased, morphine consumption decreased. Figure 5.11B
shows similar results from a similar experiment on the rat's consumption of cocaine (Pickens and Thompson 1968).

Like the rat that works directly for morphine or cocaine, the
monkey consumes less cocaine or pentobarbital as the behavioral price
of the drug rises (Goldberg et al. 1971), and alcoholic rats and humans
consume less alcohol. Rats that press a lever for a dipper of ethanol
respond to a rise in the price of buying fewer ethanol cocktails (Meisch
and Thompson 1973). A similar experiment (Bigelow and Liebson
1972) studied two humans confined to a hospital, chronic alcoholics
who pressed a lever for "screwdrivers" concocted of ethanol and
orange juice. The behavioral price of a drink ranged from 100 lever
presses to 5,000; as the price rose, total alcohol consumption fell
steadily.

FIGURE 5.11

Drug Consumption by Rats as a Function of Behavioral Price

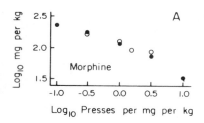 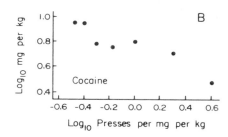

Cigarette smoking shows a similar sensitivity to its behavioral cost. In Figure 5.12 we see the daily number of cigarettes smoked by an adult male, an experimental volunteer who lived for several months in an apartmentlike laboratory setting (Findley 1966). The behavioral price of a cigarette ranged from 25 key presses to 500; as the price increased from day to day, daily consumption fell from about 25 cigarettes to 9.

According to the demand law, consumption (Q) falls in response to a rise in price (P)—an empirical relation displayed by aggregate masses of consumers under the hurly-burly conditions of the economic

FIGURE 5.12

Cigarette Consumption as a Function of Behavioral Price

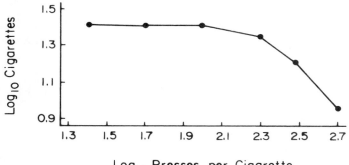

marketplace and by individual humans and animals paying a behavioral price for a great variety of rewards under the highly controlled conditions of the laboratory. We continue our empirical comparison of economic goods and laboratory rewards by looking at some of the fine-grained details of the consumer demand function, Q as a function of P. Exactly how much does Q fall in response to a rise in P? This question concerns the price elasticity of demand.

PRICE ELASTICITY OF DEMAND

Suppose a university's athletic department derives much of its annual revenue from sales of tickets to basketball games. The total number of tickets sold (Q) declines in response to periodic rises in the price of the ticket (P), in accordance with the demand law. But the total revenue on sales—the product PQ—climbs with each rise in price. Persons in charge of the soccer program eye the rising revenues from the basketball program and raise the price of admission to soccer games. Against all expectations based on the basketball experience, they discover an alarming decline in revenue on sales of soccer tickets.

Economists would describe these two contrasting cases in terms of the price elasticity of demand: Demand for basketball tickets is inelastic, but demand for soccer tickets is elastic. Price elasticity refers to the sensitivity of Q to variations in P. To say that demand is price-inelastic (elastic) is to say that the change in Q is small (large) relative to the change in P. If the rise in P occasions such a small drop in Q that PQ rises, as in the basketball example, demand is inelastic. If the rise in P occasions such a large drop in Q that PQ declines, as in the soccer example, demand is elastic. A third category, unit elasticity, describes the case in which PQ remains constant because the rise in P occasions a strictly proportional drop in Q.

Figure 5.13 presents a hypothetical example of each category, plotting Q and PQ against P. At $1 per bottle the shop manages to sell 64 bottles of perfume, for a total revenue of $64 on sales. Adventurous management quadruples the price to $4 per bottle; because the fourfold rise in price occasions only a twofold drop in consumption, to 32 bottles, revenue climbs to $128; demand is price-inelastic.

Emboldened by this discovery, management doubles the price, from $4 to $8; because this twofold rise in price occasions a twofold drop in consumption, from 32 bottles to 16, revenue holds constant at $128, illustrating unit elasticity.

What if we could derive the same revenue from still fewer sales? Think of the overhead costs we could save by storing, handling, and

FIGURE 5.13

Bottles of Perfume Sold and Revenue on Sales as Functions of
Bottle Price

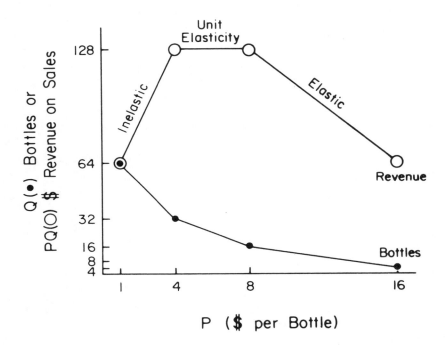

P ($ per Bottle)

selling only 8 bottles rather than 16. These entrepreneurial fantasies
lead to another exploratory price rise, from $8 to $16. Because this
next twofold rise in price occasions a catastrophic fourfold drop in
consumption, from 16 bottles to 4, revenue falls from $128 to $64.
Demand has become price-elastic.

Marketing data often reveal the general trend illustrated by
Figure 5.13: Relatively insensitive at low prices, demand grows
more price-responsive as the price rises, moving more or less
smoothly from one qualitative category to the next. Do laboratory
rewards show a similar trend?

The consumer demand functions presented earlier in this chapter plot Q against P, but omit the PQ revenue curve shown in Figure
5.13. What is the behavioral analogue of revenue on sales? Suppose
the rat buys a total of ten food pellets (Q) at a unit price (P) of two
lever presses per pellet. Then the revenue analogue is the total num-

ber of lever presses the rat exchanged for the food; $\underline{PQ} = 2(10) = 20$ lever presses. But how can we infer price elasticity from the earlier demand functions if they omit the $\underline{PQ}$ revenue curves?

In our perfume example of unit elasticity, a $\underline{b}$-fold rise in $\underline{P}$ occasioned a $\underline{b}$-fold drop in $\underline{Q}$. Logarithmic scales provide a convenient representation of these $\underline{b}$-fold changes in $\underline{P}$ and $\underline{Q}$, because each unit change on a logarithmic scale corresponds to a $\underline{b}$-fold change on the original scale.

The base-$\underline{b}$ logarithm of a number $\underline{P}$ or $\underline{Q}$ is defined as another number, $\underline{n}$, such that $\underline{b}^n = \underline{P}$ or $\underline{Q}$. For example, the base-2 log of the number 8 is 3, because $2^3 = (2)(2)(2) = 8$.

To see how each unit change on a logarithmic scale corresponds to a $\underline{b}$-fold change on the original scale, examine the base-2 logs of a doubling series of prices, $\underline{P} = 0.5, 1, 2, 4$, and 8. Inspection of the following table shows that the corresponding base-2 logs are -1, 0, 1, 2, and 3:

$\underline{P}$	$\underline{n}$	2^n	$\text{Log}_2 \underline{P}$
0.5	-1	$2^{-1} = 1/2 = 0.5$	-1
1	0	$2^0 = 1$	0
2	1	$2^1 = 2$	1
4	2	$2^2 = 4$	2
8	3	$2^3 = 8$	3

Thus, each twofold rise in $\underline{P}$ corresponds to a one-unit rise in the $\log_2$ of $\underline{P}$: Doubling $\underline{P}$ from 0.5 to 1, we raise $\log_2 \underline{P}$ by one unit, from -1 to 0; doubling $\underline{P}$ from 1 to 2, we raise $\log_2 \underline{P}$ by one unit, from 0 to 1; and so on. (More generally, $\underline{b}^n = \underline{P}$, $\underline{b}^{2n} = \underline{bP}$, $\underline{b}^{3n} = \underline{b}^2\underline{P}$, and so on; each $\underline{b}$-fold rise in $\underline{P}$ raises $\underline{n}$ by one unit.)

Figure 5.14 illustrates the use of these logarithmic transformations of the original numbers; it repeats the data of our perfume example, but shows the base-2 logs of $\underline{P}$ and $\underline{Q}$ in addition to their original values. Moving from left to right, the fourfold rise in $\underline{P}$ from \$1 to \$4 occasions only a twofold drop in $\underline{Q}$, from 64 bottles to 32: Demand is inelastic. Look at the same changes in logarithmic units: As log $\underline{P}$ runs forward from 0 to 2, log $\underline{Q}$ drops from 6 to 5. Accordingly, this first segment of the demand function falls rather gently, with a slope of $-1/2 = -.5$.

In the next segment, $\underline{P}$ doubles from \$4 to \$8, and $\underline{Q}$ shows a twofold drop from 32 bottles to 16: unit elasticity. As log $\underline{P}$ runs forward from 2 to 3, log $\underline{Q}$ drops from 5 to 4: The downward slope has steepened, $-1/1 = -1$.

In the final segment, $\underline{P}$ doubles again, from \$8 to \$16, but $\underline{Q}$ shows a fourfold drop from 16 bottles to 4: Demand is elastic. As log $\underline{P}$ runs forward from 3 to 4, log $\underline{Q}$ drops from 4 to 2: The downward slope has steepened again, $-2/1 = -2$.

FIGURE 5.14

Log$_2$ Bottles Sold as a Function of Log$_2$ Bottle Price

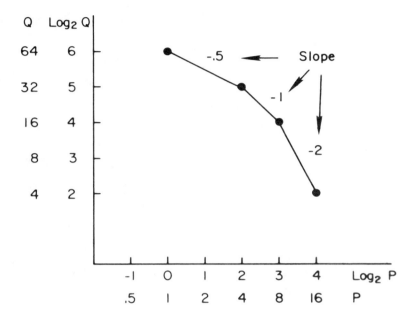

The example shows how we can infer price sensitivity from a figure that plots log $\underline{Q}$ against log $\underline{P}$: The steeper the slope of the log-log curve, the greater the sensitivity to price. If the slope = –1, we have unit elasticity. A gentler slope, less than –1, indicates inelastic demand (for example, slope = –.5). A steeper slope, greater than –1, indicates elastic demand (for example, slope = –2). Recognize that a slope of –.5 would indicate more price elasticity than a slope of –.2, although both would fall into the inelastic category.

These three numerical slope-categories have the same elasticity significates whatever the base of the logarithm might be. If we switched to the base-10 system, a tenfold rise in $\underline{P}$ would correspond to a one-unit rise in $\log_{10} \underline{P}$. Because the demand functions presented earlier in this chapter plot $\log_{10} \underline{Q}$ against $\log_{10} \underline{P}$, we can examine the relation between price and elasticity by noting how the slope varies with price. If we see that the slope steepens as price rises, we know that price elasticity increases with price.

Some information on the empirical relation between price and elasticity has come from consumer research using the "buy-response"

FIGURE 5.15

Buy-Response Curves for Ten Different Foods in Logarithmic
Coordinates

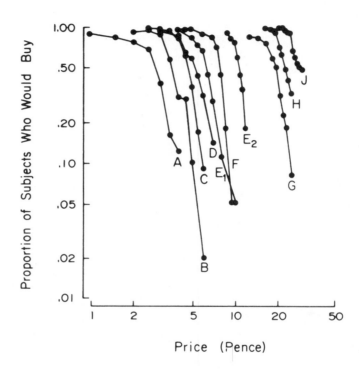

Price (Pence)

technique. The investigator asks each of many respondents whether the person would buy a particular commodity at each of several different prices. The proportion of respondents who say yes provides the measure of Q.

Ten of these buy-response curves (Lea 1978) appear in Figure 5.15, one curve for each of ten different food commodities. Notice that the figure plots Q and P on logarithmic scales. Each curve slopes downward, and generally grows steeper as the price rises; thus, consumer demand for each of the ten commodities becomes more price-elastic, more responsive to a change in price, as the price rises.

Buy-response curves are generally steeper than curves based on actual sales of commodities, but the same general relation usually appears in the actual sales figures: Demand grows more price-elastic as the price rises. The same relation can generally be seen in the consumer demand functions presented earlier in this chapter, functions based on the consumption of various laboratory rewards at various behavioral prices. Similar experiments have refined our understanding of various laboratory rewards. For example, at relatively low behavioral prices, the rat may prefer to press a lever for electrical stimulation of the brain's "pleasure center" to pressing another lever for food. But as we vary the prices, we find that the rat's demand for brain stimulation is considerably more price-elastic than its demand for food (Hursh and Natelson 1981).

There are other ways to infer price elasticity from the graphs frequently seen in the psychological literature, including the graphic analyses of schedule constraints used throughout this book. Figure 5.16A repeats the graphic representation of the behavioral constraints imposed by the structures of two reciprocal fixed-ratio schedules that require different numbers of lever presses for the same amount of drinking water. The figure plots total water consumed (milliliters) on the vertical axis, total lever presses on the horizontal. Each line of constraint includes a point that shows the rat's performance under the schedule represented by the line.

Inspection of the figure should tell you that the rat's consumption of water conformed to the demand law, with unit price elasticity. Why? Because the rat/consumer drank less water at the higher behavioral price, and the experimenter/shopkeeper derived exactly the same revenue on sales at both prices.

The first part of the trick is to recognize that the line with the steeper slope represents the lower behavioral price, $\underline{P}$ = total presses/ total milliliters. By comparing the two points on the lines, we see

FIGURE 5.16

Behavioral Analogue of Consumption, Price, and Revenue on Sales

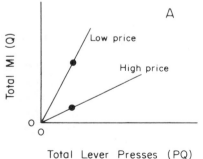
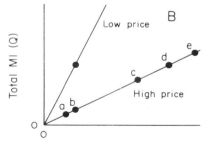

that the same lever-press total got more water on the steeper line; accordingly, the steeper line represents the lower price throughout its extent, total presses/total milliliters. Having recognized that, we see right off that the rat conformed to the demand law, drinking less water at the higher price.

The second part of the trick is to recognize total lever presses as the analogue of revenue, PQ. Clearly it is just that: If Q = total milliliters, and P = total presses/total milliliters, then PQ = (total presses/total milliliters)(total milliliters) = total presses. Because the experimenter derived the same PQ at the two different prices, we see that the rat's demand for water had unit price elasticity.

Figure 5.16B completes the picture. The five points on the shallow line show five of the possible ways in which the rat could respond to the constraints of the high-price schedule, having responded on the low-price schedule as indicated by the point on the steeper line. Points a, b, and c would conform to the demand law, less consumption at the higher price. Point c would fall into the inelastic category; b, the unit category; a, the elastic category. The other two points would violate the demand law: d, by revealing no sensitivity to price; e, by revealing more consumption at the higher price.

The key presented in Figure 5.16B works in exactly the same way for nonreciprocal schedules, schedules with an optional magnitude of reward, interval schedules, and concurrent schedules. To check your understanding of this point, look again at Figure 5.9B, which shows the rat's performance under three variable-interval schedules of the press-to-drink variety. You should see that the rat's response to the schedules established three different prices, total presses/total licks; that the lick totals conformed to the demand law; and that demand was inelastic throughout the entire range of prices. Recall, too, that the results shown in Figure 5.9B also conformed to Conservation Model 1: As total lever presses increased, total licks decreased linearly.

At this point it should come as no surprise that the very same key reveals the economic significance of the psychological models discussed in Chapter 4. For example, consider the two conservation models. Figure 5.17A reproduces the essential features of the key, but adds the paired basepoint that played such a prominent role in the creation of those models. The broken line sloping downward through the basepoint represents the theoretical constraints derived from model 1. The upward lines represent three different prices, as usual, and the point on each of the three represents the coordinate values of Q and PQ predicted by the model. In economic terms, model 1 predicts that consumption will conform to the demand law, Q falling as P rises; demand should be inelastic throughout the illustrated range of prices, because PQ should also rise as P rises. For a par-

FIGURE 5.17

Behavioral Analogues of Consumption, Price, and Revenue on
Sales: Relations Predicted by Conservation Models 1 and 2

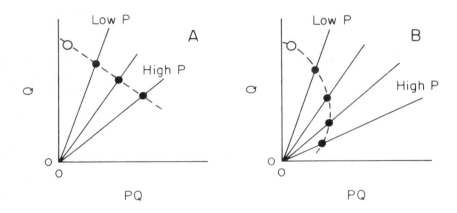

ticularly clear view of the theory's economic import, consider the
model equation for a simple fixed-ratio schedule: $\underline{N}(\underline{kI} + \underline{C}) = \underline{kO}_i +$
$\underline{O}_c = \underline{B}$. In the notation of model 1, $\underline{I/C}$ refers to the behavioral price
of the contingent reward, $\underline{P}$ (for example, lever presses/pellet); $\underline{NC}$
refers to the total amount of the contingent reward, $\underline{Q}$ (for example,
total food pellets); and $\underline{NI}$ refers to the total amount of instrumental
responding, $\underline{PQ}$ (for example, total lever presses). To verify this
translation of the model into the language of $\underline{P}$ and $\underline{Q}$, note that $\underline{PQ} =$
$(\underline{I/C})(\underline{NC}) = \underline{NI}$.

Figure 5.17B shows why one might prefer model 2 on economic
grounds. The broken curve in panel B illustrates the kind of theoretical constraint we can derive from model 2—for example, in fitting
the behavior of Teitelbaum's dynamic hyperphagic rats. Notice that
model 2 predicts the demand law—as does model 1—but also predicts
with ease the common empirical relation between price and price
elasticity. The predictions in panel B say that elasticity will increase
with price; that demand may be inelastic at relatively low prices,
have unit elasticity at intermediate prices, and become altogether
elastic at still higher prices (see the Appendix on the derivation of
price elasticity from consumer demand equations).

Unlike model 1, model 2 proposes explicitly that a rise in price
will encourage the consumer to resort to substitutes for the good
whose price is rising. Moreover, model 2 makes room for the availability of substitutes as a variable that can influence the price elasticity

of demand. If we reviewed Figures 4.6 and 4.7 in terms of elasticity, we would say that the demand for food was more price-elastic among the fat rats than the lean—perhaps in part because of their differential access to a substitute for food, energy stored as body fat. [3]

In like manner, economists recognize that price elasticity depends largely on the availability of substitutes. If only brand X of gasoline shows a rise in price, demand for brand X will be highly elastic because many other brands are readily available. But the demand for all brands of gasoline will be highly inelastic, because few of the automobile engines in present-day use can run on anything else. Similarly, the data in Figure 4.21 probably would have revealed a less elastic demand for water had I not supplied the rat with an external substitute, free access to saccharin.

INCOME ELASTICITY OF DEMAND

We already have seen that total consumption of a particular good may depend on other variables besides price. Here we examine another variable prominent in the economic analysis of consumer demand, the consumer's income.

Income elasticity of demand refers to the change in Q that occurs when we vary the consumer's income independently of other variables. If Q rises in response to a rise in income, economists classify the good in question as a normal good; but if Q falls in response to a rise in income, the good is classified as an inferior good. A study conducted in the United Kingdom in the 1920s and 1930s revealed butter as a normal good, margarine as inferior: As income increased, butter consumption rose and margarine fell. The same study revealed beef, poultry, coffee, and tobacco as normal goods and flour, bread, and beer as inferior goods (Awh 1976, p. 138).

For any particular pair of goods, a and b, we can identify each one as normal or inferior by examining what happens to Q_a and Q_b as we increase the consumer's budget—the amount of money the consumer can spare for the purchase of some combination of the two goods. Figure 5.18A plots Q_b on the vertical axis, Q_a on the horizontal. The downward sloping line is a budget line that shows how much of each good the consumer could buy on a budget of $10. Look first at the vertical intercept: Because the unit price of good b is $1, the consumer could buy none of a and ten units of b: $Q_a = 0$ and $Q_b = 10$. Now to the horizontal intercept: Because the unit price of good a is $2, the consumer could buy five units of a and none of b: $Q_a = 5$ and $Q_b = 0$. The other points on the budget line show various other consumption possibilities open to the consumer with a $10 budget, such as a "bundle" composed of $Q_a = 2$ and $Q_b = 6$. Letting M signify the

FIGURE 5.18

Consumption of Two Goods Subject to Various Budgetary Constraints

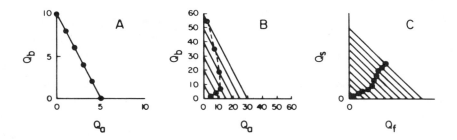

total amount of money spent on the two goods, the combination available to the consumer is subject to the following constraint: $\underline{P}_a\underline{Q}_a +$ $\underline{P}_b\underline{Q}_b = \underline{M}$, where M increases with the consumer's income, and the consumer selects $\underline{Q}_a$ and $\underline{Q}_b$ at will.

Figure 5.18B shows six different budget lines; as we move from the lowest to the highest, we increase the amount of money, $\underline{M}$, available for the purchase of the two goods. The point on each budget line shows the amount of each good purchased on that particular budget. The broken line through the six points constitutes an <u>income-consumption curve</u>, sometimes called an Engel curve. Inspection of the curve reveals good <u>b</u> as a normal good throughout the entire range of incomes: $\underline{Q}_b$ rises steadily as income rises. Good <u>a</u> is normal throughout the three lowest incomes, but becomes inferior as income rises further.

We could measure the Engel curve of a hungry rat through the use of a concurrent fixed-ratio schedule. For example, suppose we wire one lever to a dispenser of ordinary food pellets (<u>f</u>), the other lever to a sugar pellet dispenser (<u>s</u>). We set the unit behavioral price of the ordinary food pellet, presses/pellet, at $\underline{P}_f$, and the price of the sugar pellet at $\underline{P}_s$. We call the session to a halt as soon as the rat seems to have eaten its fill of pellets, at which time it will have completed a total of $\underline{M}$ lever presses. Suppose we observe that for this particular rat, $\underline{M} = 1,000$. In other words, the largest behavioral budget the rat was willing to spend on these two goods combined was $\underline{M} = 1,000$ lever presses. Its consumption for the session as a whole was subject to the following constraint: $\underline{P}_f\underline{Q}_f + \underline{P}_s\underline{Q}_s = \underline{M}$, where $\underline{P}$ signifies the behavioral price of the pellet, $\underline{Q}$ the number of pellets consumed, $\underline{PQ}$ the total number of lever presses the rat spent on that kind of pellet. For example, if each food pellet cost 2 lever presses, and the rat bought 200 food pellets, it spent 400 lever presses on food pellets; if each sugar pellet cost 10 lever presses, and the rat bought 60 sugar pellets, it spent 600 lever presses on sugar pellets: $2(200) + 10(60) = 1,000 = \underline{M}$.

We could construct a ten-point Engel curve by reviewing the rat's performance as it unfolded from the beginning of the session to the end, recording Q_f and Q_s at the 100-press mark ($\underline{M} = 100$), the 200-press mark ($\underline{M} = 200$), and so on to $\underline{M} = 1,000$. If the results came out like the hypothetical ones in Figure 5.18C, they would reveal each kind of pellet as a normal good.

Do we suspect that the shape of the Engel curve might depend on the maximum amount the rat expects it can spend on the two goods? Do the habitually poor differ from the habitually rich? Maybe we could attack such questions experimentally by examining an Engel curve derived from a slightly different experiment, one in which we test each rat repeatedly with just one preset value of $\underline{M}$, but vary $\underline{M}$ from one rat to the next. For example, if the rat learns that it can spend only 500 lever presses on the two kinds of pellet, it might come to spend its entire budget on food pellets, a monotonous but practical dietary bundle. But if it knows that it can spend as many as 1,000 lever presses, it might spend some of the first 500 on sugar pellets as well as food—a more varied and perhaps a more palatable bundle whose dietary deficiencies can always be remedied over the next 500 lever presses.

What might determine M_{max}, the number of lever presses the rat is willing to spend on the two goods, the maximum value of $\underline{M}$ the rat would spend if it could spend as much as it pleased? We would expect M_{max} to depend on the rat's motivational state; M_{max} should be relatively large among rats that have gone without food for a relatively long time. In the rat, M_{max} might well reflect the amount of its limited energetic resources the rat is prepared to allocate to the purchase and consumption of the two goods available on the terms laid down by the schedule. In terms of the performance models discussed in Chapter 4, an increase in hunger should move the measured basepoint for food and sugar pellets away from the lower left corner in Figure 5.17C and toward the upper right corner.

CROSS-PRICE ELASTICITY

Total consumption of a particular good may vary with the price of some other good as well as its own. In other words, demand may be cross-price elastic as well as own-price elastic.

Even if the price of tea holds constant, tea consumption typically rises as coffee consumption declines in response to higher coffee prices—a fact that reveals tea as a substitute for coffee (Awh 1976, p. 138). Other goods typically show the opposite pattern, one that marks them as complements. Complementary goods are generally consumed in fixed proportion to each other, like flour and shortening: Bakery recipes often call for a certain amount of each. Even if the price of flour holds constant, flour consumption falls as the price of shortening rises: If we buy less shortening because of its rise in price, we also need less flour in our reduced production of bakery goods (Awh 1976, p. 138). Hence, flour and shortening are complementary goods; so are flashbulbs and film.

Figure 5.19 illustrates the distinction between substitutes and complements. The point on budget line 1 shows how much of goods a and b the consumer selects at two unit prices, P_a and P_b. Suppose P_b holds constant, along with the budget, but P_a rises. Budget line 2 represents the new consumption possibilities. Because P_b is the same as before, budget line 2 intercepts the vertical Q_b axis at the place it did before. But P_a is higher than before, so budget line 2 must intercept the horizontal Q_a axis nearer the origin than before: Buying none of good b, the consumer can buy less of a than before.

If the consumer responds to the rise in P_a by choosing bundle x, the choice would mark b as a substitute for a: With P_b constant, Q_a falls and Q_b rises. Selection of bundle y would mark b as a complement: With P_b constant, Q_a falls and Q_b falls with it. Selection of bundle z would mark b as an independent: With P_b constant, Q_a falls but Q_b shows no change.

FIGURE 5.19

Consumption of Two Goods Subject to Various Price and
Budgetary Constraints

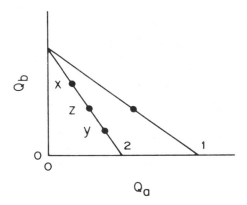

Experiments with concurrent fixed-ratio schedules have revealed that the laboratory rat treats certain beverages as mutual substitutes. For example, suppose the rat can get root beer by pressing one lever and Tom Collins mix by pressing another lever. Each beverage comes at a certain behavioral price, lever presses/milliliter. As the price of either beverage rises, the rat consumes less of that one and more of the other, as if the two beverages were mutual substitutes. Similar experiments have shown that food and water may function as complementary goods for the rat (Kagel et al. 1977; Rachlin et al. 1976).

SUBSTITUTION AND INCOME EFFECTS

If the price of good a falls relative to the price of good b, total consumption of a may change because of two different reasons. First, good a has become a better buy than before, relative to good b. Accordingly, the consumer may substitute a for b, buying more of a and less of b than before; this would illustrate the substitution effect. The second reason has to do with real income—the consumer's purchasing power, the goods and services we can get for a dollar. If a grows less expensive while the price of b remains constant, the consumer's real income has increased. Accordingly, the consumer may buy more of a in response to the rise in real wealth; this would illustrate the income effect. How can we measure the separate effect of each of these two variables?

A method suggested by J. R. Hicks (Awh 1976) makes use of an analytic device known as the indifference curve. An example appears in Figure 5.20A. Each point on the curve represents a particular bundle of the two goods, Q_a and Q_b. We call it an indifference curve because we assume that the consumer finds all points on the curve equally attractive; in other words, the consumer is indifferent as between any two points on the curve. If one point represented a bundle composed of ten apples and one banana, another two apples and eight bananas, the consumer would just as soon have one bundle as the other.

The indifference curve slopes downward because the two goods are mutually substitutable: The consumer is willing to trade some of b for more of a, or some of a for more of b.

Viewed from the origin in the lower-left corner, the curve looks convex. Look at the upper part of the curve: If we have plenty of bananas but few apples, we are willing to give up quite a number of bananas for just one more apple. The picture reverses in the lower part of the curve: If we have few bananas but plenty of apples, we will not part with even one banana unless we can get quite a number of apples in exchange.

FIGURE 5.20

Indifference Curves

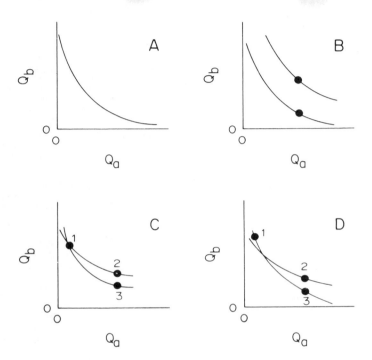

We could add any number of indifference curves to the plane defined by the two axes. Figure 5.20B shows two of the many possible curves. The analysis assumes that the consumer would prefer any point on a higher curve to any point on a lower curve. To understand the logic behind this assumption, compare the two points on the curves. The two bundles contain the same amount of good a, but the bundle on the higher curve contains more of good b. The consumer who prefers more to less will therefore prefer the point on the higher curve to the point on the lower curve. From the indifference property, it follows that the consumer will prefer any point on the higher curve to any point on the lower curve.

Do consumers truly prefer more to less? Only within limits. I could handle another dozen bananas, but not another million; King Kong or United Fruit might view the matter differently. Paired baseline measurements have also revealed some obvious limits on the preferability of more to less. Given free, unlimited access to water and a lever, even the most thirsty rat drinks only a limited amount of water. Given free, unlimited access to two different saccharin solutions, the rat drinks only a limited amount of each. 'Speculation about a less obvious case may prove instructive: Offered an unlimited amount of money, what person would accept the offer without some later regret? If I have all of the wealth in the universe, who will manufacture my automobile, and who will put food on my table? Foresight favors a sharing of the wealth and its attendant responsibilities.

Figure 5.20C shows why two indifference curves cannot intersect each other. If the person prefers point 2 to point 3, but finds points 1 and 3 equally attractive, the person cannot find 1 and 3 equally attractive. Figure 5.20D elaborates this prohibition on the intersection of indifference curves. If the person prefers point 1 to point 2, and point 2 to point 3, then the person must also prefer point 1 to point 3—which is impossible, because points 1 and 3 lie on the same indifference curve.

Thus, the Hicksian analysis, like many others in economic theory, requires that the person's choices be transitive: If x is chosen over y, and y over z, then the person must also choose x over z. If the actual choices violate the transitivity assumption, the theory does not apply. [4]

We take the next step in the Hicksian analysis by adding a budget line to the plane, as shown in Figure 5.21. As usual, the budget line meets the vertical (horizontal) axis at a place determined by the unit price of good b (a). The budgetary constraint would let the consumer buy any bundle on or below the budget line; which one should the con-

FIGURE 5.21

Indifference Analysis of the Consumer's Selection of Two Goods Subject to Price and Budgetary Constraints: The Tangency Solution

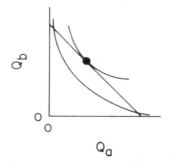

sumer actually buy? According to the theory, the consumer prefers more to less and will therefore buy the bundle marked by the point at which the budget line is tangent to an indifference curve. Any other point on or below the budget line would fall on some lower indifference curve and would therefore be less attractive than the tengency point shown in the figure.

Our original problem appears again in Figure 5.22, which shows two budget lines; the upper line with the gentler slope represents a drop in the unit price of good a, with the price of b held constant. The two points show that the consumer responded to the drop in P_a by buying more of good a than before, and less of b. Thus, when P_a fell, Q_a increased by a total of $Q_{a3} - Q_{a1}$. How much of the total increase represents the substitution effect, and how much represents the income effect?

FIGURE 5.22

Indifference Analysis of the Consumer's Response to a Change in the Price of One Good

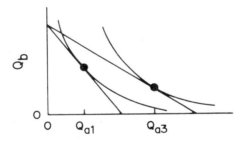

To isolate the substitution effect, we must somehow hold real income constant despite the change in price. More specifically, we must hold real income constant despite the rise in the price ratio P_b/P_a. We can do that with the help of the lower indifference curve. Recall that real income refers to the goods and services we can buy with our money. Then why not define a third budget line, wholly imaginary, that also reflects the new price ratio—a new budget line that is just high enough to finance the purchase of a bundle exactly as attractive as the old bundle?

The broken line in Figure 5.23 represents this imaginary budget line. Notice that it is tangent to the lower indifference curve and therefore permits the purchase of a bundle (B_2) just as attractive

FIGURE 5.23

Hicksian Measurement of Substitution and Income Effects,
Revealing Good a as a Normal Good

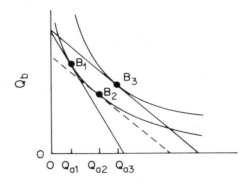

as the old one ($\underline{B}_1$). Because it runs parallel to the upper budget line
with the gentler slope, it too reflects the new price ratio. As the
consumer moves from $\underline{B}_1$ to $\underline{B}_2$, we move from the old price ratio
(steep slope) to the new (gentle slope) while holding real income con-
stant. Accordingly, $\underline{Q}_{a2} - \underline{Q}_{a1}$ measures the substitution effect, uncontaminated by any change in real income.

As the consumer moves further, from $\underline{B}_2$ to $\underline{B}_3$, we raise real
income while holding the price ratio constant. Accordingly, $\underline{Q}_{a3} -$
$\underline{Q}_{a2}$ measures the income effect, uncontaminated by any change in the
price ratio.

Thus, the rise in $\underline{Q}_a$ occasioned by the drop in $\underline{P}_a$ represents
the sum of two separate effects, the substitution effect and the income
effect:

$$\underline{Q}_{a3} - \underline{Q}_{a1} = (\underline{Q}_{a2} - \underline{Q}_{a1}) + (\underline{Q}_{a3} - \underline{Q}_{a2})$$

Economists refer to the total change in $\underline{Q}_a$ as an <u>uncompensated</u>
price change. All of the consumer demand functions presented earlier
in this chapter, based on studies of laboratory rewards, show uncompensated price changes (for example, Figure 5.2). Economists refer
to the part attributable to substitution alone as a <u>compensated</u> price
change. Thus, $\underline{Q}_{a3} - \underline{Q}_{a1}$ measures the uncompensated price change;
$\underline{Q}_{a2} - \underline{Q}_{a1}$, the compensated price change.

Notice how Figure 5.23 reveals good a as a <u>normal</u> good: Be-
cause $\underline{Q}_{a3}$ is greater than $\underline{Q}_{a2}$, $\underline{Q}_a$ rises with real income, uncontami-

FIGURE 5.24

Hicksian Measurement of Substitution and Income Effects,
Revealing Good a as an Inferior Good

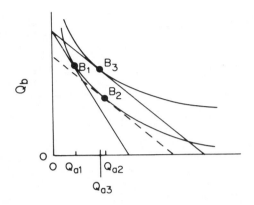

nated by any change in the price ratio. It could have come out differently. Figure 5.24 reveals good a as an inferior good: There, Q_a
shows a slight drop in response to a rise in real income, uncontaminated by any change in the price ratio.

The Hicksian solution, conceptually tidy, is often impracticable.
To apply the Hicksian method to any real example, we must know the
exact location of the two indifference curves; how else could we know
the height of our imaginary budget line? It is possible in principle,
but tedious or worse in practice, to fix the exact location of an indifference curve by experimental measurement (MacCrimmen and Toda
1969). An alternative method invented by E. Slutsky (Awh 1976),
though slightly less elegant and a trifle less accurate, proves far
more useful in practice. And one can see its merits and demerits
more readily after learning the elements of the Hicksian analysis.

The Slutskian analysis holds real income approximately constant
by giving the consumer the money needed to buy the original bundle.
An example appears in Figure 5.25, which shows the adjusted budget
as a broken line. Notice that the adjusted budget line includes the
original bundle, B_1. Thus, the consumer could buy the original B_1
on the adjusted budget, but buys B_2 instead. Once again, $Q_{a2} - Q_{a1}$
measures the substitution effect; $Q_{a3} - Q_{a2}$, the income effect.

Notice, too, that if the adjusted budget line includes the original
bundle, B_1, it cannot be tangent to the lower indifference curve, and
must be tangent to a higher indifference curve. Accordingly, the ad-

FIGURE 5.25

Slutskian Measurement of Substitution and Income Effects

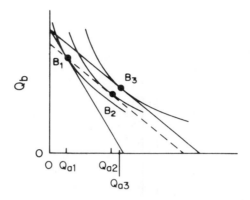

justed budget actually represents a bit more real income than the consumer had originally.

But the Slutskian approach wins the feasibility contest by a wide margin. It requires exactly three simple choices on the part of the consumer, but no measurement of indifference curves. Ask the consumer to choose $\underline{B}_1$ at the original price ratio; change the price ratio, then ask the consumer to choose $\underline{B}_3$; keep the new price ratio, cut the consumer's budget—but provide just enough money to buy $\underline{B}_1$—and ask the consumer to choose $\underline{B}_2$. The indifference curves in Figure 5.25 need not be measured; their role in the figure is to facilitate the comparison of the two different solutions proposed by Hicks and Slutsky.

The Slutskian method has had some successful applications in experimental studies of the rat's demand for nonessential goods, such as root beer and cherry cola (Kagel et al. 1975, 1977; Rachlin et al. 1976). The typical experiment uses a concurrent fixed-ratio schedule, with two levers wired to two different dispensers loaded with different kinds of soft drink, $\underline{a}$ and $\underline{b}$. Each concurrent schedule sets its two behavioral prices, $\underline{P}_a$ and $\underline{P}_b$—lever presses/milliliter—in the usual way, and the experimenter halts the session when the lever-press total reaches the budgetary limit, $\underline{M}$. Thus, $\underline{P}_a\underline{Q}_a + \underline{P}_b\underline{Q}_b = M$, where $\underline{Q}$ refers to the total milliliters consumed of each drink. Other concurrent schedules vary the price ratio, $\underline{P}_b/\underline{P}_a$, or the price ratio and $\underline{M}$, for new measures of $\underline{Q}_a$ and $\underline{Q}_b$ under the new price and budgetary constraints.

The results typically reveal a relatively large substitution effect in the total change in $\underline{Q}$. The laboratory rat, consuming one soft drink or another, thereby resembles the human in the economic market-place. In the marketplace, the substitution effect generally outweighs the income effect—probably because only a tiny portion of the average consumer's income goes toward the purchase of any particular kind of good. Thus, if we buy more coffee in response to a drop in its price, we are probably responding more to its improved standing among similar goods than the small incidental rise in our real income.

THE GIFFEN GOOD

Imagine a destitute family subsisting on a diet of bread and water. As the national rate of unemployment approaches 20 percent, the government's anti-inflationary measures finally take hold: With many fewer dollars chasing somewhat fewer goods—the classic but questionable cure for inflation—the economy finally enters a deflationary period, and the price of bread plummets. Our destitute family responds by buying less bread than before—an apparent contradiction of the demand law—and more meat than before.

This hypothetical scenario would identify bread as a Giffen good, named after the person, Sir Robert Giffen, generally credited for suggesting some conditions that might create a perfectly reasonable violation of the demand law. If a household spends a large portion of its budget on an inferior good, a drop in the price of the good might create an unusually large income effect: As real income rises, consumption of an inferior good declines, and the household buys more of some normal good, such as beef.

Figure 5.26 presents a Slutskian analysis of the situation, with good $\underline{a}$ as the inferior Giffen good and good $\underline{b}$ normal. Comparison of $\underline{B}_1$ with $\underline{B}_3$ shows that Q_a decreases in response to a drop in the price of $\underline{a}$, in violation of the demand law (Q_{a3} is less than Q_{a1}). Notice why it does: Although the substitution effect is positive (Q_{a2} is greater than Q_{a1}), it is far outweighed by the negative income effect characteristic of inferior goods (Q_{a3} is less than Q_{a2}).

Do Giffen goods actually exist? Economists seem to doubt their existence at the level of a national economy, but they might well exist at another level, the impoverished individual household. I know of no examples from experimental psychology, but it is possible to imagine experimental conditions that might reveal the existence of a Giffen good at the level of the individual animal.

For example, suppose we were to test a thiamine-deficient rat under a concurrent fixed-ratio schedule: The rat can get high-calorie but thiamine-free food pellets by pressing one lever and low-calorie thiamine-enriched food pellets by pressing another lever. On the initial budget, say $\underline{M}$ = 1,000 lever presses, each kind of food pellet

FIGURE 5.26

Slutskian Analysis of the Giffen Good: The Giffen Good a Is Inferior;
Good b, Normal

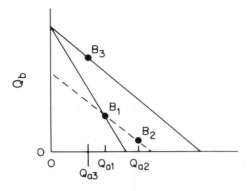

comes at a relatively high behavioral price (lever presses/pellet).
Referring to Figure 5.26, suppose we find that the rat buys bundle B_1,
which contains a total of Q_{a1} of the high-calorie pellets and Q_{b1} of the
low-calorie thiamine pellets. Next we decrease the price of the high-
calorie pellet, while holding constant the price of the thiamine pellet.
Suppose that at the new price ratio the rat buys bundle B_3. Thus, in
response to the drop in the price of high-calorie food, the rat buys
fewer high-calorie pellets and more thiamine pellets. Our third
schedule represents a smaller budget ($\underline{M}$ less than 1,000 lever presses),
just large enough to enable the rat to purchase B_1. If the rat now selects bundle B_2, the overall pattern of results would reveal high-
calorie pellets as an inferior Giffen good for the thiamine-deficient
rat and thiamine pellets as a normal good. [5]

PERFECT SUBSTITUTES AND COMPLEMENTS

The marginal rate of substitution (MRS) refers to a property of
the indifference curve, the amount of good b the consumer will give
up in exchange for one more unit of good a. On a convex indifference
curve, two of which appear in Figure 5.27A, the MRS varies as we
move along the curve: When Q_b is relatively large (small), so is the
MRS. Having a large (small) number of bananas, the consumer will
part with many (few) in exchange for one more apple. If two goods

FIGURE 5.27

Indifference Curves for Imperfect Substitutes, Perfect Substitutes, and Perfect Complements

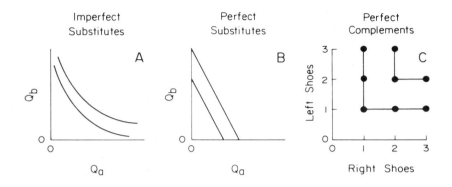

are imperfect substitutes, the indifference curve will probably be convex, and the MRS will grow smaller as we move down its slope.

The linear indifference curves in Figure 5.27B apply to perfect substitutes. Because the person will always trade two nickels for one more dime, the MRS is constant (slope = -2 = MRS). If the person will always trade one red, ripe apple for another just like it, the MRS will again be constant (slope = -1 = MRS).

What about left shoes and right shoes? If we plan to use them as projectiles, left shoes and right shoes are perfect substitutes: In flinging a slipper at the yowling cat on the fence, the left will serve as well as the right. But if we plan to use them as bipedal footwear, the indifference curves will form the 90° angles shown in Figure 5.27C. Look at the corner of the lower curve: If I have one of each kind, I gain nothing of value as footwear by getting more left shoes alone, or more right shoes alone. I can move to the higher indifference curve, representing more footwear value, only by getting at least one more left shoe and one more right shoe. Used as footwear, left shoes and right shoes are perfect complements, always consumed in the same fixed proportion, 1:1. The indifference curve for perfect complements will always form a 90° angle, but the fixed proportion need not be 1:1. The owner of a light plane with a tricycle landing gear might buy large tires and small tires in a fixed proportion of 2:1: Two large tires for the main wheels, a small one for the nosewheel.

A convex indifference curve may reflect some blend of the two properties, substitutability and complementarity. As a means of fill-ing the stomach, bananas and apples can function as substitutes; because they differ in their dietary constituents, they may also function as complements on the road to adequate nutrition.

We know already from experiments with rats that the functional relation between two different behaviors can change dramatically from one experimental setting to the next: Apparent substitutes in one setting, eating and drinking become complements in a slightly different setting.

An example (Allison and Mack 1982) appears in Figure 5.28, which scales total licks at a water tube on the vertical axis, total food consumption on the horizontal. The unfilled circle on the right shows the paired basepoint for a two-hour session, with food and water

FIGURE 5.28

Total Water Licks as a Function of Total Food Intake under Fixed-Time Schedules That Suppressed the Rats' Eating or Drinking

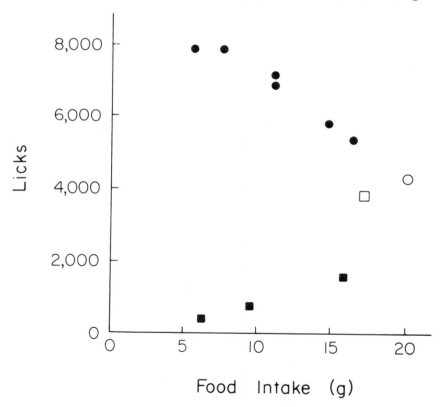

Food Intake (g)

freely available with limit. The six filled circles show what happened to their total licks at the ever-present water tube when we gave the rats less food than the baseline amount. Throughout each two-hour session, each of our six schedules made periodic deliveries of free food pellets; some delivered a larger total than others. When total food decreased, total licks increased, as if eating and drinking were substitutes.

The open square shows the paired basepoint for another group of rats. The three filled squares show what happened to the rats' intake of ever-present food when our three water-delivery schedules allowed fewer licks than the baseline number. When total licks decreased, total food intake also decreased, as if eating and drinking were complements.

It seems that if the rat has plenty of water but not enough food, eating and drinking may function as substitutes; if the rat has plenty of food but not enough water, they may function as complements. Maybe the rat can reduce some aspect of hunger by drinking more water, but cannot eat dry food without getting thirstier.

CORNER SOLUTIONS

If the two goods are perfect substitutes, economic theory predicts that the consumer will buy some of one, but none of the other. Economic jargon refers to such behavior as a corner solution, for reasons evident in Figure 5.29.

Panel A illustrates a case of imperfect substitutes: With P_b held constant, a drop in P_a results in a rise in Q_a, and some decline

FIGURE 5.29

Consumer Selections Characteristic of Imperfect Substitutes, Perfect Substitutes, and Perfect Complements: Tangency and Corner Solutions

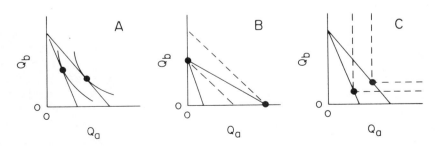

in Q_b. On the extreme right, panel C illustrates a case of perfect complements; as P_a drops, Q_a rises, and so does Q_b. Notice that each of the bundles shown in panels A and C includes some of good a and some of good b.

Panel B shows the general theoretical rule for perfect substitutes. When P_a is relatively high, the consumer can reach the highest indifference curve attainable only by buying some of good b and none of a. A drop in P_a reverses the situation: Now, the consumer can reach the highest indifference curve attainable only by buying some of good a and none of b.

If economists have evidence of corner solutions based on observations of humans, the evidence disagrees with experimental observations of animal behavior. If the rat can get expensive food by pressing one lever, and cheaper but identical food by pressing the other lever, the two identical foods should function as perfect substitutes. According to Figure 5.29B, the rat should choose a corner solution, confining all of its responding to one lever or the other—the one that offers the lower price. But we saw in Chapter 4 that the rat typically samples both levers repeatedly and thereby fails to choose a corner solution (see Figure 4.11; for similar results from the rat that presses either lever for water, and the pigeon that pecks either key for food, see Figures 4.10 and 4.12).

We see once again, this time in the context of the theoretical corner solution, how the animal experiments cast some doubt on the notion that consumer behavior maximizes utility. But perhaps the experiments are at fault. We should keep in mind that the laboratory animal has an evolutionary history that may have limited its ability to cope with our conventional laboratory schedules. In the evolutionary environment, temporal changes in the density of vital commodities may establish evolutionary pressures in favor of the animal that makes no lasting commitment to any particular location, but frequently checks the current status of other nearby locations. Thus, what appears to be a less-than-optimal response to the constraints of a conventional laboratory schedule might prove more advantageous under the constraints of a schedule more closely attuned to the animal's characteristic foraging patterns.

CONCLUSION

As promised at the start, this chapter has shown how the laboratory rewards traditionally called reinforcers bear an extraordinary resemblance to economic goods on two related levels, the definitional and the empirical. Effective laboratory procedures make the contingent reward scarce in one sense or another. In some cases, the terms of the contingency schedule specify in advance the unit behavioral price of the contingent reward; in other cases, the schedule offers so much behavioral latitude over the course of the contingency session that the behavioral price can only be calculated after the fact. In either case, uncompensated demand curves from humans and animals working directly for laboratory rewards under the terms specified by the contingency schedule generally conform to the demand law, and own-price elasticity generally rises with price. Slutsky-compensated demand functions reveal relatively large substitution effects. Animal experiments suggest that a particular pair of behaviors can function as substitutes or complements, depending on external circumstances.

We have also seen how psychological theories of adaptive response to the structural constraints of a contingency schedule can explain what amounts to various facts about the economics of consumer demand. Thus, certain varieties of psychological theory compete directly with conventional economic interpretations and may therefore offer some fresh infusions both to economic theory and the methods used in subjecting such theory to empirical test. On their side, psychologists can derive some valuable insights into their own theory and data from the economic analysis of consumer demand. In the next stage of the argument, we examine some integrative concepts from the economics of labor supply.[6]

NOTES

1. Basic concepts in the economics of consumer demand and labor supply can be found in a number of sources (Awh 1976; Lancaster 1969; Mahanty 1980; Samuelson 1976). For a relatively nontechnical account, illustrated by provocative applications to aspects of human and animal behavior that lie far beyond the economist's traditional field of application, see McKenzie and Tullock (1981). Several economists have written about the psychological basis of economic behavior from perspectives very different from the one presented here (Katona 1951, 1975; Maital 1982; Reynaud 1981; Schelling 1978; Scitovsky 1976). The psychological literature contains several papers that interpret the operant conditioning experiment in terms of the economics of consumer demand; a recent example is Hursh (1980). For an introduction to econometrics, the quantitative side of economic analysis, psychologists might consult Allen (1938), Brennan (1960), or Johnston (1963).

2. A similar relation between price and consumption has appeared in a number of other experiments that varied price by manipulating the magnitude of various rewards: food (Collier 1972; Logan

1964; Peden, Dout, and Allison 1975; Rozin and Mayer 1964), water (Logan 1964), the chance to run in an activity wheel (Klajner 1975; Premack, Schaeffer, and Hundt 1964), intragastric injection of water by means of a stomach tube (Epstein 1960), and the intravenous injection of various drugs, including morphine (Weeks 1962; Weeks and Collins 1964), cocaine, pentobarbital (Goldberg et al. 1971), and amphetamines (Goldberg 1973).

    3. The following table presents a numerical example of the contrasting predictions from the two conservation models for reciprocal fixed-ratio schedules that require different amounts of lever pressing for each contingent food pellet: I = 1, 2, 4, 8, 16, 32, 64, or 128 lever presses, and C = 1 food pellet. The behavioral price of food is the ratio I/C presses per pellet. The example assumes the following numerical values for the constants that appear in one or both models: k = 0.5, ji = 1, O_i = 5 lever presses, and O_c = 300 food pellets. From model 1, $N(kI + C) = kO_i + O_c = B$, the value predicted for the dependent variable N is

$$N = (kO_i + O_c)/(kI + C) = B/(kI + C)$$

Having calculated the predicted value of N for any particular one of the eight different schedules, we calculate the product NI to approximate the total number of lever presses the rat will perform. The product NC approximates the total number of food pellets the rat will receive under that particular schedule. From model 2, $N(kI + C) + ji(I/C) = kO_i + O_c = B$, the value predicted for the dependent variable N is

$$N = [B - ji(I/C)]/(kI + C)$$

Inspection of the table shows that both models predict the demand law. As the price of food (I/C) increases, predicted total food consumption (NC) decreases. Model 1 predicts that demand for food will be inelastic throughout the illustrated range of prices: As I/C increases, the rat will pay out an ever-increasing total number of instrumental lever presses (NI). In contrast, model 2 predicts inelastic demand over the price range from 1 to 16, unit elasticity from 16 to 32, and elastic demand in the range from 32 to 128. If we assign the proper values to the constants in model 2, we can generate performance functions that are characteristic of normal rats, rats in the dynamic weight-gain stage of hypothalamic hyperphagia, and rats in the static obese stage. Because the dynamic rat eats more free food than the normal or static rat, we would set its value of B higher than the value assumed for the normal or static rat. If we assume that the fat rat has greater access to a substitute for food than the lean rat, we would set ji higher for the dynamic or static rat than the normal rat. If we think that the sleek, mobile normal rat would find it easier to press the lever, we might model that difference by assuming a smaller value of k for the normal rat than the fatter dynamic or static rat. Numerical values that generate the right kind of performance functions for normal, dynamic, and static rats can be found in Allison (1981a).

			Model 1			Model 2		
I	C	I/C	N	NI	NC	N	NI	NC
1	1	1	201.67	202	202	201.00	201	201
2	1	2	151.25	303	151	150.25	301	150
4	1	4	100.83	403	101	99.50	398	100
8	1	8	60.50	484	61	58.90	471	59
16	1	16	33.61	538	34	31.83	509	32
32	1	32	17.79	569	18	15.91	509	16
64	1	64	9.17	587	9	7.23	463	7
128	1	128	4.65	595	5	2.68	344	3

4. Although the transitivity assumption may seem quite plausible, human behavior is often intransitive (Tversky 1969). Tversky shows how certain decision rules may generate intransitive preference orders even though the rules are perfectly reasonable. For example, suppose a personnel manager screens job applicants in terms of two separate dimensions, intelligence and motivation. The manager weighs intelligence so heavily that the decision will be made in terms of intelligence alone, if the two candidates differ sufficiently; if they do not, the manager will switch to the motivational dimension and decide in terms of the motivational difference. The following table shows how the final ordering of three different applicants, A, B, and C, could be intransitive:

Applicant	Intelligence Score	Motivation Score
A	1	6
B	2	4
C	3	2

Applicant B seems more intelligent than A, but the difference is too small to decide in terms of intelligence. Accordingly, the manager switches to the motivational dimension, sees that A is clearly more motivated than B, and therefore ranks A ahead of B: A > B. Similarly, B and C are too close in terms of intelligence, but B is clearly more motivated than C; accordingly, B > C. But C is clearly more intelligent than A; accordingly, C > A. Notice that the final ordering of A, B, and C forms an intransitive triple. If A > B, and B > C, transitivity implies that A > C. Instead, C > A—an intransitive triple.

(In this particular example, the intransitivity resulted because the two dimensions, intelligence and motivation, were negatively correlated. If the two dimensions were positively correlated, the same decision rule would result in a transitive triple:

Applicant	Intelligence Score	Motivation Score
A	1	2
B	2	4
C	3	6

From the same decision rule as before, $C > B$ and $B > A$ on the basis of motivation, and $C > A$ on the basis of intelligence—a transitive triple.) Tversky has demonstrated such intransitivities experimentally. The existence of such examples, the perfectly reasonable consequence of certain decision rules, shows that transitive preference orders are not a necessary consequence of rational decisions. Some economists (for example, Maital 1982) have suggested that the existence of such intransitivities raises serious questions about the mathematical theory of risky decisions that has dominated economic theory for nearly 40 years (von Neumann and Morgenstern 1944).

5. I thank Edda Thiels for her suggestion of this hypothetical possibility.

6. For some recent accounts in the popular press of the economic import of laboratory experiments with animals, see Alexander (1980) and Simison (1982).

Chapter 6

Labor Supply

A few years ago the popular press reported an interview with
the owner of a furniture store in Oakland, California. Distraught
over labor problems—too many acrimonious squabbles over wages,
too much absenteeism, premature resignations bringing too many new
workers to train, the new ones no more promising than the old—the
owner decided to try for a simpler, calmer life. He informed his
staff that each employee would henceforth set his or her own wage
rate by dictating it in person. Each individual employee was to tell
the owner the employee's own valuation of his or her services and
would get exactly that amount in return for services rendered.

The newspaper report of the experimental results lacked detailed
facts and figures, but left no doubt about the owner's delight with the
outcome: The employees chose reasonable wage rates for themselves,
with minimal fuss all around—maybe a little higher than the owner
would have chosen for them, but well worth the incidental gains: less
grief, less time and energy spent in fussing with the wage rate, less
absenteeism, less employee turnover, and a staff more pleasant toward owner and customers alike. (For a related example, see Knickerbocker 1979.)

Pure Utopian fantasy, too good to be true? Maybe so; but keep
it in mind as we discover later on that laboratory rats, allowed to
choose their own wage rates, often choose lower ones than they might.

WAGE RATE, LABOR SUPPLY, AND INCOME

Imagine a worker paid at some hourly wage rate—$/hour—with
freedom to choose the amount of labor supplied and the total number
of hours to be spent on the job each day. The product of two variables
will determine the worker's daily income from labor:

Total daily income = (Wage rate)(Daily work hours)

Thus, if each variable exceeds zero, income rises with the wage rate and the amount of labor the worker chooses to supply.

Figure 6.1 displays these relations graphically, scaling daily income from labor on the vertical axis, daily hours worked on the horizontal. The five lines rising from the origin represent five different wage rates; each line rises with a slope equal to the wage rate, rise/run = $/hour. Each wage rate line confines the worker to the income possibilities that lie on the line. At any particular wage rate greater than zero, the worker gains more income by supplying more labor; for any amount of labor greater than zero, income rises with the wage rate. Although the example expresses labor supply in terms of the work performed by the individual laborer, the analysis also applies to other aggregate measures, such as the percentage of the national work force willing to offer its services in the labor supply market.

How much labor will the worker supply at any particular wage rate? Enough to hold daily income constant, despite variations in the wage rate? A reasonable supposition, but it happens to disagree with economic theory and evidence.

To understand the economic approach to the question, recognize, first, that the worker's decision involves a choice between two mutually exclusive alternatives, labor and leisure. Allowing some time for sleep and other biological necessities, the worker has perhaps 15

FIGURE 6.1

Daily Income as a Function of Daily Work Hours and the Hourly
Wage Rate

Daily Work Hours

FIGURE 6.2

Daily Income as a Function of Wage Rate, Daily Work Hours, and
Daily Leisure Hours

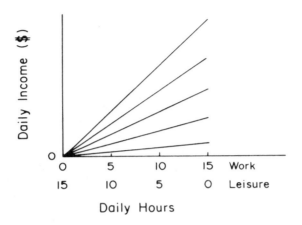

hours in the day for the two remaining categories, labor and leisure—
movies, television, a drive in the country, an afternoon at the beach,
an hour in the hammock with a good book. To labor one more hour,
the worker must therefore sacrifice one hour of leisure.

To the anthropocentric observer of the laboratory rat, working
for all of its daily food (income) by pressing a lever, the leisure time
activities afforded by the typical test cage would surely seem impoverished. But the typical rat takes a large measure of those activities:
rest, grooming, sniffing, general exploration of the cage's interior
features—lever, food cup, light fixtures, screwheads, nooks and cran-
nies in the floor, walls, and ceiling. If the rat is particularly fortunate, this room of its own may also enable it to peer through a trans-
parent Plexiglas wall into the space outside the cage. But their specific differences should not obscure the fact that the rat faces the same
general constraint as the human: Time spent pressing the lever is
time that cannot be spent on leisure time activities.

The labor/leisure alternatives faced by the worker appear in
Figure 6.2, on the horizontal axis. The work scale runs from left to
right; leisure, right to left. In choosing one more hour of work or
leisure, the worker must forgo one hour of the other. Thus, each
point on the horizontal axis represents a unique combination of work
and leisure hours. In predicting the amount of labor supplied at any

particular wage rate, economic theory deals with money and leisure
as two different goods, imperfect substitutes. If applied to the example of the laboratory rat, the theory would deal with food and leisure
as imperfect substitutes.

MONEY AND LEISURE AS IMPERFECT
SUBSTITUTES

Figure 6.3 is the same as 6.2, but replaces the wage rate lines
with five indifference curves, mirror images of the curves for imperfect substitutes presented in Chapter 5. Each point on a curve represents a unique bundle composed of two goods, a certain amount of
daily leisure time, and a certain amount of daily income. Viewed
from the leisure origin on the right, the curves look convex. Having
a large daily income but little leisure time, the worker will sacrifice
a good deal of money for some extra leisure time; having little daily
income but much leisure time, the worker will trade little money for
extra leisure. In other words, the marginal rate of substitution diminishes as we move down each curve.

Like the consumer in Chapter 5, the worker will try to stand on
the highest indifference curve attainable, given the structural con-

FIGURE 6.3

Indifference Curves for Money and Leisure as Imperfect Substitutes

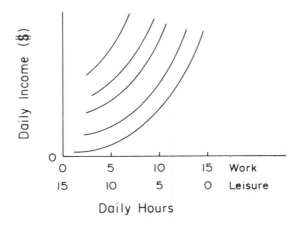

straints of the situation. The consumer's constraints came from
prices and budgets; next we see that the worker's constraint comes
from the worker's wage rate.

FIGURE 6.4

A Backward–Bending Labor Supply Curve

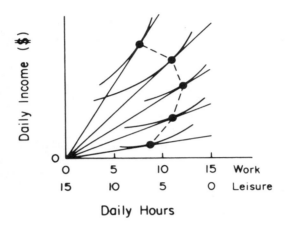

Figure 6.4 puts the two preceding figures together and completes the standard economic analysis of labor supply. In response
to the constraints of the prevailing wage rate, the worker will climb
the proper wage rate line to the highest indifference curve attainable,
supplying more daily labor and gaining more daily income along the
way. The worker will halt at a unique point, the point at which the
wage rate line is tangent to an indifference curve. That point represents the best the worker can do under the constraint of the wage rate,
the best available bundle of money and leisure. By stopping short of
that point, or climbing beyond it, the worker would stand on some
lower indifference curve that we could add to the money/leisure plane.
Standing on the lower indifference curve, the worker would hold a less
attractive bundle.

Each of the five points in the figure is called an equilibrium
point, a point that represents a balance among the forces that induce
the worker to move along the wage rate line. Only if the forces are
out of balance will the worker continue to move up or down the line.

The broken line that joins adjacent equilibrium points forms a
backward–bending labor supply curve. As the wage rate drops, daily

income falls steadily, but the greatest supply of labor comes at an intermediate wage rate.

There are several ways of understanding why the curve might bend as it does in Figure 6.4. Consider how a drop in the wage rate will affect the income derived from an hour of labor. As we reduce the wage rate, we reduce the money gained from an hour's work. This income effect will induce us to work longer in order to maintain our purchasing power, in order to keep up those monthly payments on the boat. But consider, too, how the same drop in the wage rate will affect the cost of leisure. The price of a leisure hour is the money we lose by using the hour for leisure instead of for work; in the commercial idiom, time is money. Thus, the price of a leisure hour is the wage rate itself, $/hour. It represents an opportunity cost, the money we lose from the lost opportunity to work. In accordance with the demand law, this price effect should lead us to consume more leisure, and perforce work less, as the wage rate drops. For the unemployed, leisure is very cheap indeed (time is not money), but perhaps also low in quality.

Notice that these two effects work in opposite directions as far as the supply of labor is concerned: The income effect of a lower wage rate would induce more labor, the price effect less. If its income effect outweighs its price effect, a drop in the wage rate will induce more work on balance, so the labor supply curve will slope downward from left to right. But if its price effect outweighs its income effect, a drop in the wage rate will induce less work on balance, so the curve will slope downward from right to left.

For a slightly different view of the situation, imagine the worker's decision as the resolution of a psychological approach-avoidance conflict. If we start at an extremely high wage rate, we can easily resolve the conflict created by a slight drop in the wage rate: We can keep our purchasing power by working just a little more; leisure, though cheaper than before, remains pretty costly; thus, we choose to work more than before, but less than we would if leisure had not become cheaper. Starting at a relatively low wage rate, we resolve the conflict just as easily, but differently: Already cheap, leisure cheapens even more; to keep our purchasing power we would have to work a great deal more, so we decide to work less than before, but more than we would in the absence of a challenge to our purchasing power.

Does the curve in Figure 6.4 provide an accurate factual account of the relations among wage rate, labor supply, and income? Yes and no. Economic studies of labor supply in the United States generally reveal only the top part of the curve, the part dominated by income effects. As the wage rate drops, income falls steadily, but the supply of labor rises steadily (Watts and Rees 1977). Perhaps

American wage rates are simply too high to allow price effects to dominate.

To help settle this issue, we turn to some experimental studies of labor supply in rats. Laboratory experiments with animals can provide a convenient if preliminary way of attacking the issue empirically. Their convenience derives from the fact that we can pay laboratory animals practically any wage rate we please, from extremely high to extremely low, without serious risk to the health and welfare of labor or management.

EMPIRICAL LABOR SUPPLY CURVES: ANIMALS

Writing in 1953, B. F. Skinner suggested that for the rat pressing a lever for each food pellet on some fixed-ratio schedule, the pellets/press ratio corresponds to the human's wage rate: $/hour for the worker paid on an hourly basis, or $/unit of production of the piece-rate worker. If we extend Skinner's suggestion to its logical conclusion, we arrive at two further points of correspondence. First, the total number of lever presses performed over the course of the contingency session—the workday—measures the amount of labor supplied at any particular wage rate. Second, the total food received measures the rat's total income from its labor. Thirty years later we have abundant experimental support for Skinner's speculation, support we can appreciate most fully after we have understood the rudiments of labor supply theory.

Figure 6.5 shows a backward-bending labor supply curve based on five rats that pressed a lever for all of their daily water in daily one-hour test sessions (Allison and Boulter 1982). The experiment tested each rat with three different fixed-ratio schedules. Notice that the three schedules covered an extremely broad range of wage rates, milliliters/press. As the wage rate dropped so did total milliliters, the analogue of income. At the same time, total lever presses, the analogue of labor supply, rose and then fell. Thus, the intermediate wage rate resulted in a significantly greater supply of labor than the highest or lowest rate. In terms of labor supply theory, the high range of wage rates revealed a dominant income effect; the low range, a dominant price effect—the dominant price effect that generally fails to appear in economic studies of the supply of labor in the United States.

Figure 6.6 shows another backward-bending curve, this one from rats that pressed a lever for sucrose solution (sugar water) in one-hour sessions (Kelsey and Allison 1976). Each of the eight fixed-ratio schedules required a certain number of instrumental lever presses for each ten-lick access to the sucrose solution. Because the instrumental requirement ranged from 1 lever press to 128

FIGURE 6.5

Total Water Earned by Rats as a Function of Total Lever Presses
at Three Different Wage Rates
(milliliters/press)

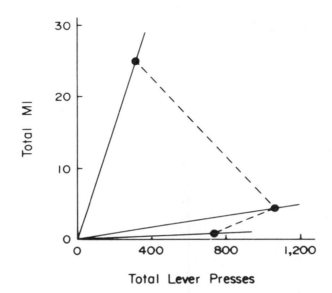

Total Lever Presses

presses, the wage rate ranged from 10 licks/press down to 0.08 licks/press. Notice again that the curve shows no dominant price effect until the wage rate becomes extremely low.

In the two experiments portrayed in Figures 6.5 and 6.6, the leisure-time alternatives offered little more than the chance to rest, groom, explore the inside of the cage, peer through the Plexiglas door, and eat the free food pellets scattered about the floor of the cage. Because the price effect refers to the consumption of more leisure as its price declines, one might expect to see a greater price effect as we improve the quality of the leisure-time alternatives to work.

To illustrate that possibility, Figure 6.7 reproduces the results of an experiment already discussed in Chapter 4, one in which a thirsty rat licked a dry tube for each contingent access to water, but had free access to food and saccharin solution. Five schedules varied the wage rate, water licks/dry lick. As the wage rate fell, total dry licks—the measure of labor supply—rose and then fell, with one minor exception at the lowest wage rate. The steady decline in total water

FIGURE 6.6

Total Sucrose Licks Earned by Rats as a Function of Total Lever
Presses at Eight Different Wage Rates
(licks/press)

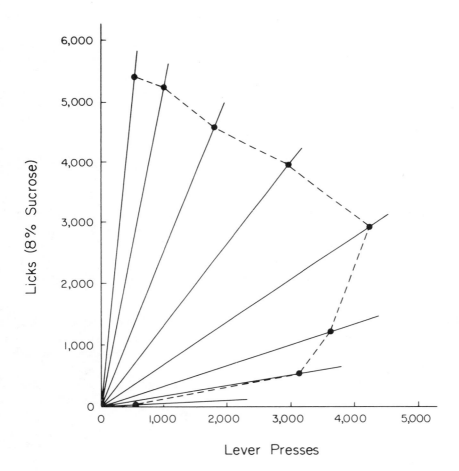

licks, the measure of income, was generally accompanied by a compensatory rise in licks at the free saccharin solution. Perhaps the
rat's labor supply curve would not have bent quite so sharply as it did
if the leisure-time alternatives to work had not included the chance to
drink saccharin. I know of no animal experiments that have studied
systematically the dependence of the price effect upon the quality and
quantity of leisure-time activities.

FIGURE 6.7

Total Earned Water Licks or Free Saccharin Licks as a Function
of Total Dry Licks at Five Different Wage Rates
(water licks/dry licks)

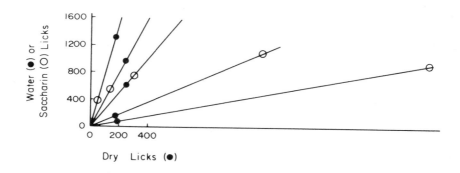

If you will review Figures 4.6 and 4.7 in terms of the economics of labor supply, you will see that the price effect may also depend
on endogenous characteristics of the laborer: Working for food, fat
hyperphagic rats show a more pronounced price effect than normal
controls. The prospect of living off the fat of the land may seem
more attractive to the fat than the lean.

Recent reviews of similar experiments with rats and pigeons
have revealed many additional examples of the backward-bending
labor supply curve (for example, Staddon 1979). Other experiments
with rats and pigeons working for water or food have made a fairly
persuasive case for another phenomenon that economists have found
elusive, the effect of <u>nonlabor income</u> on the supply of labor.

Imagine two laborers identical in every way save one. Worker
<u>A</u> derives all income directly from personal on-the-job labor. Over
and above that source of income, worker <u>B</u> gets some amount of nonlabor income—interest on a savings account, proceeds from stocks
and bonds, annuity payments, retirement benefits, food stamps, an
inheritance—any income besides the money derived directly from personal on-the-job labor.

Figure 6.8 presents a standard economic analysis of their
situation, plotting total income on the vertical axis, daily hours of
work and leisure on the horizontal. One of the two wage rate lines
intercepts the vertical income axis at the origin; it represents the
situation faced by worker <u>A</u>, who receives no nonlabor income. The
other worker gets exactly the same wage rate, but starts each workday

FIGURE 6.8

Daily Income as a Function of Work, Leisure, and Nonlabor Income

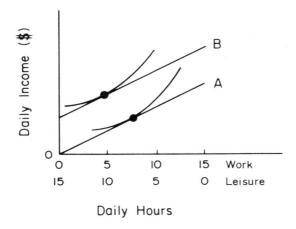

Daily Hours

with a certain amount of nonlabor income. Accordingly, the wage rate line for worker B intercepts the vertical income axis above the origin; the higher the intercept, the greater the amount of daily non-labor income.

The two equilibrium points show that in this particular exam-ple, nonlabor income should cut the supply of labor but raise total income, the sum of labor and nonlabor income. Worker B can get the best available bundle of money and leisure by working less than the less fortunate A, whose best available bundle is substantially worse than the one available to B. According to the theory, any amount of nonlabor income greater than zero should cut the supply of labor. By imagining other indifference curves, or other amounts of nonlabor income than the one shown in the example, the reader can easily see that nonlabor income might increase, decrease, or have no effect on total income.

In the 1960s the U. S. government financed the first of several projects intended to measure the empirical effects of nonlabor in-come. The New Jersey Income Maintenance Project targeted 735 families for the periodic receipt of nonlabor income payments—"free" money. The project sought evidence that might prove useful in eval-uating such politically touchy proposals as a negative income tax, automatic cash payments from the government to persons below a certain income level—a relatively simple, efficient form of social welfare. The elaborate controls included 632 closely comparable families that received no such payments. A valiant effort, and many would agree that its final product was well worth the $7.9 million that went into the project. But we can easily imagine the formidable difficulties involved in conducting such a large-scale study under field conditions and in making sense of the final results. The final verdict, by no means undebatable, seems to be that nonlabor income generally reduced the supply of labor, but that the effect was surprisingly small and mysteriously nonexistent among black households (Watts and Rees 1977).

One can always wonder about their wider applicability, but animal experiments leave little doubt about the effects of nonlabor income upon the behavior of rats or pigeons (Battalio, Green, and Kagel 1981; Green, Kagel, and Battalio 1980). If the contingency schedule will deliver water in return for a certain number of instrumental lever presses, any water delivered freely at the start of the session would serve as an analogue of nonlabor income. The experiment discussed earlier (Allison and Boulter 1982) tested each of its five rats with a fourth condition, a nonlabor income condition, that has no representation in Figure 6.5. We started the session for that condition by giving the rats about 4.5 milliliters of free water. They had to earn all subsequent water by working at the intermediate wage rate.

Figure 6.9 represents that fourth condition as a line of intermediate slope that intercepts the vertical axis at about 4.5 milliliters. The large unfilled circle on the fourth line shows the results. Compare that point with the large filled circle on the parallel line just below, the line that represents the same wage rate, but with no free water. The comparison shows that free water produced a significant decrease in total lever presses, but a significant increase in total water intake, relative to the same schedule that offered no free water. In economic terms, nonlabor income cut the supply of labor and raised total income, the sum of earned and nonlabor income. Notice, too, that the results could have been quite different: The structural constraints of the free-water schedule allowed the rats to climb as much or as little as they pleased up their line of constraint, which heads straight up the vertical axis to 4.5 milliliters, then bends abruptly and runs past the point for which they settled on the no-free-water schedule.

The off-line symbols in Figure 6.9 represent predictions derived from Conservation Model 2 for ten other wage rates. Filled circles stand for performance under schedules that offer no nonlabor income; unfilled circles stand for the rats' predicted performance under the same ten schedules, given that the rats have already drunk 4.5 milliliters of free water. The off-line points show that the model

FIGURE 6.9

Total Water Received by Rats as a Function of Total Lever Presses,
Wage Rate, and the Amount of Water Received Freely at the Start
of the Test Session
(wage rate in milliliters/press)

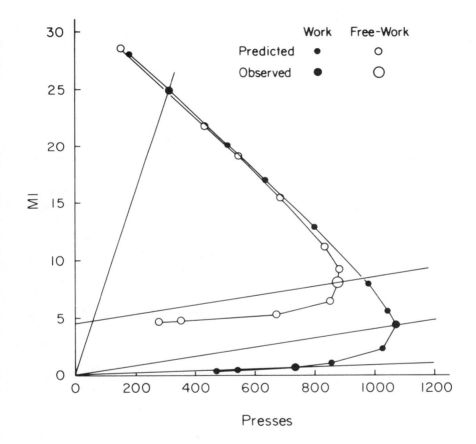

predicts both the backward-bending labor supply curve and the effects
of nonlabor income seen in this experiment: less labor and more
total income.

By comparing the filled with the unfilled circles, we see in addition that the model's predictions depend on the wage rate: Nonlabor
income should have its greatest effects at the relatively low wage
rates. Similar experiments have confirmed these predictions, show–

ing that the animal analogues of nonlabor income produce the largest decrease in the supply of labor, and the largest increase in total income, at relatively low wage rates. [1]

In summary, if we accept the animal analogues of wage rate, labor supply, and income, the animal experiments leave little doubt about the empirical status of the backward-bending labor supply curve, or its perturbations from nonlabor income. The key facts can be explained in terms of the price and income effects of labor supply theory; they can also be explained by psychological models of the adaptive response to the constraints imposed by the contingency schedule. [2]

HARDSHIP PAY

During the construction of the Alaskan pipeline in the 1970s, multitudes of construction workers were lured to the frozen north to work under the extreme hardships of the Alaskan wilderness. Presumably a major attractant was the promise of pay rates far higher than they could get anywhere else in the United States. A recent experiment confirms the supposition that human endurance of hardship depends on the pay rate.

Johnson and Cabanac (1983) paid each of five adult males, each clad only in bathing suit and shoes, for each minute he chose to stay inside a cold climatic chamber. Adapted to an outside air temperature of 25° Celsius, the person stepped into a 15° C. chamber that gradually approached 0° C. over the next two hours. Each person, tested individually, was paid for each minute spent inside the chamber. He understood that he could leave the chamber whenever he pleased, but that any exit would be final, as it would terminate the test session for that particular day. Thus, the "leisure" alternative to "work" was time outside the chamber, in warm air rather than in cold.

Each person was tested on five different days, with a different pay rate on each day: 2, 5, 10, 20, or 40 cents per minute. A cumulative counter inside the chamber showed the person the total amount of money earned throughout the test session. Each person got the five different pay rates in a different sequence. While inside the chamber, the subject was not allowed to exercise or change posture in an effort to keep warm.

Figure 6.10 shows my replot of the data in the form of a labor supply curve. The group data appear in panel A, which plots total pay received as a function of pay rate and median time spent inside the chamber. Notice that the lowest pay rates were extremely low. In general, as the pay rate increased, time inside the chamber increased, along with total pay. Thus, the group data conform to the

FIGURE 6.10

Total Dollars Earned as a Function of Total Time in the Cold at
Five Different Wage Rates
(dollars/minute)

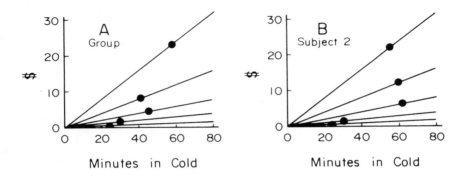

lower part of a backward-bending labor supply curve, the part dominated by the price effect. Larger financial incentives generally induced a larger supply of labor, more endurance of cold.

The authors note that one of the five subjects behaved quite differently from the others in the region of the highest pay rates. His
data appear separately in Figure 6.10B and reveal a backward-bending
labor supply curve: He spent more time in the cold at the intermediate
pay rate than at higher or lower pay rates. Thus, his data indicate a
dominant income effect at the highest pay rates and a dominant price
effect at the lowest rates.

If we accept these results as a guide, we should expect some
individual differences in the labor-supply response to variations in
the wage rate. For a discussion of physiological differences that
might be expected to affect the response in this particular setting,
see Johnson and Cabanac (1983). An economic interpretation might
translate physiological variables into individual differences in the substitutability of money for leisure. Such differences would take the
form of individual differences in the shape of the indifference curve
with respect to money and leisure.

THE SALARY SYSTEM

In the piece-rate and hourly systems described in the preceding
sections the firm sets the wage rate, and the worker decides how much

labor to supply: the more labor, the greater the current income. But there is another widespread system of compensation in which the worker's current income does not depend on current productivity. Here we examine a theoretical analysis of this alternative system and an empirical study of its effects on the amount of labor supplied by psychology professors. Although the study focuses on an academic setting, the same basic system appears in a great variety of nonacademic settings where the person receives a salary for the performance of some professional, managerial, or executive function.

The typical professor awaits each summer an important letter from the office of the university president. When the letter finally arrives, the practiced eye moves quickly to the line that states the total salary to be received for whatever services the professor may choose to provide in the coming academic year. Thus, in any particular year the professor's income ($) does not depend on the amount of academic labor ($\underline{L}$) supplied during that year. The system allows the professor to supply more labor or less, within reasonable limits: Those who often miss class, or fail to publish scholarly research, or evade service on departmental committees, risk ostracism, reprimand, or an intolerably small raise next year. The nontenured ones risk, in addition, an eventual loss of employment. But the system it self imposes no contractual relation between current salary and current productivity. Next year's salary, the amount stated in the letter, is safely insulated from next year's productivity. Consequently, variations in current productivity will not affect current income but will only affect the current wage rate, the ratio $/$\underline{L}$. Because the $ numerator is fixed, the professor can achieve a relatively high wage rate by supplying relatively little labor. What is the rational response to the constraints of this system?

Figure 6.11 presents an answer in terms of labor supply theory, plotting the current year's salary against the current year's labor and leisure. The two horizontal lines represent a senior professor with a relatively high salary and a junior professor with a lower salary. Point $\underline{L}$ on the horizontal axis signifies the amount of labor the average professor must supply in order to remain in good graces with the employer and to assuage the professional conscience. According to the theory, each person should strive toward the upper left portion of the space between the two axes, because the upper left corner represents both more money and more leisure than the lower right corner.

As the figure shows, the one with the higher salary can reach a higher indifference curve than the one with the lower salary. But both can reach the highest indifference curve attainable by following exactly the same strategy: Supply the amount of labor marked by point $\underline{L}$ as we climb to our respective salary lines set for the coming year. The two continuous lines sloping upward from the origin define the rational

FIGURE 6.11

Current Salary as a Function of Current Labor and Leisure:
Theoretical Indifference Analysis of the Salary System

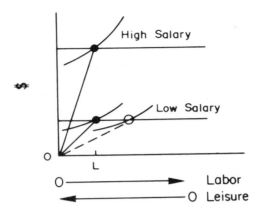

strategies; the slope of each line shows the resulting wage rate selected by the professor, the ratio $/L. If the person supplies more
labor than amount L, the person will end on a lower indifference
curve and receive a lower wage rate. This hypothetical selection of
a lower wage rate is illustrated by the broken wage rate line for the
low-salaried professor who chooses to supply more labor than amount
L, choosing instead the amount marked by the unfilled circle.

   If the workers in such a system behave in the manner prescribed
by the figure, the data will reveal no consistent relation between income and labor. For example, the filled circles in the figure show
that the high-salaried professor supplies the same amount of labor as
the low-salaried professor. But the same data should reveal a strong
positive relationship between income and wage rate. If both supply
the same amount of labor, the one with the higher salary will have a
higher wage rate, $/L, than the one with the lower salary, as illus-
trated in Figure 6.11. How does the theory fare against the evidence?

   Most universities recognize three major components of professorial productivity: teaching, service, and research. A 1982 study
(Allison in press) focused on these three components of the labor supplied by the 38 faculty members, 34 males and 4 females, in the
psychology department of a state university in the midwestern United
States. The sample included 24 full professors, 10 associate professors, and 4 assistant professors, all holding the Ph.D. degree. A
panel of four psychologists rated the performance of each of their col-

leagues over the most recent three-year period. Each panelist made three separate ratings, one for each of the three productivity categories. Each rating scale ranged from 1 (substandard) to 4 (outstanding); a rating of 2.5 signified satisfactory performance. The four panelists showed excellent agreement among themselves, rarely differing by more than 0.3 scale points. Their ratings were averaged to form each person's productivity profile, one number on each of the three dimensions of productivity.

In their evaluations of teaching, the panelists considered such information as the number of courses taught, class enrollments, service on thesis committees, textbooks published, evaluations by students, creation of new courses, academic counseling, honorary awards for teaching, and financial awards for the development of innovative techniques. Their evaluations of service took account of editorships, reviewing of manuscripts and research proposals, service on editorial boards, election to office in professional organizations, efforts in organizing professional conferences, service on departmental and university committees, and service rendered to community mental health organizations. In evaluating research they attended to the quantity and quality of scholarly publications, papers presented at professional meetings, invited talks and papers, research grants, and honorary awards in recognition of distinguished research.

The three numbers on each person's profile were averaged to form a single composite measure of productivity ($\underline{L}$) as the measure of the amount of labor supplied over the rating period. Income ($) was defined as the person's average annual salary over the same three-year period. To examine the empirical relation between income and productivity, the 38 psychologists were listed in order on the income variable. The ordered list was scissored into seven nonoverlapping income groups, with five psychologists in each of the four highest groups, six in each of the three lowest.

The results appear in Figure 6.12A, which scales each group's median income ($) on the vertical axis, mean productivity ($\underline{L}$) on the horizontal. In agreement with the theory, the seven points in the figure reveal no statistically significant relation between current income and current productivity.[3] Because the seven different income groups supplied essentially the same amount of labor, the higher income groups got higher wage rates than the lower income groups. Figure 6.12B reveals this relation more clearly than Figure 6.12A, plotting mean wage rate ($/$\underline{L}$) against median income ($). Wage rate increased linearly as income increased, and the relation was highly significant statistically.[4]

The data presented in Figure 6.12A show that the professor's income has essentially no value as a predictor of the professor's productivity. Our best guess of any particular person's productivity in-

FIGURE 6.12

Productivity (A) and Wage Rate (B) as a Function of Income among
Seven Groups of Psychology Professors with
Nonoverlapping Incomes

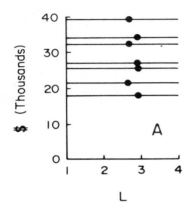
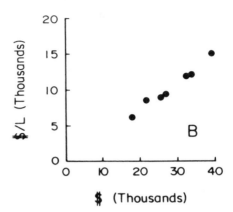

dex is simply the group mean for the 38 individuals, $\underline{L}$ = 2.81.
Knowledge of the professor's income does not improve this guess to
any significant degree. But what about the wage rate variable, $\$/\underline{L}$,
as a possible predictor of $\underline{L}$? Although the high income groups
showed the same productivity as the low, the members of each income group showed a substantial amount of variability among them-
selves on all three measures: $\$$, $\underline{L}$, and the wage rate $\$/\underline{L}$. Thus,
we cannot infer from Figure 6.12A the general relation between wage
rate and productivity. If we cannot predict $\underline{L}$ from $\$$, maybe we can
predict both $\$$ and $\underline{L}$ from the wage rate. In the labor supply analysis
of the piece-rate system, where the firm sets the wage rate, the
theory has some success in predicting $\$$ and $\underline{L}$ from the ratio $\$/\underline{L}$.
What relations might we see in the salary system, where the firm
sets $\$$ and the worker sets $\$/\underline{L}$? How might $\$$ and $\underline{L}$ vary as the pro-
fessors themselves vary $\$/\underline{L}$?

Figure 6.13 presents all of the possibilities permitted by the
structure of the wage rate ratio, $\$/\underline{L}$. Panel A portrays two profes-
sors with different wage rates. The professor who sits on the steeper
line has the higher wage rate. Both have the same salary, but one
achieves a higher wage rate by being less productive than the other.
To fix it firmly in mind, the reader might imagine the pattern in
panel A as the worker-drone pattern, a vivid if unfair simile.

Panel B shows another possibility: The two are equally productive but one has a higher salary, and thus a higher wage rate.

FIGURE 6.13

Income and Productivity as Functions of the Wage Rate
(Income/Productivity): Possible Relations (A, B, C, D, and E)
and Relations Observed among Seven Groups of Psychology
Professors with Nonoverlapping Wage Rates (F)

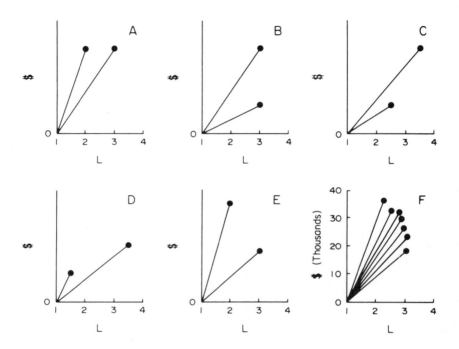

Panel C shows that the one with the higher wage rate might also
have the higher salary and the greater productivity, the Horatio Alger
pattern. Panel D shows the opposite pattern: high wage rate, low
income, low productivity. The final possibility appears in panel E:
high wage rate, high income, low productivity.

To examine the actual distinction between those with high and
those with low wage rates, the 38 psychologists were listed in order
on the wage rate variable, $/\underline{L}$. The ordered list was divided into
seven nonoverlapping wage rate groups, with five persons in each
of the four highest groups and six in each of the three lowest. Figure
6.13F shows the results. As the wage rate increased, income rose
and productivity fell significantly. Thus, the actual results generally
conformed to the pattern shown in panel E: high wage rate, high income, low productivity.

Notice how the empirical function in Figure 6.13F resembles
the top part of the backward-bending labor supply curve, the part dominated by the income effect. In light of that resemblance, the results
presented here and in the preceding sections suggest the following
conclusion: As long as the lowest wage rate is none too low the income effect will exceed the price effect, no matter who sets the wage
rate—the firm in the case of the piece-rate system, the worker in
the case of the salary system. A similar pattern is suggested by the
results of Dalton and Thompson (1971), who studied pay and productivity among 2,500 engineers and managers employed by several different companies (see Maital 1982, p. 97, for a graphic summary of
their findings).

THE WORKER-SELECTED WAGE RATE

In the example cited at the beginning of this chapter human employees, allowed to set their own wage rates, allegedly chose lower
ones than they might have chosen. Our study of psychology professors
may provide a similar example, because none of the 38 received a
substandard productivity rating. However, professorial behavior may
say more about the screening of employees than it says about the motivation of workers chosen at random. A strong academic department
will probably do its best to avoid hiring or keeping the exploitative
drone, the one who gets an exorbitant wage rate by supplying practically no labor in return for the preset salary. To clarify this issue,
we turn once again to laboratory experiments with animals.

We already have discussed (in Chapter 4) a number of experiments that show that animals often choose lower wage rates than they
might. Some of the pertinent experiments use a concurrent fixed-ratio
schedule that allows the individual a choice between two alternative
wage rates, one substantially higher than the other. Figure 6.14 presents an example, one seen earlier as Figure 4.10. The unfilled circle shows total licks at a water tube and total lever presses under the
paired baseline condition. The two wage-rate lines represent the constraints of the schedule: Lever A offered a wage rate of 30 licks/
press; lever b, only 7.5 licks/press. The rat could have had the
highest wage rate available by responding exclusively on lever A. Instead, the rat sampled both levers extensively and thereby selected
an intermediate wage rate, the one defined by the broken line passing
through the filled circle. For several additional examples of the same
kind, see Figures 4.11 and 4.12.

Other pertinent examples come from the fixed-ratio schedule
with an optional magnitude of reward. In that type of schedule the experimenter sets the instrumental work requirement, but the animal

FIGURE 6.14

Total Water Licks as a Function of Total Lever Presses by a Rat
Tested with a Concurrent Fixed-Ratio Schedule: Selection of a
Lower Wage Rate (Licks/Press) than the Highest One Available

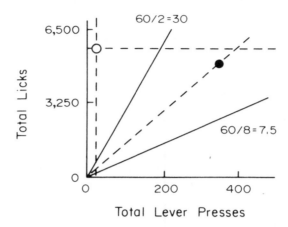

sets the size of the contingent meal or drinking bout. Because the
wage rate analogue is grams/press or milliliters/press, the rat can
select the highest wage rate available by taking the largest meals or
drinking bouts it can manage. As we saw in Chapter 4, rats tested
with that type of schedule typically take meals or drinking bouts
smaller than the ones we know they can manage and thereby choose
considerably less than the highest wage rate available. For one of
many such examples, see Figure 4.15B.

A controversial phenomenon known as contrafreeloading also
supports the contention that animals often choose lower wage rates
than they might. The typical setup tests a rat or a pigeon in a cage
divided into two separate chambers joined by a passageway. In the
work chamber, the animal can get food by pressing a lever or pecking
a key; in the freeloading chamber, food is "freely" available. The
complete freeloader would get all of its food from the freeloading
chamber, none from the work chamber. The complete contrafree-
loader would show the opposite pattern, getting all of its food from
the work chamber. (Whether the contrafreeloading pattern would illustrate the Protestant work ethic in rat or pigeon is a matter of
some dispute.) Because the typical animal actually falls somewhere
between these two extremes, the typical animal chooses a wage rate

lower than the one it could have had by getting all of its food from the freeloading chamber.

By putting "freely" in quotation marks, as if the term were faintly disreputable, I acknowledge the recent discovery by experimental psychologists that there is truly no such thing as a free lunch, even in the freeloading chamber. In some of the earlier experiments in the genre, the working animal could get the food it had already earned at a negligible cost, the cost of bending down to the food receptacle near the floor of the work chamber. The freeloading chamber imposed a slightly higher cost, the cost of reaching into a food receptacle a little taller than the one in the work chamber. Recent work has shown that the rat is quite sensitive to this subtle difference in cost, eating more "free" food from a short receptacle than a tall one. But even when the rat can feed from a conveniently short receptacle it still strays a bit from the pure freeloader ethic, getting some of its food from the work chamber, too (Mitchell, Fish, and Calica 1982).

Take note of the problems these data present for models that view the paired basepoint as a behavioral ideal and for models that view the organism as a maximizer of utility. Is there some utility in work, or in switching from one chamber to the other?

Some investigators have discounted the utility of work, concluding that earned food has no special attraction in comparison with free food. The pertinent experiments have identified another subtle source of attraction to the work chamber: the stimulus change normally attendant on work, but normally missing from the free-food chamber (Wallace et al. 1973). If the instrumental key-peck briefly opens and illuminates the grain cup with an audible click, and briefly darkens the key light and the overhead house lights, the pigeon typically does a great deal of key pecking for food in the presence of another cup that offers free food but no stimulus change. If we reverse these conditions, the pigeon soon loses its inclination to peck for food: When the key peck gains only food, but the entry into the free-food cup is accompanied by a click, an illumination of the cup, and a darkening of the house lights, the pigeon soon deserts the key in favor of the free food. Given a choice between two free-food cups, the bird typically enters more frequently the cup that offers more stimulus change, but eats about the same amount of food from each cup.

The original experiments on contrafreeloading gained widespread notice because they demonstrated a clear preference for the work chamber over the free chamber. Later experiments often revealed the opposite result, a clear preference for the free side and more eating there, but considerable eating in both sides (Morgan 1974). For some investigators, the real question is why the animal spends any time at all on the work side. As we have just seen, one possible explanation is the stimulus change normally available on the work side, but not on the free side. Some have suggested in addition that even if we could equate the two sides in terms of external stimulus change, the animal might still derive more benefit from switching sides from time to time than from standing pat. The exact origin and character of this hypothetical benefit remain to be delineated.

GENDER DIFFERENCES: EQUAL
PAY FOR UNEQUAL WORK?

The title of this section plays on an egalitarian slogan whose rightness few Americans would deny: Equal pay for equal work! Yet, labor statistics from the U.S. economy suggest widespread violations of this egalitarian rule.

For one outstanding example, females generally earn somewhere between half and two-thirds of the earnings received by males. Much of this difference might arise from some segregation process that tended to place the males in the more lucrative occupations. But what about two workers employed in comparable occupations? Employers have been known to claim, perhaps less often or less vocally now than a few years ago, that the male should get the higher wage rate because the male is more productive than the female. How could we test the claim experimentally?

Recently, a team of economists attacked the problem by comparing the labor supplied by males and females working at the same piecework job for identical wage rates (Battalio, Kagel, and Reynolds 1977). The volunteer participants in the experiment, otherwise unemployed, lived for 98 days in an institutional setting that permitted the detailed recording of production, earnings, and consumption in the experimental economy. Semiprivate rooms were provided without charge, along with heat, lighting, and cleaning services. The participants had to buy all other goods from the earnings derived from labor—meals, recreation, alcoholic drinks—and could keep any savings at the end of the experiment. The job consisted of the weaving of woolen belts on portable hand looms, at a piecework rate of $2.50 (Canadian) for each acceptable belt, with all means of production provided free of charge. Each participant could work any time, any place, and for any amount of time the worker pleased.

The mean amount of money earned by the female participants came to 69.5 percent of the amount earned by the males—a statistically significant difference, comparable to the gender difference seen at the level of the national economy. But we cannot explain the experimental difference in terms of some gender-biased assignment to different occupations.

We can easily think of many other ways of explaining the difference. For example, maybe the difference was simply job dependent: Other jobs, such as the assembly of transistor radios, might favor a delicate, dexterous touch that would give most females the productive advantage over the average sausage-fingered male.

An alternative possibility: In the spirit of labor supply theory, the female may be more willing than the male to sacrifice cash for a little extra leisure. More formally, the female's indifference curve may fall more steeply than the male's, indicating a higher marginal rate of substitution. The two indifference curves in Figure 6.15 illustrate this kind of gender difference: Even if both receive the same wage rate, the best bundle available to the female contains more leisure and less money than the best one available to the male. In consequence, the female would work less than the male. If the explanation is correct, we should be able to find some wage rate for the female, lower than the wage rate shown in the figure, that would induce her to work just as much as the male works at the wage rate shown in the figure. We should not be able to equalize their productivity by giving her some wage rate higher than the male's. But if our goal is to equalize income rather than productivity, then indeed we must give the female some wage rate higher than the male's.

Figure 6.16 illustrates three possible explanations in the spirit of conservation theory. If males generally consume more food, beer, or commercial recreation than females, they will need more cash than females do to finance their baseline levels of consumption—the

FIGURE 6.15

A Gender Difference in Labor Supply Explained as a Gender Difference in the Substitutability of Money and Leisure

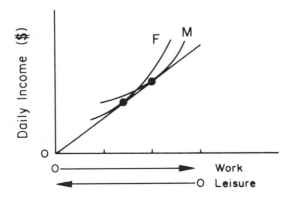

FIGURE 6.16

A Gender Difference in Labor Supply Explained in Terms of
Conservation Theory

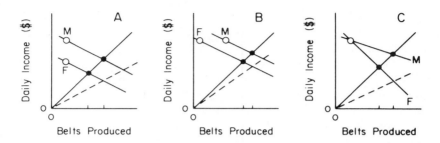

levels whose cash equivalents are shown as the unfilled circles in
panel A. Accordingly, the males will produce the larger number of
belts and, thus, earn more money, even though both work at the wage
rate shown as the continuous line in panel A. If the explanation is correct, the females will turn out the same number of belts as the males
if we test the females at a lower wage rate, the wage rate shown as
the broken line in panel A. Once again, we should not be able to
equalize their production by giving females a higher wage rate than
the males.

Panel B illustrates another possibility. Maybe the weaving of
belts simply holds more intrinsic attraction for males than for females: In a paired baseline condition, males would make more belts
than females would. Then males will make more belts for pay than
the females will for the same wage rate, and we can equalize their
production only by giving the females a lower wage rate.

Our third possibility: Maybe females simply find the work more
difficult than males do. Panel C illustrates this possibility. Notice
how the male-female difference illustrated in panel C resembles the
easy-hard difference shown in Figure 4.19: Pressing a lever for
water at a constant wage rate, rats supplied more lever presses when
the work was easy than they did when the work was hard.

Notice, too, that all of the explanations illustrated by Figures
6.15 and 6.16 prescribe the very same curative wage-rate adjust-
ment: To equalize their productivity, pay the females a lower wage
rate than the males, for exactly the same job. If a similar experiment
could equalize production by paying females the higher wage rate, it
would contradict all of these explanations.

Recognize that the theories behind the various explanations take
an entirely neutral stance with respect to males and females. Should

a similar experiment happen to use a job that gave the productive advantage to females, the same theories would imply that the males could be raised to the females' standard of productivity by giving the males a lower wage rate than the females.

The theories are also silent on the question of goals: Although the firm may have an intense interest in getting equal productivity from males and females, the workers themselves may advocate other goals, such as the equalization of income. A pertinent example of "advocacy economics" has come from the Institute for Labor Education and Research (1982). Noting that the major U.S. corporations have recently intensified the advocacy of their cause through use of the mass media, the authors counter with a popular introduction to economic issues that frankly seeks to articulate and advance the interests of workers and consumers against corporate interests—often through the device of a fictional cartoon character named Arthur "Dupe" Dagain, an employee of Short Circuit Electrical Corporation, Heartland, Ohio.

SOCIAL SECURITY BENEFITS

Our social security system pays the participant a certain amount of nonlabor income. It also allows the participant to earn further income without penalty, up to a certain limit. Beyond that limit, the worker incurs a loss in social security benefits, $0.50 for every $1 earned beyond the limit. In effect, the worker who exceeds the limit actually gets only half of the income earned on the job: If the nominal wage rate is $4/hour, the net is only $2/hour: $4 - $2 = $2/hour. When the worker reaches some further limit, the social security payments are discontinued, and the net wage rate returns to its nominal value, $4/hour. How should this system affect the supply of labor?

Figure 6.17 analyzes the system in terms of labor supply theory. The spline on the bottom, with three distinct limbs, is a wage-rate function that identifies the worker's income possibilities. It intercepts the vertical income axis at a point that marks the worker's nonlabor income. The first limb rises with a slope equal to the nominal wage rate, but only until the worker has earned a certain amount. The second limb represents the penalty for further work by rising with a slope equal to half of the nominal wage rate. The third limb rises with the same slope as the first: No further social security payments and no further penalty.

The straight line represents an alternative system, one that imposes no penalty for work, no reduction in social security payments when the earnings exceed some limit. The two equilibrium points show

FIGURE 6.17

Indifference Analysis of the Social Security System

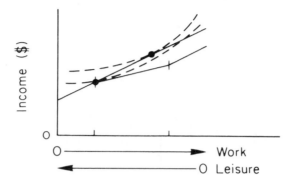

the theoretical predictions: A prospective loss of benefits should dis-
courage labor and cut total income. On the spline function, the best
available bundle of leisure and money contains more leisure and less
money than the best one available on the straight line function.

It would not be difficult to test the theory experimentally, using
rats as laborers. We could simulate nonlabor income by dispensing
free food at the start of the experimental session. When the rat has
finished the free food, we introduce the lever. Our first wage rate,
pellets/press, is $\underline{W}$; the no-penalty system maintains $\underline{W}$ throughout
the entire duration of the session, like the straight line function in
Figure 6.17. The penalty system maintains $\underline{W}$ until the rat has earned
a certain number of food pellets, at which time we cut the wage rate
in half, to $\underline{W}/2$. We signal the switch from $\underline{W}$ to $\underline{W}/2$ by turning on a
light above the lever. We maintain $\underline{W}/2$ until the rat has earned a
certain number of additional food pellets, at which time we return
the wage rate to its original value, $\underline{W}$, and extinguish the light. Once
they have learned the terms of their schedules, the rat tested under
the penalty system should quit pressing the lever in response to the
light that signals the switch from $\underline{W}$ to $\underline{W}/2$, and supply fewer lever
presses than the rat tested under the no-penalty system.

Would the results generally conform to labor supply theory?
Perhaps not. My doubts arise from two different sources: familiar-
ity with the behavior of hungry laboratory rats and psychological
theories whose predictions oppose the ones derived from labor supply
theory.

Figure 6.18 analyzes the rat experiment in terms of conservation theory. Look first at panel A, which shows the paired basepoint

as an unfilled circle. The two filled circles, equilibrium points predicted by the conservation model, plainly contradict the predictions of labor supply theory: The rat tested with the penalty schedule should supply more lever presses than the rat tested with the no-penalty schedule.

Panel B shows that if the experimental conditions were just right, the two rats might supply the same number of lever presses. But as long as the wage rates are relatively high, under no condition would the model predict more lever presses under the no-penalty schedule than the penalty schedule.

I know of no such experiment. Its results might hold some interest for the social engineers in charge of the social security system.

FIGURE 6.18

Conservation Analysis of an Experimental Analogue of the Social Security System: Total Food Earned as a Function of Total Lever Presses and a Wage Rate That Remains Constant or Diminishes When the Rat Has Earned a Prescribed Amount of Food

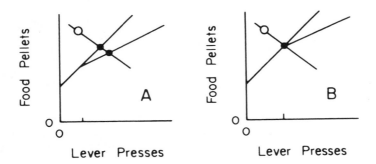

LABOR SUPPLY AND THE LAFFER CURVE

On a backward-bending labor supply curve, we see the greatest supply of labor at some intermediate wage rate. Our workers do not work very much at extremely high or extremely low wage rates. It is time to relate that microeconomic phenomenon to a macroeconomic problem: How does the rate of taxation affect the government's tax revenues?

The worker actually faces two wage rate lines, one expressing the gross (before taxes) wage rate, another expressing the net (after taxes) wage rate. Let us assume that the worker attends to the second of these two lines in making the personal labor-leisure decision. It is the after-taxes wage rate, multiplied by the amount of labor supplied, that determines the worker's take-home pay, hence the goods and services the worker can buy in the private sector of our economy.

If the tax rate is zero, the two lines are identical: gross income = net income. As the tax rate increases, the line that expresses the net wage rate slopes ever more gently, while the gross wage-rate line remains firmly in place. In effect, an increase in the tax rate simply decreases the wage rate that the worker attends to in deciding how much labor to supply. Our assumption thus allows us to treat a low tax rate as the analytic equivalent of a high wage rate and a high tax rate as the analytic equivalent of a low wage rate.

If the tax rate is zero, the government will collect no taxes on any amount of labor supplied by the national work force. As the tax rate approaches 100 percent, the net wage rate approaches zero; now the government will collect practically no tax revenues because the supply of labor has practically vanished: A confiscatory tax rate reduces the private financial incentive for work. By the logic of exclusion, we conclude that the government will collect its largest tax revenues at some intermediate rate of taxation—in other words, at some intermediate wage rate, perhaps one very close to the wage rate that will also maximize the supply of labor.

Figure 6.19 shows these general relations in graphic detail. Each panel includes two wage-rate lines; the slope of the steeper one, the same in all three panels, represents the gross wage rate. The slope of the other line represents the net wage rate. As the tax rate increases, the two wage-rate lines diverge more sharply: Panel A shows a lower tax rate than B, and B a lower tax rate than C. The filled circles in the figure conform to a backward-bending labor supply curve: As we move across the panels from left to right we have a steady decline in the net wage rate, a steady decline in net income, and a rise followed by a fall in the supply of labor. Notice what happens to tax revenues, the difference between gross income and net income: As the tax rate increases, tax collections rise and then fall. Thus, the government collects its largest tax revenues at an intermediate rate of taxation.

Demand-side economists in the Keynesian tradition attend to the stimulational effects of wealthy consumers chasing after huge quantities of consumer goods and services. A trickle-up process will stimulate others to invest in new enterprises intended to supply the desired goods and services.

Supply-side economists, more influential now than they were a few years ago, attend to the stimulational effects of the entrepreneur with plenty of money to invest in new enterprises. In turn, these new

FIGURE 6.19

Theoretical Effect of the Tax Rate upon Labor Supply, Tax
Revenues, and Net Income

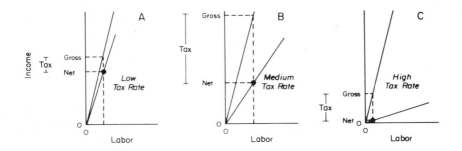

enterprises create new jobs and an eventual trickle-down effect, more
consumer dollars chasing more goods and services.

Because the entrepreneurial money must come from somewhere,
some supply-siders point to the Laffer curve (McKenzie and Tullock
1981) as a basis for advocating lower tax rates. The Laffer curve,
which appears in Figure 6.20, says nothing more than we have already
learned from the backward-bending labor supply curve. The function
shown in the figure is perfectly symmetrical, but could assume many
other shapes without distorting its fundamental message: As the tax
rate increases from 0 to 100 percent, tax collections rise from zero

FIGURE 6.20

Tax Collections as a Function of Tax Rate: The Laffer Curve

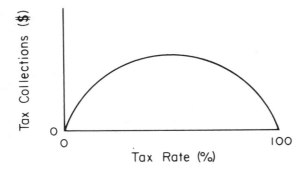

to a peak at some intermediate rate, then head back down toward zero as the tax rate approaches 100 percent. The Laffer curve belongs to a large family of curves with the same general implications.

Because no one can specify our present location on the Laffer curve, it is safe enough to claim that our present location is right of center; if we will only move leftward, the entrepreneurs will get to keep more of their money for financing their new enterprises, and the government will get more money to spend on public goods and services. Thus, lower taxes will benefit everyone all around. But if we happen to be left of center already, a tax reduction will threaten the welfare of those who value public goods and services and benefit those who do not.

The fundamental issue, like many others in economics, relates to the concept of Pareto optimality. We can improve social welfare by making any change that leaves at least one person better off than before and none worse off. A Pareto optimal or Pareto efficient welfare situation is one in which we cannot make anyone better off without harming someone else.

The debate outlined above may strike some readers as a bit myopic for its lack of attention to taxation effects on the supply of labor, a vital contributor to the health of the macroeconomy. We might feel a little more comfortable with a model that could relate the tax rate to three dependent variables: public tax collections, private income, and the supply of labor. If the same model could also predict a backward-bending labor supply curve, the effects of nonlabor income, the demand law, and the relation between price and price elasticity of demand, so much the better for our confidence in the model's applicability to the present problem.

The three functions in Figure 6.21 represent predictions derived from Conservation Model 2. The exact shape of each function depends on the numerical values assigned to the model's constants, but its general form does not. All three functions were generated by selecting one numerical value for the gross wage rate and by varying the tax rate over a wide range of values. [5]

Panel A shows the predicted relation between tax rate and tax collections. Its two scales were normalized by expressing each tax rate or each tax collection as a proportion of the largest rate considered, or the largest collection predicted. The curve in panel A bears the desired family resemblance to the Laffer curve: As the tax rate rises from zero, tax collections should rise from zero to a peak and decline again to zero with a further rise in the tax rate. Thus, Conservation Model 2 predicts the Laffer curve.

Panels B and C show the two different aspects of the backward-bending labor supply curve. In panel B, private income falls steadily as the tax rate rises. In panel C, the supply of labor rises to a peak, then declines as the tax rate rises further.

FIGURE 6.21

Tax Revenues (A), Private Income (B), and Labor Supply (C) as
Functions of the Tax Rate: Predictions Derived from
Conservation Model 2

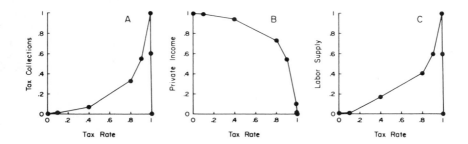

The graphic scale is too small to show the difference, but in
this particular example the tax rate that would maximize tax collection (panel A) is a trifle higher than the one that would maximize the
supply of labor (panel C). By comparing panel B with the others, we
are led to suspect that we cannot select a tax rate that maximizes
private income without losing alarming amounts of tax revenue and
labor.

Can we select some compromise tax rate that will give us
"enough" of each dependent variable? How much is "enough?" I
have seen no persuasive answer, but models can help us to fully see
and understand the problem by sketching its interrelated parts in
realistic detail.

NOTES

1. The concept of nonlabor income predates, and seems to in-
corporate, Hursh's (1980) distinction between closed and open economies (Allison and Boulter 1982). Hursh suggests that in a closed
economy—that is, one that offers no nonlabor income—demand will
generally be inelastic. Results like those in Figure 6.5 seem to contradict that generalization: Viewed as a demand curve, the rats' demand for water was inelastic in the region of the two lowest prices,
but elastic in the region of the two highest prices. Possibly true in
principle, it would be formidably difficult to close the economy against
vital commodities as tightly as Hursh's generalization would seem to
require. Even if all external water must be bought at a behavioral

price, the rat still has large bodily reserves of water stored in extra- and intracellular space.

2. For further discussion of experiments with animals in terms of the economics of labor supply, see Green and Green (1982) and Rachlin et al. (1981).

3. With respect to the seven points in Figure 6.11A, the linear regression of productivity ($\underline{L}$) on salary (\$) was $\underline{L} = 2.97 - .0000060\$$, $r^2 = .11$. Applied to the 38 individuals, $\underline{L} = 3.01 - .0000074\$$, $r^2 = .016$.

4. With respect to the seven points in Figure 6.12B, the linear regression of wage rate (\$/$\underline{L}$) on salary (\$) was \$/$\underline{L} = -526.55 + .39\$$, $r^2 = .97$. Applied to the 38 individuals, \$/$\underline{L} = -758.34 + .39\$$, $r^2 = .72$.

5. We can express Conservation Model 2 as

$$\underline{w} = [\,\underline{b} - (\underline{ji}/\underline{n})\,]/(\underline{k} + \underline{n})$$

where $\underline{w}$ signifies labor supply; $\underline{b}$, $\underline{j}$, $\underline{i}$, and $\underline{k}$ are positive constants; and $\underline{n}$ signifies the net after-tax wage rate. Note that $\underline{g} = \underline{n} + \underline{t}$, where $\underline{g}$ signifies the gross wage rate, $\underline{t}$ the tax rate. The values on which Figure 6.21 is based were calculated by setting $\underline{b} = 100$, $\underline{ji} = \underline{k} = \underline{1}$, $\underline{g} = 10$, and varying $\underline{t}$ from 0 to 9.99. If $\underline{w}$ is the supply of labor, then $\underline{wn}$ is personal income and tax collections are $\underline{wt}$. Figure 6.21 shows the normalized values of $\underline{w}$, $\underline{wn}$, and $\underline{wt}$ calculated from the model.

Chapter 7

Things to Come

The two preceding chapters dealt mainly with well-established parallels between the adaptive response to the constraints of a laboratory schedule and the behavior of the human in the world of economics. This chapter has a more programmatic character, dealing mainly with new points of correspondence that might emerge from further research and new theoretical developments.

SUPPLY, DEMAND, AND EQUILIBRIUM PRICE

In a competitive market, what determines the equilibrium price of any particular commodity? At any particular time, why does coffee sell for a market price of $X/pound instead of $Y/pound?

The conventional economic analysis predicts the equilibrium market price as the point of intersection between two curves, a downward-sloping consumer demand function and an upward-sloping supply function. The analysis appears in Figure 7.1, which reverses the economist's convention by scaling Q (total quantity) on the vertical axis and P (unit price) on the horizontal. Curve d is the consumer demand function; curve s, the supply function.

At the price shown in panel A, P_a, consumers are willing to buy more coffee than suppliers are willing to provide at such a low price: Q_d is greater than Q_s. Thus, a price as low as P_a would create a market shortage of coffee. Needy consumers willing to pay a higher price than P_a would bid for coffee at some higher price, and their bids would create an upward pressure on the market price of coffee.

At the price shown in panel B, P_b, consumers are willing to buy less coffee than suppliers are happy to provide at such a high

FIGURE 7.1

Supply–Demand Determinants of Equilibrium Price and Quantity
in a Competitive Market

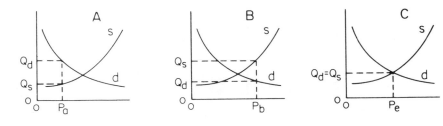

price: Q_d is less than Q_s. Thus, a price as high as $\underline{P_b}$ would create
a market surplus of coffee. The surplus would create a downward
pressure on price as suppliers attempt to clear the market of coffee.

Panel C shows the equilibrium market-clearing price. The two
curves cross at $\underline{P_e}$, where the amount consumers are willing to buy
matches the amount suppliers are willing to provide: $Q_d = Q_s$.

We can apply a similar analysis to an economy consisting of
one individual who acts as both consumer and supplier. Our application will introduce two useful analytic concepts, marginal cost and
marginal benefit.

The shipwrecked Robinson Crusoe, hungry for strawberries,
swims out to the wreck and returns with a handful of strawberry seeds.
He selects the most cultivable soil on the island and starts his first
strawberry patch. It costs him relatively little to produce the first
few berries: In that best-of-all-possible patches, the already fertile
soil requires no extra fertilizer, the plants can grow conveniently
near one another, and the nearby stream provides a handy source of
fresh water. But if Crusoe wants to expand his production, the next
few berries will eventually cost him more than the last. The next
patch will occupy soil that is perhaps less fertile, perhaps not so
close to the stream. The plants will have to be spread further apart,
requiring a longer walk between plants in the course of weeding, water-
ing, and harvesting; and the necessary water will cost more time and
effort in the longer haul from stream to patch. Thus, the marginal
cost of production—the cost of producing one more strawberry—will
eventually increase with the number of strawberries already produced.
In other words, strawberry output will follow a principle of diminishing marginal returns: A fixed amount of time, energy, and other factors of production will bring ever fewer strawberries. But how many
berries should Crusoe supply for himself?

FIGURE 7.2

Marginal Cost or Marginal Benefit as a Function of the Amount
Already Produced or Consumed in the One-Person Economy

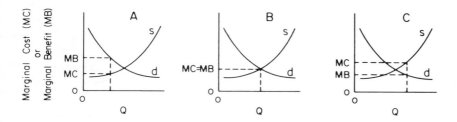

The answer depends partly on Crusoe-the-consumer's taste
for strawberries. Aside from that, his consumption of strawberries
will probably follow a principle of diminishing marginal benefit, or
diminishing marginal utility, akin to a satiety effect. The first strawberry would taste very good indeed; so would the next, but maybe not
quite so good as the first; and the one-thousandth, definitely not so
good as the tenth. Thus, the marginal benefit—the benefit derived
from eating one more strawberry—will eventually decrease as the
number of strawberries already eaten rises.

Figure 7.2 assembles the elements of Crusoe's situation, his
one-person economy. The vertical axis refers to marginal cost or
benefit. The horizontal Q axis refers to total strawberries produced
or consumed. Crusoe's marginal-cost curve slopes upward, and his
marginal-benefit demand curve slopes downward. In panel A, Crusoe
faces a strawberry shortage: Because the marginal benefit is greater
than the marginal cost, he should produce and consume another strawberry. He should continue producing strawberries until he reaches
the situation shown in panel B, where the marginal cost equals the
marginal benefit. Panel C shows why he should go no further than the
amount shown in panel B: He will produce no strawberry whose marginal cost exceeds its marginal benefit; thus, he will never face a
strawberry surplus.

Optimal foraging models deal with a similar problem: How much
of its limited resources should the animal predator spend on the search
for food in its wild habitat? Some of these models (Rapport and Turner
1977) use cost-benefit concepts in analyzing the predator's production
of offspring, one index of biological fitness. In theory, high-quality
foods (like Crusoe's best soil) can be converted into offspring (Crusoe's strawberries) more efficiently than low-quality foods. Accord-

ingly, the predator gets decreasing marginal benefits as it continues its foraging, moving from the high-quality foods to the low. As it continues to forage, it also incurs ever-greater marginal opportunity costs: The more time and energy it allocates to foraging, the less it can spend on the other necessary reproductive activities—courting, mating, and building and defending the nest. Thus, in theory, the optimal forager will forage up to the point where the marginal benefit matches the marginal cost, and no further.

About 20 years ago an economist, Vernon Smith (1962), described a way to determine experimentally whether a miniature market would truly arrive at the equilibrium price predicted by economic theory, the price defined by the intersection of supply and demand curves. Its simplicity and its success eventually won its admission to a select academic collection, the arsenal of surefire classroom demonstrations.

Each member of the group is assigned to one of two roles, buyer or seller, and receives a card bearing one number. The number specifies the highest price the buyer can bid for the commodity, or the lowest price the seller can accept as a bid. By giving different numbers to different buyers, and different numbers to different sellers, the experimenter defines in advance the exact shapes of the demand and supply curves.

Each participant is instructed to try to maximize profit. The buyer's profit is the highest bid the buyer is allowed to make, minus the bid actually accepted by some seller. To make any profit, the buyer must announce a bid high enough to attract some seller, but lower than the price printed on the buyer's card. Similarly, the seller profits by announcing a selling price low enough to attract some buyer, but higher than the price printed on the seller's card.

After the participants receive their instructions, the market opens in the style of a double oral auction; the offers to buy or sell continue until the trading period comes to an end for the apparent lack of any further acceptable offers. For the sake of simplicity, each person is allowed to consummate no more than one transaction during any one trading period. Presumably more attuned to the harsh realities of the market, the participants then move on to the next trading period and repeat the auction procedure with the same cards they held before. Thus, each trading period results in a variable number of transactions, Q, and a variable, P, that consists of the mean price of the Q transactions.

Figure 7.3 shows a typical set of results from an experiment that conducted five training periods in succession (Smith 1978). The predicted equilibrium price was a bit more than $2, and the predicted equilibrium quantity was eight units. The actual Ps and Qs fell a little off the mark in the first two trading periods, came much closer in

FIGURE 7.3

Number of Transactions and the Mean Price of the Transaction:
Five Successive Trading Periods in a Miniature Experimental
Market

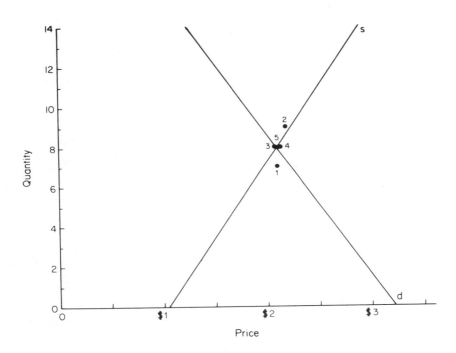

the third and fourth, and practically coincided with the predicted
equilibria in the fifth and final period. The actual profits of the group
came close to 100 percent of the total possible profits.

If we intend to measure the market equilibria established
through the cooperative interactions of buyers and sellers, we had
best use organisms more skillful than rats at the business of symbolic
communication. But we can think of other experimental procedures,
well suited to the capacities of the common laboratory animals, that
would allow us to test the theoretical predictions about equilibrium
price and quantity.

Imagine a test cage equipped with three levers lined up in a row
along one wall, each lever wired to its own food dispenser. The first
phase of the experiment measures the individual rat's demand curve.
We start each session in the demand phase of the experiment by pre-

senting one of the three levers by itself, holding the other two in re-
serve for subsequent sessions. In the demand phase, we load the
dispenser with more food pellets than the rat could possibly eat.
Throughout the entire session, the rat can get food at a particular
behavioral price, presses/pellet, established by the terms of the
fixed-ratio schedule for that particular lever. When the rat settles
on some stable amount of food consumption, Q_d pellets, for several
sessions in a row, we switch to a new lever and measure the stable
Q_d at the new behavioral price, $\underline{P}$. When we finish with the demand
phase, we will have measured Q_d at each of three different $\underline{P}$s, and
we can then specify the rat's demand curve by plotting Q_d against $\underline{P}$.
Notice that the demand phase gave the rat ample opportunity to learn
which lever offered which price.

Next we specify the a priori supply curve. We do that by load-
ing each dispenser with fewer pellets than the rat could possibly eat
and by varying the load—Q_s—from one dispenser to the next. Specifically, we increase Q_s as we move from a low-price lever to a high-
price lever. By plotting Q_s against $\underline{P}$, we specify our a priori supply
curve. At this point in the experiment we would probably want to conduct some pretraining sessions to teach the rat the supply-curve relation between $\underline{P}$ and Q_s.

Now comes our experimental measurement of the equilibrium
$\underline{P}$ and $\underline{Q}$. In the equilibrium phase, we start each session by presenting two levers at once. As soon as the rat presses either one, we
retract the other lever and thereby commit the rat to the chosen price
for the remainder of the session. We continue the equilibrium phase
until the rat settles on some stable equilibrium price, the lever of
consistent choice, and some stable equilibrium $\underline{Q}$.

Figure 7.4 illustrates several predicted equilibria. The filled
circles represent the hypothetical demand curve that we measured
beforehand. The unfilled circles represent various a priori supply
curves. The three supply curves in the left panel were chosen deliberately so as to predict an interesting pattern of choices. Test comparison 1 offers the rat a choice between the two lowest prices, $\underline{P}_a$
and $\underline{P}_b$. Because the supply and demand curves cross at the lower
of the two prices, $\underline{P}_a$, the rat should choose the lever that offers the
lower price. But the theory predicts precisely the opposite choice
in test comparison 2. There, the supply and demand curves cross at
the higher price, $\underline{P}_b$; thus, by shifting the supply curve downward, we
should induce the rat to reverse its earlier preference, choosing the
lever that offers the higher price, $\underline{P}_b$ rather than $\underline{P}_a$.

Test comparisons 3 and 4 reveal a similar reversal in the predicted choice, for the same reason. Thus, the theory implies that
the rat's choice of an equilibrium price will depend on the relation
between Q_d and $\underline{Q}_s$: In test comparisons 1 and 3, the rat will choose

FIGURE 7.4

Number of Food Pellets Consumed as a Function of Behavioral
Price (Pellets/Lever Press): Hypothetical Measurement of
Equilibrium Price and Quantity in the Individual Rat

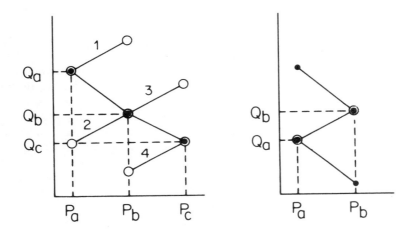

the low-price lever because Q_s happens to match Q_d at the low-price
lever; in test comparisons 2 and 4, the rat will choose the high-price
lever because Q_s happens to match Q_d at the high-price lever. In
test comparisons 1 and 3, the extra food available at the higher price
is not worth the higher price; in test comparisons 2 and 4, the extra
food is worth the higher price.

In the left panel, the predicted reversals arise from our direct
experimental manipulation of the a priori supply curve. The right
panel shows how a shift in the demand curve should lead to similar
reversals. We might try to shift the demand curve downward by pro-
viding the rat with a competitive source of food, perhaps several free
food pellets in a fourth receptacle—roughly analogous to an attractive
new restaurant across the street that draws some patrons away from
the college cafeteria. With no free food available, the rat should
choose the higher price, P_b; if the free food shifts the demand curve
downward, the rat should choose the lower price, P_a.

I leave to the reader's ingenuity the problem of devising a feasible experiment, parallel to Vernon Smith's, in which each member of
a group of rats acts as either a buyer or seller of food under the constraints of demand and supply curves specified beforehand.

DEFERRED CONSUMPTION

Self-control often comes down to the selection of one alternative over another, such as a large reward later over a small reward now. The dieting fashion model with a box of candy at hand may face two such alternatives. Eating the candy right now would provide a small early reward in comparison with the alternative: If she does not eat the candy, the weight loss on which her livelihood depends may not show up until many hours or many days later, if it shows up at all. The cigarette smoker gets a small early reward by smoking the cigarette at hand; the better health, the larger reward that comes from not smoking, comes much later if it comes at all. The student can go to the movies right now or get, much later, the better grade that might come from more study and fewer movies. We sometimes characterize the selection of the small, immediate reward as impulsive behavior and the selection of the larger delayed reward as an instance of self-control.

Humans may achieve this kind of self-control by doing something now that commits them more or less irrevocably to the larger delayed reward. The compulsive candy eater or the chain smoker may put the candy or the cigarettes into a box equipped with a time lock. The worker may put some cash into the equivalent of a safe equipped with a time lock, a certificate of savings that carries a heavy financial penalty for early withdrawal.

Pigeons may handle their prospective temptations in essentially the same way (Ainslie 1974). Faced with a plastic key on the wall, illuminated from behind by a green light bulb, the pigeon may or may not peck at the key. The schedule is programmed in such a way that if it chooses not to peck in green, the bird gets into a choice between a small immediate reward and a larger delayed reward. The unpecked green key goes briefly dark, then red for three seconds. If it pecks in red, it gets a 2-second access to grain right away. But if it waits out the 3 seconds of red without pecking, it then gets a larger but later reward, a 4-second access to grain. Confronted with that red-key choice, the pigeon typically selects the small, immediate reward more than 95 percent of the time.

But let us return to the green key and examine the scheduled consequence of pecking in green. If the pigeon chooses to peck in green, it thereby commits itself to a large delayed reward: The key goes dark and the reward comes 15 seconds later, a 4-second access to grain. Some pigeons develop the commitment behavior, consistently pecking the key in green. By pecking in green, they commit themselves to a large delayed reward and foreclose any interim red-key chance to go for a small, immediate reward. (Color controls show that their behavior does not reflect a simple preference for pecking a green key.)

Similar experiments have shown that pigeons and humans are likely to commit themselves to the large delayed reward when there is no immediate prospect of either reward. But if the two alternatives are not such distant prospects, pigeons and humans alike show an overwhelming tendency to choose the small immediate reward over the larger delayed reward (Rachlin and Green 1972; Solnick et al. 1980).

Economists who worry about inflation also worry about ways of inducing consumers to defer their consumption, to save their money for later instead of spending it now. One plausible remedy would attempt to encourage consumers to defer their consumption by raising the interest rate for savings. If the interest rate exceeds the rate of inflation, consumers may choose to save now and buy later. But the economic evidence suggests a more complex situation: At higher interest rates some persons save more, some save less, and some save the same amount as they do at lower rates (Samuelson 1976).

Laboratory experimentation might well reveal similar complexities in the rat's response to variations in interest rate. If we use an optional magnitude of reward, the rat will readily increase the rate at which it consumes the food or water in front of it, as the experimenter increases the behavioral price of access to food or water. But consider a situation in which the receipt of more food or water later on depends on the rat's voluntary refusal to eat the food, or drink the water, it has just now earned. Could the rat manage that kind of self-control, deferring consumption now in return for more at some future time? If it could manage it at all, would the tendency to defer increase systematically with the interest rate? With the amount of food or water already packed away?

With the help of a laboratory microcomputer, it would not be difficult to execute such an experiment or interpret its results. We start each session by presenting a lever; upon the rat's Ith press of the lever, we retract the lever; at the same time, we present the drinking tube for C contingent licks, the rat's bank deposit, and start a clock that runs each moment the rat fails to lick at the tube. Each lick reduces by one the current value of C, the size of the rat's bank account. But for each no-lick second accumulated on the clock, the computer multiplies the current value of C by an interest rate factor, r, and adds the result to the current value of C. If the rat exhausts its bank account, we retract the tube and present the lever again.

Thus, the rat becomes eligible for interest payment by deferring its consumption; the interest compounds at a rate of r for each second of eligibility, the compounding period. If we set r equal to zero, we have a thoroughly conventional fixed-ratio schedule and an unambiguous standard of comparison. All we need do is record the number of interest payments the rat would have received had r been greater than zero and compare that number with the number received when r is greater than zero. If interest works the way it is supposed to work with humans, the number of interest payments should rise with r, ceteris paribus.

Notice that if r is greater than zero, the rat could perform the minimum number of lever presses and get more water than it could possibly drink, merely by deferring consumption from time to time. But I doubt that the rat would achieve that optimal level of performance. Upon its very first access to water, the thirsty rat will probably not defer consumption to any significant degree; consequently, the thirsty rat will probably waste its chance to perform optimally. Optimal performance is probably reserved to those who have already achieved a comfortable level of consumption; others must defer too heroically.

But we should also prepare to discover that the achievement of optimal performance depends on other related variables that we can manipulate at will, such as I, C, r, and the compounding period. Optimal performance should be more accessible under one combination than another, but the best combination is open to speculation. For example, the instrumental requirement I stands firmly between the thirsty rat and its water. As I increases, so may the rat's impatience to drink as soon as it has the chance to drink. However, the behavioral price of water also increases with I; and, as the behavioral price of water rises, the rat may grow more sensible of the advantage of deferring consumption and putting its bank deposit to work instead.

Similarly, if C is relatively small, the behavioral price of water is relatively high. Conversely, if C is sufficiently large, the rat may become sufficiently satiated to pause from time to time before it has exhausted its current account, and may thereby gain more interest than it would if C were smaller.

The probable effects of the other two variables are not so debatable: Optimal performance should be most accessible when the rate of interest, r, is relatively large and the compounding period short.

How could we simulate various rates of inflation? By reducing the current value of C by an inflation rate factor applied periodically. As the inflation rate rises, the rat should grow less inclined to defer consumption. In the limiting case, the rat that has just earned C licks at the tube will lose them all if it defers even the first of the licks it has earned.

Several related experiments on the deferment of consumption have already been reported by psychologists concerned with laboratory simulations of foraging (Abarca and Fantino 1982; Collier and Rovee-Collier 1980; Lea 1979, 1981). The typical schedule starts with a "search" component in which the animal performs some instrumental response, such as pressing a lever or pecking a key. As a contingent consequence of each completed search, the animal comes upon one or the other of two different patches of food, but has no way of knowing in advance which patch it will find at the end of any particular search. In the dense patch, the schedule makes food relatively abundant by means of one scheduling device or another. For example, in a fixed-ratio patch the schedule would charge a relatively low behavioral price for the food; in an interval patch the schedule would deliver response-contingent food relatively soon. In the thin patch, response-contingent food would come later or at a higher behavioral price. But when the animal finally arrives at the patch, whether the patch be dense or thin, the animal must make a choice: It can accept that patch, exhaust the food there, then resume its search for the next patch; or, it can reject that patch and quickly resume its search, without bothering to feed from the patch already at hand. Experiments with rats and pigeons have shown that the animal's decision at the choice point depends on the cost of the search. Specifically, if the search costs the animal a relatively large amount of time or effort, the animal is more likely to accept the thin patch instead of resuming the risky search for the dense patch. Indeed, if the search cost is sufficiently high, the animal accepts any patch that comes its way. Thus, as the search cost rises, the animal grows more inclined to settle for second best.

EXPECTATIONS GREAT AND SMALL

Economists have called attention to various psychological factors that may influence consumption independently of the current price of the commodity (for example, Scott and Nigro 1982). For example, all else equal, if consumers expect prices to rise in the future, they may buy more at present than they would otherwise; if they expect prices to fall, they may buy less at present than they would otherwise.

Expectational factors might also influence the behavior of a laboratory animal tested with an ascending series of prices. By raising the behavioral price of food from one session to the next, we might eventually induce an expectation of rising price that would influence current food consumption, Q, independently of the current value of $\underline{P}$. The experiment should include different groups of controls tested with the same set of $\underline{P}$s as the experimental group, but only one value of $\underline{P}$ for each separate control group. A second experimental condition would cut the price of food from one session to the next. If expectations influence Q independently of $\underline{P}$, then the plot of Q against $\underline{P}$ should reveal significant differences between the two experimental groups and the controls.

I know of no definitive test of the role of expectations in the animal's consumption of laboratory rewards. But some experiments, designed with other purposes in mind, have tested the individual rat with two separate series of water prices, an ascending series followed by a descending series of the same prices, with no apparent difference between the two series (for example, Allison and Boulter 1982). The field is open for a more intensive study with the proper controls included, controls that experience only one value of $\underline{P}$.

Labor supply theory gives a slightly different perspective on similar variations over the course of an individual work session. Usually we would hold the wage rate, pellets/press, constant over the course of the session. That is why we can normally represent the wage rate as a line with a constant slope. Alternatively, we could link the current wage rate to the total amount of labor already supplied, raising or lowering the wage rate as we move along the labor-supply axis.

Figure 7.5 presents an analysis of the situation in terms of labor supply theory. Each of the two splines in panel A represents the worker's income possibilities. The upper spline shows the case in which the wage rate drops as the supply of labor rises, and the lower lower spline shows the case in which the wage rate rises with the amount of labor already supplied. The equilibrium points predict more labor and less income on the lower spline than the on the upper spline.

The broken lines in panel B represent the conventional arrangement, constant wage-rate lines that pass through the original points of equilibrium and thereby allow the worker to get the same bundles of leisure and income the worker chose under the variable wage-rate system. The theory predicts that the conventional system will produce

FIGURE 7.5

Indifference Analysis of the Labor-Supply Response to Supply-Dependent Changes in the Wage Rate

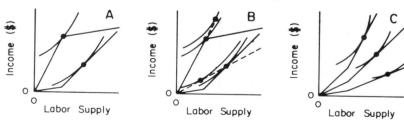

less labor than the rising wage-rate system, but more labor than the falling wage-rate system.

I know of no experimental tests of those predictions. But the theory has been used to explain how management can get rid of the backward bend in the labor supply curve. The firm offers labor a "package deal," an all-or-none arrangement that works as follows: The worker will get the lower of two wage rates until the worker has supplied some minimum amount of labor; subsequent work is paid at the higher wage rate. In response to the promise of a higher wage rate after a certain amount of labor, the worker should supply more labor than the amount supplied under the constant wage-rate system. The constant system allows the worker to reach a higher indifference curve than the variable system. The two lower wage-rate functions in panel B show the expected effect of this package deal. Panel C shows how the package deal should remove the backward bend from the the labor supply curve.

Let us review the theoretical predictions concerning the package deal that is supposed to remove the backward bend in the labor supply curve. Look again at the two lower functions in panel B. We have two wage-rate functions, one straight, the other splined. The two functions cross at a point that represents a particular bundle of money and leisure, but the spline function steepens abruptly before the crossing point. Labor supply theory predicts that the worker will respond to the sharp rise in the wage rate by supplying more labor. The one who works under the constant wage-rate system will stop short of the crossing point, because the crossing point lies on a lower indifference curve—a curve that happens to be the highest one available to the worker who gets the package deal.

A diabolical invention—the package deal! However, I am not so sure that rats working for food would respond to the package deal as the theory claims they should. An alternative theory predicts exactly the opposite result, more labor under the constant wage-rate system.

Figure 7.6 shows a hypothetical experiment pertinent to both theories. The unfilled diamond near the upper left corner shows a paired basepoint, total lever presses and total food pellets consumed under the paired baseline condition. The three unbroken splines represent three different package deals. Each one enforces a relatively low wage rate, food pellets/press, until the rat has supplied a total of 100 lever presses. At the 100-press mark, each of the three wage rates doubles; it remains doubled throughout the rest of the session. Each spline passes through a filled circle, an equilibrium point predicted from an appropriate version of Conservation Model 2. Notice that the model predicts a standard labor supply curve, fully equipped with a backward bend, under the package deal system.

The three broken lines represent three conventional fixed-ratio schedules, the constant wage-rate system; each would allow the rat to

FIGURE 7.6

Conservation Analysis of a Hypothetical Experiment in Which the
Wage Rate (Pellets/Lever Press) Remains Constant or Doubles
after the First Hundred Lever Presses

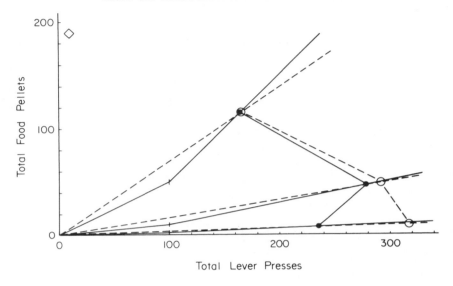

get the bundle chosen under the package deal system. Each broken
line passes through an unfilled circle, an equilibrium point predicted
from Conservation Model 2. In this particular example the model
predicts a bend, but not a backward bend, in the labor supply curve
under the constant wage-rate system.

Most important, compare the unfilled circles and the filled. In
direct opposition to labor supply theory, Conservation Model 2 predicts that the constant wage-rate system will yield more labor than
the package deal system. Moreover, the difference should increase
as the wage rate decreases. [1]

BEHAVIORAL SUBSTITUTES AND COMPLEMENTS

If the rat can get root beer by pressing one lever, and Tom Collins mix by pressing another, the rat consumes less of either drink
as its behavioral price rises, in accordance with the demand law. At
the same time, the rat consumes more of the other drink. This pat-

tern of results would lead an economist to classify the two drinks as mutual substitutes, like coffee and tea in the human economy. The pattern reflects the kind of process that economists have in mind when they derive the demand law from the notion that the organism maximizes utility: All else equal, when the price of good A rises we may maximize utility by buying less of A and more of B, a substitute for A. Similar examples come from experiments that allow the rat to get food by pressing either of two levers; there, the rat consumes more food at the source that offers the lower behavioral price.[2]

Biologists use similar concepts as a means of understanding the manner in which the animal forages for its food in the wild. In the ecological analysis of predator strategy, the foraging animal selects a particular combination of two different kinds of prey, A and B (for example, the coyote feeds on rabbit and lamb). Optimal foraging— the best selection—depends partly upon relative prey abundance, an analogue of relative price. It also depends on the time and energy available for foraging, analogous to the consumer's budgetary constraint. It depends, too, on the substitutability of A and B as contributors to the predator's biological fitness, an analogue of the consumer's utility.

Figure 7.7A illustrates the application of the familiar economic analysis to the situation facing the foraging predator (Rapport and Turner 1977). The continuous line separates all possible combinations of the two kinds of prey into two categories: The predator has time and energy enough to get any combination on or below the line, but not enough to get any combination above the line. The slope of the line depends on the relative abundance of the two kinds of prey. The broken curve is analogous to an indifference curve; because a higher curve represents more biological fitness than a lower curve, the optimal forager will select the prey combination that sits on the highest curve attainable. In panel A the predator selects a tangency solution—some of prey A, and some of prey B—because the curve is convex to the origin, a property that identifies A and B as imperfect substitutes. If the coyote has plenty of rabbits, it will trade many rabbits for just one taste of lamb; but if it has only a few rabbits, it will part with very few in return for one taste of lamb.

Panel B shows what might happen if prey A grew more abundant: Another tangency solution, but the predator's new selection contains more of prey A and less of B than the old.

The broken lines in panel C represent a different case, prey A and prey B as perfect substitutes. Now the optimal selection is a corner solution: If A grows a little more abundant, the predator's selection may shift dramatically, from a pure-B diet to a pure-A diet.

Panel D shows A and B as perfect complements. When A grows more abundant, the optimal forager eats more of both A and B.

FIGURE 7.7

Indifference Analysis of Optimal Foraging for Two Different Kinds
of Prey: Imperfect Substitutes (A and B), Perfect Substitutes (C),
and Perfect Complements (D)

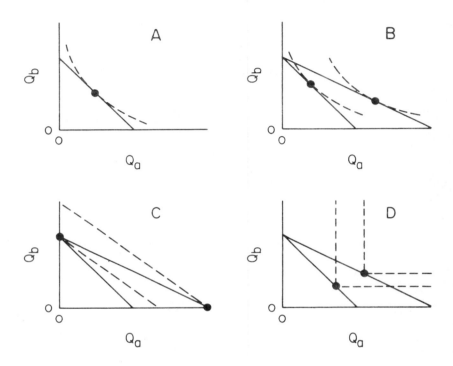

Although economists have taken the rational human as their
proper object of study, one needs no brain—indeed, no nervous system
of any description—to conform to the principles of economics. Stentor
coeruleus, a minute one-celled creature that abounds in stagnant
water, feeds on both algal and nonalgal prey. Experiments have shown
that if one acceptable type of prey becomes more abundant than another,
Stentor shifts its consumption toward the more abundant type, as if the
two were mutual substitutes. In terms of reproduction, Stentor may
thrive well enough on a diet composed purely of one prey type or the
other. But if we let Stentor choose some combination of the two, it
chooses a mixture that allows it to thrive even better than it does on
a pure diet of either, as if the two prey types were complementary
goods. Only by consuming more of each type does Stentor achieve a
higher degree of biological fitness (Rapport and Turner 1977).

BASELINE AND SCHEDULE FRONTIERS

As mutual substitutes in the economic sense, either of two behaviors will tend to rise as the other one falls. As mutual complements, the two behaviors will tend to rise or fall together. We saw
in Chapter 5 that eating and drinking may function as substitutes when
the rat has plenty of water but not enough food: As the rat ate less,
it also drank more. They function more as complements when the
rat has plenty of food but not enough water: As the rat drank less, it
also ate less. If neither behavior varies with the other we would assign them to a third category, mutual independents.

How might we measure experimentally the intrinsic relations
between any two behaviors—substitutability, complementarity, or independence? The simplest approach I can imagine would use a baseline condition in which we allow one behavior to vary freely, but manipulate the other behavior systematically.

As a specific example, consider a pair of rat behaviors: licking
a water tube and licking a saccharin tube. Each baseline session
starts with the presentation of both tubes. The water tube stays freely
available throughout each session. But we withdraw the saccharin tube
for good as soon as the rat's saccharin-lick total reaches some number prescribed in advance, and we vary that number from one session
to the next. A second series of baseline sessions reverses the procedure: free access to saccharin, but controlled access to water. If
the water total falls (rises, remains constant) as the saccharin total
rises, we classify the two behaviors as substitutes (complements,
independents).

This experimental procedure will generate a baseline function
that may lack some of the properties of an indifference curve, but
will tell us what we want to know: the marginal rate at which the individual substitutes a "free" behavior for the one that we vary systematically. If the baseline function turns out to have all of the properties of an indifference curve, so much the better. If it is truly an indifference curve, it will also be the highest curve in the baseline set,
marking all along its frontier the greatest amount of utility the individual can achieve under the baseline conditions.

Figure 7.8 illustrates three hypothetical outcomes of our experimental baseline measurements, plotting total water licks against total
saccharin licks. Panel A illustrates the two behaviors as perfect
substitutes. The measured baseline function has a slope of -2. Thus,
the marginal rate of substitution (MRS) has a constant value, +2:
Throughout the entire function, an extra saccharin lick is worth two
water licks and vice versa.

Sheer logic cannot tell us whether the measured baseline function in panel A is or is not an indifference curve. The question is

FIGURE 7.8

Three Hypothetical Baseline Frontiers: Water Licks and Saccharin
Licks as Perfect Substitutes (A), Perfect Complements (B), and
Independents (C)

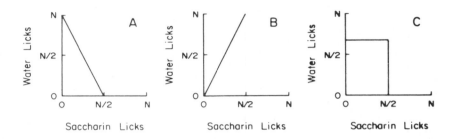

purely empirical, one that can be answered only by further experimentation. For example, imagine a follow-up experiment in which we present the rat on each of several trials with a choice between two particular points on the measured baseline function. Two such points would be $\underline{N}$ water and zero saccharin licks (point 1) versus zero water and $\underline{N}/2$ saccharin licks (point 2). If the rat chooses point 1 on half of the trials and point 2 on the other half, we would conclude that the rat seems to be indifferent as between these two points—an essential empirical feature of an indifference curve. But should the rat generally choose one point in preference to the other, we would conclude that these two points do not lie on the same indifference curve.

The same cautionary note would apply to panel B, which illustrates the two behaviors as perfect complements. The baseline function has a slope of +2 throughout, which means a constant MRS of -2: An extra saccharin lick induces a need for two extra water licks, a two-lick water deficit.

Panel C illustrates the two behaviors as independents. When we vary the number of saccharin licks on the horizontal axis, the rat shows no variation in its licks at the ever-present water tube; the measured baseline function is perfectly horizontal. As we vary the number of water licks on the vertical axis, the rat shows no variation in its licks at the ever-present saccharin tube; the measured baseline function is perfectly vertical.

We have already examined some psychological models of the response to the constraints of a contingency schedule—models based on reinforcement, probability-differential, response deprivation, minimum-deviation, and conservation theory. Our new baseline procedure has laid the groundwork for a new theoretical approach.

FIGURE 7.9

Hypothetical Response to the Constraints of Five Different
Contingency Schedules: Baseline and Schedule Frontiers Reveal
Water Licks and Saccharin Licks as Perfect Substitutes (A) or
Imperfect Substitutes (B)

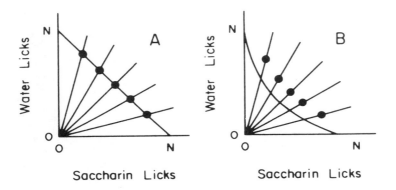

Figure 7.9 illustrates the new approach by combining various
hypothetical baseline functions, all measured beforehand, with upward
sloping lines that represent the constraints imposed by five different
reciprocal fixed-ratio schedules. Unlike the situations we dealt with
before, each schedule has its very own tailor-made basepoint, the
point where the schedule's line of constraint crosses the baseline
function.

In panel A, each schedule requires some instrumental saccharin
licks for each contingent opportunity to lick water. The baseline function in panel A portrays water licks and saccharin licks as perfect substitutes, with MRS = +1: If the rat makes one more lick at either solution, it makes one less lick at the other solution. The five filled circles represent the rat's hypothetical response to the behavioral constraints imposed by the five schedules. Notice how the intrinsic relation between the two behaviors, measured beforehand, constitutes a
complete explanation of the rat's response to the five schedules: All
five points fall on the baseline frontier. Relative to its tailor-made
basepoint, none of the schedules has facilitated or suppressed the two
behaviors. The rat's experience with the schedules has had absolutely
no effect upon the substitutability of one behavior for the other. In the
contingency phase, as in the baseline phase, the MRS = +1.

Panel B portrays water licks and saccharin licks as imperfect
substitutes: The MRS is always positive, but diminishes steadily as

FIGURE 7.10

Hypothetical Baseline and Schedule Frontiers for Water Licks
and Dry Licks

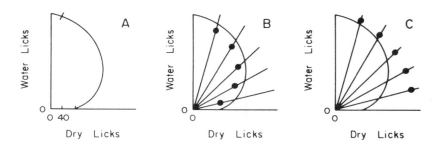

we move down the convex baseline function. Notice that each schedule
facilitated the two behaviors, relative to its basepoint. But the schedules collectively had absolutely no effect on substitutability: The five
filled circles lie above the baseline frontier, but follow a convex
schedule frontier with the same curvature as the convex baseline
frontier.

Figure 7.10 refers to a different behavioral pair, water licks
and licks at an empty metal tube (dry licks). Panel A portrays a
slightly more complicated baseline function, concave when viewed
from the origin. Substitutes in the top part of the baseline curve, the
two behaviors next become independents, and finally complements in
the lower part of the curve.

Its backward bend would surely lead us to question this baseline
curve's status as an indifference curve. Is it plausible to suppose
that the rat would show no preference between 100 dry licks plus
10 water licks (point 1) and 100 dry licks plus 300 water licks (point
2)? Plausible or not, the question remains an empirical one, to be
answered by a further experiment whose results might or might not
reveal the concave baseline function as an indifference curve.

To understand how the baseline measurements might generate
a concave curve, imagine the steps we would take in measuring the
intrinsic baseline relations. The full description of the procedure
should make it apparent that our measured baseline curve is practically guaranteed to pass through the basepoints crucial to earlier
theories: the paired basepoint and the single basepoint of each behavior.

Suppose we decide to deal first with the horizontal dry-lick axis,
sweeping the axis from left to right. Because the first value on the

horizontal axis prescribes zero licks at the empty tube, we start the first session by presenting the water tube alone, leaving it there throughout the session—the single baseline condition. We find that the thirsty rat performs a large number of water licks during this first session—the single basepoint for water licking.

Suppose the next value on the horizontal axis prescribes five dry licks. Accordingly, we start the next session by presenting both tubes together; water stays there throughout, but we retract the empty tube when and if the rat completes the prescribed five-lick total. We find in this second session that the rat does perform the five dry licks, but not quite so many water licks as it did in the first session.

We manage to continue our rightward sweep until we hit a prescribed total of 45 dry licks; the rat was willing to complete as many as 40 such licks with water freely available—the paired baseline condition—but not as many as 45. We have now measured the top part of the curve, the small part that lies above the hash mark on the curve, and the hash mark identifies the paired basepoint.

To measure the rest of the curve we switch to the water-controlled, empty-free condition and sweep the vertical axis. We start our first session in the new series by presenting the empty tube alone, leaving it there throughout. This first session in the new series tells us that if the rat has no chance to lick water, it performs more dry licks than it does with water available. Thus, the single basepoint for dry licks is greater than the paired basepoint. As we continue our upward sweep of the vertical axis the two lick totals rise together, up to a point. Beyond that point, the dry total falls as the water total continues its rise. At the hash mark we hit the largest number of controlled water licks the rat is willing to make with the empty tube freely available—the paired basepoint again—and complete our baseline measurements at that point.

Panel B represents one hypothetical response to the constraints of the five schedules. Each schedule suppressed the two behaviors, relative to the tailor-made basepoint, but the schedules again had absolutely no effect upon the relations measured beforehand. Thus, the backward bend in the labor supply curve shown in panel B reflects the intrinsic relations between the two measured behaviors, and nothing more than that.

Panel C represents another possible result. At last we see some schedule effects that transcend all of the intrinsic baseline relations between the two behaviors. The five points that represent the rat's performance under the schedules do not follow the same curvature as the concave baseline curve. Where the two behaviors acted before as substitutes, they still act as substitutes; but where they acted before as independents or complements, they act now as substitutes instead. Somehow, the rat's experience with the schedules has caused an extrinsic change in the intrinsic baseline relations measured beforehand.

This new approach implies that we cannot understand the organism's response to the schedule constraints without some knowledge of intrinsic baseline relations—the two behaviors' roles as substitutes, complements, or independents. Effects that we would normally interpret in terms of reinforcement, response deprivation, a paired basepoint ideal, or conservation may really reflect no more than the intrinsic baseline relations. Experience with the schedules may alter those relations for one reason or another, but we cannot tell whether it does without measuring them beforehand in a more comprehensive manner than we have ever done before. Timberlake (1979b, p. 287) has suggested that performance under the constraints of a contingency schedule may represent some composite effect of learned (extrinsic) and unlearned (intrinsic) substitution. The present approach extends that possibility to two additional relations, complementarity and independence, and provides a way of measuring all three.

The proposed approach requires no commitment to one theory rather than another; it can provide a great variety of theorists with a firm benchmark for their favorite interpretations of schedule effects. For example, a utility theorist might feel that the measured baseline function is closely akin to an indifference curve, marking all along its frontier the greatest amount of utility the rat can achieve under the baseline conditions. Suppose further that the schedules prove to suppress the two behaviors relative to the tailor-made basepoints (for example, Figure 7.10B). What would such a result tell us? It would simply say that the rat derived more utility from the way it behaved under the baseline condition than it did from the behavioral pattern enforced by the contingency schedule. If the schedule requires more frequent switching from one behavior to the other than the rat would do in baseline, maybe the rat finds some disutility in switching so frequently. Accordingly, it follows a contingency curve lower than the baseline curve.

Behavioral interventionists may find more attractive the theoretical interpretation of facilitation effects (for example, Figures 7.9B and 7.10C). Facilitation effects tell us that the rat discovered more utility in the behavioral pattern enforced by the schedule than it derived from its unfettered baseline pattern.

All bets are off if the necessary trip is unusually long; otherwise, maybe rat or pigeon does indeed discover some unforeseen utility in moving more often than normal from tube to tube, lever to lever, key to key, lever to tube, or lever to food bin. How else can we explain the provocative departures from optimal performance that we see so often under the concurrent fixed-ratio schedule and the schedule with an optional magnitude of reward?

The baseline frontier would have other implications for a conservation theorist. A linear frontier like the one in Figure 7.9A would signify that the organism allocates a constant amount of some dimension, such as energy expenditure, to the two behaviors all along the baseline frontier. A baseline curve like the one in Figure 7.10 would mean that the dimensional total does not remain constant, but changes as we move along the frontier. If a particular contingency schedule fails to facilitate or suppress the two behaviors relative to its tailor-made basepoint, we conclude that the schedule constraints induced no change in the amount of the dimension the organism chose to allocate to the two behaviors. Should a schedule prove to facilitate (suppress) the two behaviors, we conclude that the schedule induced the organism to allocate more (less) of the dimension to the two behaviors than it did in the baseline condition.

Minimum deviationists might also get some help from the baseline frontier. Although minimum deviation theory has focused on the paired basepoint as the behavioral ideal toward which the organism strives under the constraints of the schedule, the paired basepoint is only one among many basepoints on the entire frontier. Thus, an animal that seems to stray further than it should from the paired basepoint may actually hit some other measured basepoint exactly on target.

Figure 7.11 illustrates this possibility in the context of a concurrent fixed-ratio schedule. The unfilled circle on the concave baseline frontier represents the paired basepoint. The animal can come as

FIGURE 7.11

Response to the Constraints of a Concurrent Fixed-Ratio
Schedule as a Minimum Deviation from a Baseline Frontier

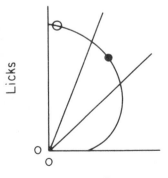

Lever Presses

close as possible to the paired basepoint by responding exclusively on the schedule represented by the steeper line of schedule constraint. But animals often stray from that strategy; that is, they sample both schedules during the course of the session, as indicated by the filled circle. But notice that the filled circle does sit squarely on the measured baseline frontier. Thus, the animal that strays from the paired basepoint may simply be governed by some other basepoint ideal.

The baseline frontier might also explain why certain contingent behaviors seem incapable of facilitating certain instrumental behaviors. For example, in the hamster contingent food reward readily facilitates instrumental digging for food, but does not facilitate instrumental face washing (Shettleworth 1975). Figure 7.12A shows how

FIGURE 7.12

"Constraint on Learning" Explained in Terms of the Measured
Baseline Frontier: Eating Facilitates a Substitute (Digging, A),
but Does Not Facilitate an Independent (Face Washing, B)

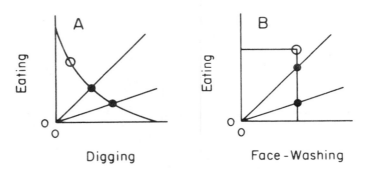

contingent eating might facilitate instrumental digging relative to the paired basepoint if eating and digging are substitutes. But if eating and face washing are independents, as in Figure 7.12B, then contingent eating might not facilitate instrumental face washing. Thus, the measured baseline frontier might illuminate one of the more puzzling problems in contemporary research on animal learning, the constraints-on-learning problem. Perhaps if the two behaviors are intrinsically independent throughout the baseline frontier, no contingency schedule will facilitate either one.

NOTES

1. The conservation model for this experiment can be expressed as

$$N_1(kI_1 + C) + ji(I_1/C) + N_2(kI_2 + C) + ji(I_2/C) = kO_i + O_c$$

where the subscripts 1 and 2 signify the first and second lever-press requirements and O_i and O_c signify the paired baseline number of lever presses and food pellets. In this particular example, $N_1I_1 = 100$ lever presses altogether before the change to I_2, $I_1 = 2$, 10, or 50 lever presses and $I_2 = I_1/2$. The response-contingent reward is $C = 1$ food pellet. The constants are set at $k = .5$, $ji = 1$, and $kO_i + O_c = 200$. After entering the appropriate numerical values into the model equation, the equation is solved for N_2. Then, the total number of lever presses predicted by the model is $100 + N_2I_2$, and total food pellets is $N_1 + N_2$.

2. Animal experiments on substitutability appear in Lea and Roper (1977), Rachlin et al. (1976), and Shapiro and Allison (1978).

Chapter 8

Retrospect

Although all of life is not just one big contingency session, much
of it is. In attempting to explain the behavioral effects of the pervasive
contingency schedule, several generations of psychological theorists
both defined and answered the question in terms consonant with Thorndike's law of effect: What is it about the response–contingent event
that strengthens (or weakens) the response?

The enduring popularity of the Thorndikian view is readily apparent in the accepted jargon of the contemporary behaviorist: We
used food as a reinforcer; we reinforced the pigeon (sic) with grain;
correct responses were reinforced with water (food, tokens, "right").
Many contemporary behaviorists find such language entirely acceptable, and some would hotly deny that the language itself carries any
significant theoretical connotations.

The statement of Premack's theory contained no explicit threat
to the Thorndikian view: Any (contingent) behavior will reinforce
another (instrumental) behavior if, and only if, it is more probable
than the other. These words still focus our attention on the response–
contingent event. Their revolutionary import derives from something
else, the implication that one and the same behavior may or may not
function as a reinforcer. Accordingly, its power to reinforce another
behavior cannot reside in any of its intrinsic properties. If contingent
drinking may or may not reinforce instrumental running, then the act
of drinking has no intrinsic property, no intrinsic effect, that guarantees the strengthening of the instrumental behavior.

It was a serendipitous failure that eventually exposed the fallacy
of the narrow Thorndikian focus on the response–contingent event.
If the rat can perform its normal amount of (contingent) drinking
merely by performing its normal amount of (instrumental) running,
then the high-probability drinking response does not reinforce the
low-probability running response. Thus, the probability-differential

condition is not sufficient for the manifest occurrence of a reinforcement effect. Eisenberger and his collaborators delivered the final blow, showing that the probability-differential condition is not necessary for reinforcement: Regardless of their relative probability, a behavior will reinforce another if, and only if, the contingency schedule deprives the individual of the other behavior.

Mark well the crucial change in the necessary language. Reinforcement does not proceed from any particular feature of either behavior, nor from any particular probabilistic relation between the two behaviors. It is incomplete at best, and misleading at worst, to say that drinking reinforced running. It was not the drinking that increased the running, but rather, the antecedent response deprivation condition. Instrumental running rose above its paired baseline level because of the constraint the schedule placed on drinking: In performing only the normal amount of running, the rat would have fallen short of its normal amount of drinking. To forecast the behavioral effects of the schedule, we must compare its constraints with the organism's free performance of the behaviors controlled by the schedule.

In the 1970s several psychologists, some heavily influenced by the research on response deprivation, broke away from the confines of the traditional unit of analysis: the instrumental response and its immediate consequence. A valuable legacy of the associationist approach to the psychology of learning, the traditional unit of analysis had become too restrictive.

Many of the theoretical models that emerged from that period were or can be expressed in language totally free of the terminology of reinforcement. The typical model in this new generation incorporated some reference to how the organism behaves in the absence of schedule constraints, a detailed analysis of the structural constraints imposed by various types of contingency schedule, and the supposition that the behavioral effects of the schedule represent a particular kind of adaptive response to the schedule constraints. Different models postulated different kinds of adaptive response.

Because many of these models were expressed mathematically, they offered the possibility of a significant advance in our ability to deal with the quantitative details of the behavior at hand. It was one such model, the conservation model, that led me to see the economic content of the behavior under experimental study. Others, such as the psychologists Rachlin and Green and their economist collaborators, were led to similar insights by economic theory.

In one sense, the laboratory animal working away at its lever is a consumer buying food at a behavioral price established in whole or in part by the terms of the contingency schedule. If it worked instead for tokens, later exchanging these tokens for some bundle of various goods chosen at will at various rates of exchange, its resem-

blance to economic man might become more obvious, but no more
fundamental. Once we understand how to measure the behavioral
price of the good, the rest is relatively easy. Does the rat's consumption of food conform to the demand law? To discover the answer,
vary the behavioral price of the food, measure total food consumption,
and see whether it falls as the price rises. Does the uncompensated
demand for food become more price-elastic as the price rises? Plot
the same data in log-log coordinates, and see whether the demand
curve steepens as the price rises. Does the psychological model for
such experiments predict these empirical relations? Analyze the
model mathematically; if we can solve the model equation for consumption in terms of price, we are more than halfway home. Does the
animal's consumption of two different goods reveal a relatively large
substitution effect and a relatively small income effect, like the typical consumer in the economic marketplace? Apply the Slutskian procedure: See which bundles the animal selects as we vary the behavioral price ratio and the size of the behavioral budget. Do we wonder
whether the individual human under laboratory test, like the anonymous
masses in the marketplace, conforms to the economic theory of consumer demand? Replace rat with human, replace the cage and its
levers with a computer keyboard terminal, and vary the behavioral
prices and budgets for various visual or auditory displays. If theory
survives such a test, well and good. If theory fails under such simple, antiseptic laboratory conditions, perhaps we reconsider its applicability to the more complex world of the marketplace.

In another sense, the same experimental subject is a supplier
of labor at a wage rate specified in whole or in part by the terms of
the same schedule. In place of the consumer paying a behavioral
price for one contingent good, we see instead a space composed of
two coordinate goods, leisure and income. Where we saw before a
consumer demand curve that may grow more elastic as the price
rises, we see in its place a labor supply curve that may bend back
on itself as the wage rate declines: Falling from left to right in the
region of inelastic demand, the labor supply curve reverses direction
and falls from right to left in the region of elastic demand. The labor
supply analogy readily suggests some additional pertinent variables,
such as nonlabor income, the difficulty of the work, the quantity and
quality of leisure-time alternatives to work, and income- or labor-
dependent changes in the prevailing wage rate. Economic theory can
predict the effects of some of these variables, and so can various
psychological models; where the predictions conflict, one can imagine
feasible experiments that would help to resolve the issue empirically.

Both advocate and critic would probably agree that the laboratory experiment can provide at best only a pale approximation of its
initial inspiration and its ultimate target, the world outside the labora-

tory. Nevertheless, to the extent that history permits such judgments, history substantiates the ultimate success of the laboratory sciences. It remains practically impossible to predict the exact path a particular leaf will follow as it flutters to the ground. All the same, its behavior can violate no natural law revealed in simpler cases: When the falling leaf begins to rise, we look for wires or thermals, not witches. Perhaps we face a similar difficulty in predicting the behavior of the factory worker, the grocery shopper, or the wild animal foraging for its food. But the behavior will defy none of the natural laws we might learn through meticulous study of its simpler forms.

Appendix

PRICE ELASTICITY OF DEMAND

Price elasticity of demand refers to a ratio of two ratios: the relative change in Q relative to the relative change in P. We can express this ratio more gracefully with the help of some new notation. Let ΔQ signify a change in Q, ΔP a change in P. Then the ratio $\Delta Q/Q$ denotes the relative change in Q, and the ratio $\Delta P/P$ denotes the relative change in P. Price elasticity, E, is defined as follows:

$$E = (\Delta Q/Q)/(\Delta P/P) \tag{1}$$

Thus, if consumption follows the demand law, E will be negative: As price increases (ΔP is positive), quantity consumed will fall (ΔQ will be negative).

Notice that the units of measurement cancel out of the numerator and the denominator of equation 1. Accordingly, the E defined by the equation is a pure ratio, a number that does not depend on the units we happen to use in our measurements of P and Q. It follows that the absolute value of E, denoted $|E|$, corresponds to our three qualitative categories. If the relative change in Q equals the relative change in P, then $|E| = 1$ and demand has unit price elasticity. If the relative change in Q is less than the relative change in P, then $|E| < 1$ and demand is inelastic. If the relative change in Q is greater than the relative change in P, $|E| > 1$ and demand is elastic.

We can calculate elasticity with respect to two points on an empirical demand curve by resorting to the arc elasticity coefficient, defined as

$$\text{Arc } E = \frac{(Q_1 - Q_2)/\tfrac{1}{2}(Q_1 + Q_2)}{(P_1 - P_2)/\tfrac{1}{2}(P_1 + P_2)}$$

$$= \frac{\Delta Q/(Q_1 + Q_2)}{\Delta P/(P_1 + P_2)} \tag{2}$$

where the two subscripts refer to two different values of P and the corresponding values of Q. For example, if $P_1 = 10$, $Q_1 = 10$, $P_2 = 20$, and $Q_2 = 8$, then

$$\text{Arc } \underline{E} = \frac{(2/18)}{(-10/30)} = -1/3 = -.33$$

Thus, $\underline{Q}$ fell as $\underline{P}$ increased, and demand was inelastic.

With the help of differential calculus, we can examine the general relation between price $(\underline{P})$ and price elasticity of demand $(\underline{E})$. For example, suppose we have a theory of consumer demand that says that $\underline{Q} = \underline{P}^n$. Does the theory predict the demand law? What does the theory imply about the relation between $\underline{P}$ and $\underline{E}$? In the notation of differential calculus, equation 1 is

$$\underline{E} = (d\underline{Q}/\underline{Q})/(d\underline{P}/\underline{P})$$

from which

$$\underline{E} = (d\underline{Q}/d\underline{P})(\underline{P}/\underline{Q}) \tag{3}$$

where $\underline{Q} = \underline{u}(\underline{P})$. Thus, to examine $\underline{E}$ as a function of $\underline{P}$, equation 3 tells us to differentiate $\underline{Q}$ with respect to $\underline{P}$ and multiply the result by $\underline{P}/\underline{Q}$, substituting for $\underline{Q}$ the function of $\underline{P}$ specified by the theoretical demand equation.

For example, consider the theoretical demand equation $\underline{Q} = \underline{P}^n$. Differentiating $\underline{Q}$ with respect to $\underline{P}$, we get

$$d\underline{Q}/d\underline{P} = \underline{nP}^{n-1}$$

from which

$$\underline{E} = \underline{nP}^{n-1}(\underline{P}/\underline{Q})$$

Substituting for $\underline{Q}$ the expression $\underline{P}^n$, we arrive at

$$\underline{E} = \underline{nP}^{n-1}\underline{P}/\underline{P}^n \tag{4}$$

$$= \underline{n}$$

Thus, the theory predicts that $\underline{E}$ will not depend on $\underline{P}$; instead, $\underline{E}$ will be constant and the constant will equal $\underline{n}$. If $\underline{n}$ is negative, $\underline{E}$ will be negative and consumption will therefore conform to the demand law. If $\underline{n} = -1$, $\underline{E} = -1$, and the demand function will have unit elasticity throughout the range of prices. If $\underline{n} = -.5$, demand will be inelastic throughout the range of prices and an $\underline{x}$-fold rise in $\underline{P}$ will occasion an $\underline{x}/2$-fold drop in $\underline{Q}$. If $\underline{n} = -2$, demand will be elastic throughout and an $\underline{x}$-fold rise in $\underline{P}$ will occasion a $2\underline{x}$-fold drop in $\underline{Q}$.

For our second example, we consider a consumer demand equation that predicts that elasticity will increase systematically as price increases—a common occurrence in the real world. According to our second equation, $Q = 100 - 5P$. Differentiating Q with respect to P, we get

$$dQ/dP = -5$$

from which

$$E = -5(P/Q) = 5P/(100 - 5P)$$
$$= -1/[(20/P) - 1]$$

(5)

Thus, our second demand equation predicts the demand law, because the predicted E is negative. It predicts, in addition, that demand will have unit elasticity if $P = 10$; if P is less than 10, demand will be inelastic; if P is greater than 10, demand will be elastic. (Notice that the demand equation excludes any value of P greater than 20, because a negative value of Q is meaningless; note that equation 5 excludes $P = 20$, because we cannot divide by zero.)

Similar analyses have been applied to the mathematical versions of the two conservation models discussed in Chapter 4, each of which can be interpreted as a theoretical consumer demand equation. Because both models predict a negative value for E, both predict the demand law. Both models predict, in addition, that price elasticity will increase systematically with the behavioral price of the commodity. The chief advantage of model 2 over model 1 is that it allows a relatively smooth progression through the qualitative categories as price increases—inelastic at low prices, elastic at high prices, and unit elastic at intermediate prices. Model 1 predicts a sharp transition from inelastic to elastic, with no gradations in the elastic category and no transition through the unit category. Further details can be found in Allison et al. (1979) and Allison (1981a).

Bibliography

Abarca, Nureya, and Edmund Fantino. 1982. "Choice and Foraging."
Journal of the Experimental Analysis of Behavior 38:117-23.

Ainslie, G. W. 1974. "Impulse Control in Pigeons." Journal of the
Experimental Analysis of Behavior 21:485-89.

Alexander, T. 1980. "Economics according to the Rats." Fortune,
December 1, pp. 127-32.

Allen, R. G. D. 1938. Mathematical Analysis for Economists.
New York: St. Martin's Press.

Allison, James. In press. "Behavioral Substitutes and Complements."
In Animal Cognition and Behavior, edited by Roger L. Mellgren.
New York: North Holland Press.

_____. 1982. "Constraints on Performance in Two Elementary
Paradigms." In Quantitative Analyses of Behavior, vol. 2:
Matching and Maximizing Accounts, edited by Michael L. Com-
mons, Richard J. Herrnstein, and Howard Rachlin. Cambridge,
Mass.: Ballinger.

_____. 1981a. "Economics and Operant Conditioning." In Advances
in Analysis of Behaviour, vol. 2: Predictability, Correlation,
and Contiguity, edited by Peter Harzem and Michael D. Zeiler,
pp. 321-53. Chichester: Wiley.

_____. 1981b. "Paired Baseline Performance as a Behavioral Ideal."
Journal of the Experimental Analysis of Behavior 35:355-66.

_____. 1980. "Conservation, Matching, and the Variable-Interval
Schedule." Animal Learning and Behavior 8:185-92.

_____. 1979a. "Demand Economics and Experimental Psychology."
Behavioral Science 24:403-15.

_____. 1979b. "Remarks on Staddon's Comment." Journal of Ex-
perimental Psychology: General 108:41-42.

_____. 1976. "Contrast, Induction, Facilitation, Suppression, and Conservation." Journal of the Experimental Analysis of Behavior 25:185–98.

_____. 1971. "Microbehavioral Features of Nutritive and Nonnutritive Drinking in Rats." Journal of Comparative and Physiological Psychology 76:408–17.

_____. 1964. "Strength of Preference for Food, Magnitude of Food Reward, and Performance in Instrumental Conditioning." Journal of Comparative and Physiological Psychology 57:217–23.

Allison, James, and Peter Boulter. 1982. "Wage Rate, Nonlabor Income, and Labor Supply in Rats." Learning and Motivation 13:324–42.

Allison, James, and N. John Castellan, Jr. 1970. "Temporal Characteristics of Nutritive Drinking in Rats and Humans." Journal of Comparative and Physiological Psychology 70:116–25.

Allison, James, and Roy Mack. 1982. "Polydipsia and Autoshaping: Drinking and Lever Pressing as Substitutes for Eating." Animal Learning and Behavior 10:465–75.

Allison, James, Melinda Miller, and Mark Wozny. 1979. "Conservation in Behavior." Journal of Experimental Psychology: General 108:4–34.

Allison, James, and William Timberlake. 1975. "Response Deprivation and Instrumental Performance in the Controlled-Amount Paradigm." Learning and Motivation 6:122–42.

_____. 1974. "Instrumental and Contingent Saccharin-Licking in Rats: Response Deprivation and Reinforcement." Learning and Motivation 5:231–47.

_____. 1973. "Instrumental and Contingent Saccharin-Licking in Rats: Response Deprivation and Reinforcement." Bulletin of the Psychonomic Society 2:141–43.

Arkes, Hal R., and John P. Garske. 1982. Psychological Theories of Motivation. 2d ed. Monterey, Calif.: Brooks/Cole.

Atkinson, John W. 1964. An Introduction to Motivation. Princeton, N.J.: Van Nostrand.

Awh, Robert Y. 1976. Microeconomics: Theory and Applications. Santa Barbara, Calif.: Wiley/Hamilton.

Ayllon, T., and N. H. Azrin. 1965. "The Measurement of Reinforcement of Behavior of Psychotics." Journal of the Experimental Analysis of Behavior 8:357-83.

Baer, D. B. 1962. "Laboratory Control of Thumbsucking by Withdrawal and Representation of Reinforcement." Journal of the Experimental Analysis of Behavior 5:525-28.

Bandura, Albert. 1969. Principles of Behavior Modification. New York: Holt, Rinehart and Winston.

Bandura, Albert, and B. Perloff. 1967. "Relative Efficacy of Self-Monitored and Externally Imposed Reinforcement Systems." Journal of Personality and Social Psychology 7:111-16.

Battalio, R. C., L. Green, and J. H. Kagel. 1981. "Income-Leisure Tradeoffs of Animal Workers." American Economic Review 71:621-32.

Battalio, Raymond C., John H. Kagel, and Morgan O. Reynolds. 1977. "Income Distributions in Two Experimental Economies." Journal of Political Economy 85:1259-71.

Bernstein, Daniel J. 1973. "Structure and Function in Response Repertoires of Humans." Ph.D. dissertation, University of California at San Diego.

Bernstein, Daniel J., and Ebbe B. Ebbesen. 1978. "Reinforcement and Substitution in Humans: A Multiple-Response Analysis." Journal of the Experimental Analysis of Behavior 30:243-53.

Bexton, W. H., W. Heron, and T. H. Scott. 1954. "Effects of Decreased Variation in the Sensory Environment." Canadian Journal of Psychology 8:70-76.

Bigelow, G., and I. Liebson. 1972. "Cost Factors Controlling Alcoholic Drinking." Psychological Record 22:305-14.

Blodgett, H. C. 1929. "The Effect of the Introduction of Reward upon the Maze Performance of Rats." University of California Publications in Psychology 4:113-34.

Brennan, M. J. 1960. Preface to Econometrics. Cincinnati: South-Western.

Buchwald, Alexander M. 1969. "Effects of 'Right' and 'Wrong' on Subsequent Behavior: A New Interpretation." Psychological Review 76:132-43.

Castro, B., and K. Weingarten. 1970. "Toward Experimental Economics." Journal of Political Economy 78:598-607.

Cole, Susan, F. Reed Hainsworth, Alan C. Kamil, Terre Mercier, and Larry L. Wolf. 1982. "Spatial Learning as an Adaptation in Hummingbirds." Science 217:655-57.

Collier, G. H., and C. K. Rovee-Collier. 1980. "A Comparative Analysis of Optimal Foraging Behavior: Laboratory Simulations." In Foraging Behavior: Ecological, Ethological, and Psychological Approaches, edited by Alan C. Kamil and Theodore D. Sargent. New York: Garland.

Collier, George. 1972. "Reinforcement Magnitude in Free Feeding." Paper presented at the meeting of the Psychonomic Society, St. Louis.

Collier, George H., E. Hirsch, and P. H. Hamlin. 1972. "The Ecological Determinants of Reinforcement in the Rat." Physiology and Behavior 9:705-16.

Cowles, J. T. 1937. "Food Tokens as Incentives for Learning by Chimpanzees." Comparative Psychology Monographs 14:5, whole no. 71.

Dalton, Gene, and Paul H. Thompson. "Accelerating Obsolescence of Older Engineers." Harvard Business Review 49:57-67.

Deci, Edward L. 1975. Intrinsic Motivation. New York: Plenum.

Dember, William N. 1956. "Response by the Rat to Environmental Change." Journal of Comparative and Physiological Psychology 49:93-95.

Dreyer, Paul, and K. Edward Renner. 1971. "Self-Punitive Behavior—Masochism or Confusion?" Psychological Review 78:333-37.

Dunham, Philip. 1977. "The Nature of Reinforcing Stimuli." In Handbook of Operant Behavior, edited by Werner K. Honig and J. E. R. Staddon, pp. 98-124. Englewood Cliffs, N.J.: Prentice-Hall.

Eisenberger, Robert, Michael Karpman, and James Trattner. 1967. "What Is the Necessary and Sufficient Condition for Reinforcement in the Contingency Situation?" Journal of Experimental Psychology 74:342-50.

Ellson, D. G. 1937. "The Acquisition of a Token-Reward Habit in Dogs." Journal of Comparative Psychology 24:505-22.

Epstein, A. N. 1960. "Water Intake without the Act of Drinking." Science 131:497-98.

Estes, W. K. 1969. "Reinforcement in Human Learning." In Reinforcement and Behavior, edited by Jack T. Tapp, pp. 63-94. New York: Academic Press.

Findley, Jack D. 1966. "Programmed Environments for the Experimental Analysis of Human Behavior." In Operant Behavior: Areas of Research and Application, edited by Werner K. Honig, pp. 827-48. New York: Appleton-Century-Crofts.

Goldberg, S. R. 1973. "Comparable Behavior Maintained under Fixed-Ratio and Second-Order Schedules by Food Presentation, Cocaine Injection or d-Amphetamine Injection in the Squirrel Monkey." Journal of Pharmacology and Experimental Therapeutics 186:18-30.

Goldberg, S. R., F. Hoffmeister, U. U. Schlichting, and W. Wuttke. 1971. "A Comparison of Pentobarbital and Cocaine Self-Administration in Rhesus Monkeys: Effects of Dose and Fixed-Ratio Parameter." Journal of Pharmacology and Experimental Therapeutics 179:277-83.

Green, J. K., and L. Green. 1982. "Substitution of Leisure for Income in Pigeon Workers as a Function of Body Weight." Behaviour Analysis Letters 2:103-12.

Green, L., J. H. Kagel, and R. C. Battalio. 1980. "Ratio Schedules and Their Relationship to Economic Theories of Labor Supply." Working Paper 80-15, Department of Economics, Texas A. & M. University.

Herrnstein, R. J. 1970. "On the Law of Effect." Journal of the Experimental Analysis of Behavior 13:243-66.

Herrnstein, R. J., and D. H. Loveland. 1975. "Maximizing and Matching on Concurrent Ratio Schedules." Journal of the Experimental Analysis of Behavior 24:107-16.

Heth, C. Donald, and A. G. Warren. 1978. "Response Deprivation and Response Satiation as Determinants of Instrumental Performance." Animal Learning and Behavior 6:294-300.

Hilgard, Ernest R., and Gordon H. Bower. 1975. Theories of Learning. 4th ed. Englewood Cliffs, N.J.: Prentice-Hall.

Hogan, J. A., S. Kleist, and C. S. L. Hutchings. 1970. "Display and Food as Reinforcers in the Siamese Fighting Fish (Betta Splendens)." Journal of Comparative and Physiological Psychology 70:351-57.

Holstein, S. B., and A. G. Hundt. 1965. "Reinforcement of Intracranial Self Stimulation by Licking." Psychonomic Science 3:17-18.

Hursh, Steven R. 1980. "Economic Concepts for the Analysis of Behavior." Journal of the Experimental Analysis of Behavior 34:219-38.

Hursh, Steven R., and Benjamin H. Natelson. 1981. "Electrical Brain Stimulation and Food Reinforcement Dissociated by Demand Elasticity." Physiology and Behavior 26:509-15.

Institute for Labor Education and Research. 1982. What's Wrong with the U.S. Economy? A Popular Guide for the Rest of Us. Boston: South End Press.

Johnson, K. G., and M. Cabanac. 1983. "Human Thermoregulatory Behavior during a Conflict between Cold Discomfort and Money." Physiology and Behavior 30:145-50.

Johnston, J. 1963. Econometric Methods. New York: McGraw-Hill.

Kagel, J. H., R. C. Battalio, H. Rachlin, and L. Green. 1977. "Demand Curves for Animal Consumers." Unpublished manuscript available from John H. Kagel, Department of Economics, Texas A. & M. University, College Station, Texas 77840.

Kagel, J. H., R. C. Battalio, H. Rachlin, L. Green, R. L. Basmann, and W. R. Klemm. 1975. "Experimental Studies of Consumer Demand Behavior Using Laboratory Animals." Economic Inquiry 13:22-38.

Kamil, A. C., and T. D. Sargent, eds. 1981. Foraging Behavior: Ecological, Ethological, and Psychological Approaches. New York: Garland.

Katona, G. 1975. Psychological Economics. New York: Elsevier.

_____. 1951. Psychological Analysis of Economic Behavior. New York: McGraw-Hill.

Kazdin, Alan E. 1977. The Token Economy. New York: Plenum.

Kelsey, John E., and James Allison. 1976. "Fixed-Ratio Lever Pressing by VMH Rats: Work vs. Accessibility of Sucrose Reward." Physiology and Behavior 17:749-54.

Kimble, Gregory A. 1961. Hilgard and Marquis' Conditioning and Learning. 2d ed. New York: Appleton-Century-Crofts.

Klajner, Felix. 1975. "The Relations among Instrumental Performance, Reinforcement, and Contingent-Response Deprivation in the Instrumental Conditioning Paradigm." Ph.D. dissertation, University of Toronto.

Knickerbocker, Brad. 1979. "A Capitalist Company Whose Workers Set Their Own Pay." Christian Science Monitor, March 5, p. 7.

Konarski, Edward A., Jr., Charles R. Crowell, Moses R. Johnson, and Thomas L. Whitman. 1982. "Response Deprivation, Reinforcement, and Instrumental Academic Performance in an EMR Classroom." Behavior Therapy 13:94-102.

Konarski, Edward A., Jr., Moses R. Johnson, Charles R. Crowell, and Thomas L. Whitman. 1980. "Response Deprivation and Reinforcement in Applied Settings: A Preliminary Analysis." Journal of Applied Behavior Analysis 13:595-609.

Lancaster, Kelvin. 1969. Introduction to Modern Microeconomics. Chicago: Rand-McNally.

Lea, S. E. G. 1979. "Foraging and Reinforcement Schedules in the Pigeon: Optimal and Non-Optimal Aspects of Choice." Animal Behaviour 27:875-86.

_____. 1978. "Psychology and Economics of Demand." Psychological Bulletin 85:441-66.

Lea, S. E. G., and T. J. Roper. 1977. "Demand for Food in Fixed-Ratio Schedules as a Function of the Quality of Concurrently Available Reinforcement." Journal of the Experimental Analysis of Behavior 27:371-80.

Lea, Stephen E. G. 1981. "Correlation and Contiguity in Foraging Behaviour." In Advances in Analysis of Behaviour, vol. 2: Predictability, Correlation, and Contiguity, edited by Peter Harzem and Michael D. Zeiler, pp. 355-406. Chichester: Wiley.

Logan, Frank A. 1964. "The Free Behavior Situation." In Nebraska Symposium on Motivation, edited by David Levine, pp. 99-128. Lincoln: University of Nebraska Press.

MacCrimmen, K. R., and M. Toda. 1969. "The Experimental Determination of Indifference Curves." Review of Economic Studies 36:433-51.

Machlis, Lee. 1977. "An Analysis of the Temporal Patterning of Pecking in Chicks." Behaviour 63:1-70.

Mackintosh, N. J. 1974. The Psychology of Animal Learning. London: Academic Press.

Mahanty, Aroop K. 1980. Intermediate Microeconomics with Applications. New York: Academic Press.

Maital, Shlomo. 1982. Minds, Markets, and Money: Psychological Foundations of Economic Behavior. New York: Basic Books.

March, Robert H. 1978. Physics for Poets. 2d ed. New York: McGraw-Hill.

Marwine, Alan, and George Collier. 1979. "The Rat at the Waterhole." Journal of Comparative and Physiological Psychology 93:391-402.

McKenzie, Richard B., and Gordon Tullock. 1981. The New World of Economics. 3d ed. Homewood, Ill.: Irwin.

Mazur, James E. 1975. "The Matching Law and Qualifications Related to Premack's Principle." Journal of Experimental Psychology: Animal Behavior Processes 4:374-86.

Meisch, R. A., and T. Thompson. 1973. "Ethanol as a Reinforcer: Effects of Fixed-Ratio Size and Food Deprivation." Psychopharmacologia 28:171-83.

Menzel, E. W., Jr., and Charles Juno. 1982. "Marmosets (Saguinus Fuscicollis): Are Learning Sets Learned?" Science 217: 750-52.

Mitchell, Denis, Robert C. Fish, and David R. Calica. 1982. "Rats Respond for Food in the Presence of Free Food: How Free Is the 'Free' Food?" Learning and Motivation 13:257-63.

Morgan, M. J. 1974. "Do Rats Like to Work for Their Food?" Learning and Motivation 5:352-68.

Morrison, S. D. 1968. "The Constancy of the Energy Expended by Rats on Spontaneous Activity, and the Distribution of Activity between Feeding and Nonfeeding." Journal of Physiology 197: 305-23.

Neumann, John von, and Oskar Morgenstern. 1944. Theory of Games and Economic Behavior. Princeton, N.J.: Princeton University Press.

Norris, Eugenia B., and David A. Grant. 1948. "Eyelid Conditioning as Affected by Verbally Induced Inhibitory Set and Counter Reinforcement." American Journal of Psychology 61:37-49.

O'Leary, K. D. 1978. "The Operant and Social Psychology of Token Systems." In Handbook of Applied Behavior Analysis, edited by A. C. Catania and T. A. Brigham. New York: Irvington.

Olton, D. S. 1979. "Mazes, Maps, and Memory." American Psychologist 34:583-96.

Pavlov, I. P. 1927. Conditioned Reflexes, translated by G. V. Anrep. London: Oxford University Press.

Peden, Blaine, Debra Dout, and James Allison. 1975. "Fixed-Ratio Responding by Pigeons: Further Tests of the Conservation Model." Paper presented at the meeting of the Psychonomic Society, Denver.

Pickens, R., and T. Thompson. 1968. "Cocaine-Reinforced Behavior in Rats: Effects of Reinforcement Magnitude and Fixed-Ratio Size." Journal of Pharmacology and Experimental Therapeutics 161:122-29.

Podsakoff, Philip M. 1982. "Effects of Schedule Changes on Human Performance: An Empirical Test of the Contrasting Predictions of the Law of Effect, the Probability-Differential Model, and the Response-Deprivation Approach." Organizational Behavior and Human Performance 29:322-51.

_____. 1980. "Performance Models, Microeconomics and Schedule Responding in Humans." Ph.D. dissertation, Indiana University.

Premack, David. 1965. "Reinforcement Theory." In Nebraska Symposium on Motivation, edited by David Levine, pp. 123-80. Lincoln: University of Nebraska Press.

_____. 1963. "Rate Differential Reinforcement in Monkey Manipulation." Journal of the Experimental Analysis of Behavior 6:81-89.

_____. 1962. "Reversibility of the Reinforcement Relation." Science 136:255-57.

_____. 1959. "Toward Empirical Behavior Laws: I. Positive Reinforcement." Psychological Review 66:219-33.

Premack, David, R. W. Schaeffer, and A. Hundt. 1964. "Reinforcement of Drinking by Running: Effect of Fixed Ratio and Reinforcement Time." Journal of the Experimental Analysis of Behavior 6:91-96.

Rachlin, Howard, R. C. Battalio, J. H. Kagel, and L. Green. 1981. "Maximization Theory in Behavioral Psychology." Behavioral and Brain Sciences 4:371-88.

Rachlin, Howard, and Barbara Burkhard. 1978. "The Temporal Triangle: Response Substitution in Instrumental Conditioning." Psychological Review 85:22-47.

Rachlin, H., and L. Green. 1972. "Commitment, Choice and Self-Control." Journal of the Experimental Analysis of Behavior 17:15-22.

Rachlin, Howard, Leonard Green, John H. Kagel, and Raymond C. Battalio. 1976. "Economic Demand Theory and Psychological Studies of Choice." In The Psychology of Learning and Motivation, edited by Gordon H. Bower, vol. 10, pp. 129-54. New York: Academic Press.

Rapport, D. J., and J. E. Turner. 1977. "Economic Models in Ecology." Science 195:367-73.

Restle, Frank. 1979. Personal communication.

Reynaud, Pierre-Louis. 1981. Economic Psychology, translated by Stephen E. G. Lea. New York: Praeger.

Robbins, L. 1930. "On the Elasticity of Demand for Income in Terms of Effort." Economica 10:123-29.

Roitblat, H. L., William Tham, and Leonard Golub. 1982. "Performance of Betta Splendens in a Radial Arm Maze." Animal Learning and Behavior 10:108-14.

Rozin, P., and J. Mayer. 1964. "Regulation of Food Intake in the Goldfish." American Journal of Physiology 206:1430-36.

Samuelson, Paul A. 1976. Economics. 10th ed. New York: McGraw-Hill.

Schelling, Thomas C. 1978. Micromotives and Macrobehavior. New York: Norton.

Schwartz, Barry, and Hugh Lacey. 1982. Behaviorism, Science, and Human Nature. New York: Norton.

Scitovsky, Tibor. 1976. The Joyless Economy: An Inquiry into Human Satisfaction and Consumer Dissatisfaction. London: Oxford University Press.

Scott, Robert H., and Nic Nigro. 1982. Principles of Economics. New York: Macmillan.

Segal, E. F. 1962. "Exteroceptive Control of Fixed-Interval Responding." Journal of the Experimental Analysis of Behavior 5:49-57.

Shapiro, Neil, and James Allison. 1978. "Conservation, Choice, and the Concurrent Fixed-Ratio Schedule." Journal of the Experimental Analysis of Behavior 29:211-23.

Shettleworth, S. J. 1975. "Reinforcement and the Organization of Behavior in Golden Hamsters: Hunger, Environment, and Food Reinforcement." Journal of Experimental Psychology: Animal Behavior Processes 1:56-87.

Simison, R. L. 1982. "Why Are Auto Sales Strictly for the Birds? Just Ask Any Pigeon." Wall Street Journal, December 15, p. 1.

Skinner, B. F. 1953. Science and Human Behavior. New York: Macmillan.

Smith, Adam. 1776. An Inquiry into the Nature and Causes of the Wealth of Nations, vol. 1. London: Strahan and Cadell.

Smith, M. F. 1939. "The Establishment and Extinction of a Token-Reward Habit in the Cat." Journal of General Psychology 20: 475-86.

Smith, Vernon. 1962. "An Experimental Study of Competitive Market Behavior." Journal of Political Economy 70:111-37.

Smith, Vernon L. 1978. "Relevance of Laboratory Experiments to Testing Resource Allocation Theory." In Evaluation of Econometric Models, edited by J. Kmenta and J. Ramsey. New York: Academic Press.

Solnick, Jay V., Catherine H. Kannenberg, David A. Eckerman, and Marcus B. Waller. 1980. "An Experimental Analysis of Impulsivity and Impulse Control in Humans." Learning and Motivation 11:61-77.

Staats, Arthur W. 1975. Social Behaviorism. Homewood, Ill.: Dorsey Press.

Staddon, J. E. R. 1979. "Operant Behavior as Adaptation to Constraint." Journal of Experimental Psychology: General 108:48-67.

Stern, Sander, Leonid Margolin, Bernard Weiss, Shin-tsu Lu, and Sol M. Michaelson. 1979. "Microwaves: Effect on Thermoregulatory Behavior in Rats." Science 206:1198-1201.

Teitelbaum, Philip. 1957. "Random and Food-Directed Activity in Hyperphagic and Normal Rats." Journal of Comparative and Physiological Psychology 50:486-90.

Thorndike, Edward L. 1911. Animal Intelligence. New York: Macmillan.

_____. 1898. "Animal Intelligence: An Experimental Study of the Associative Processes in Animals." Psychological Review Monograph Supplement, vol. 2, no. 8.

Timberlake, William. 1979a. "A Molar Equilibrium Theory of Learned Performance." In The Psychology of Learning and Motivation, edited by Gordon H. Bower, vol. 14, pp. 1-58. New York: Academic Press.

_____. 1979b. "Licking One Saccharin Solution for Access to Another in Rats: Contingent and Noncontingent Effects in Instrumental Performance." Animal Learning and Behavior 7:277-88.

Timberlake, William, and James Allison. 1974. "Response Deprivation: An Empirical Approach to Instrumental Performance." Psychological Review 81:146-64.

Tversky, Amos. 1969. "Intransitivity of Preferences." Psychological Review 76:31-48.

Veblen, Thorstein. 1898. "Why Is Economics Not an Evolutionary Science?" Quarterly Journal of Economics 12:373-97.

Wallace, R. F., S. Osborne, J. Norborg, and E. Fantino. 1973. "Stimulus Change Contemporaneous with Food Presentation Maintains Responding in the Presence of Free Food." Science 182:1038-39.

Wasik, B. H. 1968. "A Postcontingency Test of the Effectiveness of Reinforcement." Psychonomic Science 13:87-88.

Watts, H. W., and A. Rees, eds. 1977. The New Jersey Income Maintenance Experiments, vol. 2: Labor-Supply Responses. New York: Academic Press.

Weeks, J. R. 1962. "Experimental Morphine Addiction: Method of Automatic Intravenous Injections in Unrestrained Rats." Science 138:143–44.

Weeks, J. R., and R. J. Collins. 1964. "Factors Affecting Voluntary Morphine Intake in Self-Maintained Addicted Rats." Psychopharmacologia 6:267–79.

Weiss, Bernard, and Victor G. Laties. 1960. "Magnitude of Reinforcement as a Variable in Thermoregulatory Behavior." Journal of Comparative and Physiological Psychology 53:603–8.

Wolfe, J. B. 1936. "Effectiveness of Token Rewards for Chimpanzees." Comparative Psychology Monographs 12:5, whole no. 60.

Wozny, Mark C. 1979. "Models and Microeconomics of Performance under Fixed Ratio Schedules." Ph.D. dissertation, Indiana University.

Author Index

Subject Index

About the Author

JAMES ALLISON, Professor of Psychology at Indiana University, holds a Ph.D. from the University of Michigan (1963), an M.A. from the Claremont Graduate School (1960), and an A.B. from the University of California at Berkeley (1954). His research on learning, motivation, and behavioral economics has appeared in several books and journals, including Psychological Review, Behavioral Science, Journal of Experimental Psychology, Journal of Comparative and Physiological Psychology, Learning and Motivation, and Animal Learning and Behavior, among others. Coauthor of a psychology laboratory manual, his honors include awards in recognition of distinguished teaching and creativity in research. He has served on the editorial board of the Journal of the Experimental Analysis of Behavior.

DATE DUE

APR 11 '85			
MAY 2 4 2007			
GAYLORD			PRINTED IN U.S.A.